PLUG-N-PLAY MOSAIC

Plug-n-Play Mosaic

for Windows

Angela Gunn

SAMS PUBLISHING

201 West 103rd Street
Indianapolis, IN 46290

For my parents, Cheryl and Donald Gunn; my grandparents, Beulah and Melvin Schoenfeld and Ellen Gunn; and my brother Darrin. Now can I get you guys online?

FIRST EDITION

International Standard Book Number: 0-672-30627-1

Library of Congress Catalog Card Number: 94-68266

98 97 96 95 4 3

Interpretation of the printing code: the rightmost double-digit number is the year of the book's printing; the rightmost single-digit, the number of the book's printing. For example, a printing code of 95-1 shows that the first printing of the book occurred in 1995.

Composed in Palatino and MCPdigital by Macmillan Computer Publishing

Printed in the United States of America

Trademarks

Publisher
Richard K. Swadley

Acquisitions Manager
Greg Wiegand

Managing Editor
Cindy Morrow

Acquisitions Editor
Sunthar Visuvalingam

Development Editor
Mark Taber

Software Development Specialist
Wayne Blankenbeckler

Production Editor
Matthew Usher

Editorial Coordinator
Bill Whitmer

Editorial Assistants
Carol Ackerman
Sharon Cox
Lynette Quinn

Technical Reviewer
Andrew Busey

Marketing Manager
Gregg Bushyeager

Cover Designer
Jay Corpus

Book Designer
Alyssa Yesh

Director of Production and Manufacturing
Jeff Valler

Imprint Manager
Juli Cook

Manufacturing Coordinator
Paul Gilchrist

Production Analysts
Dennis Hager
Mary Beth Wakefield

Graphics Image Specialists
Tim Montgomery
Dennis Sheehan
Susan VandeWalle

Production
Stephen Adams
Carol Bowers
Elaine Brush
Kim Cofer
Mary Ann Cosby
Karen Gregor
Kimberly K. Hannel
Donna Harbin
Louisa Klucznik
Ayanna Lacey
Brian-Kent Proffitt
SA Springer
Jacqueline Thompson
Marcella Thompson
Jill Tompkins
Scott Tullis
Dennis Wesner

Indexers
Jeanne Clark
Greg Eldred
Michael Hughes

Overview

Contents

Acknowledgments

Without my family putting up with my dragging the computer home on every trip to see them (not to mention various other forms of love and support), none of this would have happened. I promise I'll get that vacation thing under control one of these days.

Every writer has stories to tell about her editors. My stories are all happy ones. Respect to Sunthar Visuvalingam for his infinite patience, good humor, and the occasional well-placed threat; to Mark Taber for his wise direction; and to Andrew Busey for mighty (and mighty timely) tech-editing support. And major gratitude is due Joe Salemi for his wisdom in the formative days of this project.

Thanks always to my crack Disaster Recovery Team: Arminda Thomas, Tony Fascé, Gayle Ehrenman, Mike Zulich, Cindy Wolf, Keven McKenny, Molly Rhodes, Jon Espenschied (for special commando e-mail support), Kristian Chronister, and Dan Slott. You know.

Many thanks to all the net.citizens who gave me advice, suggestions, and commentary on the content and focus of this book, with special thanks to Scott Alexander and Sandra Gross for keeping the e-mail flowing. Special thanks to the many people who have graciously allowed me to reprint and comment on their home pages—I appreciate your generosity (both for your permission and for putting up such great pages in the first place)—and to Patrick Pecorelli at FTP Software and the many tech folk who patiently answered questions on deadlines that were not their own. (I'll be mortified if I miss anyone, so I'm not even going to start listing names now....) And BIG thanks to the writers of Mosaic for letting me forget every damn thing I know about UNIX, or at least letting me block it.

The soundtrack for this book, for those craving a multimedia-type reading experience: Jello Biafra/Dead Kennedys, Liz Phair, Lucinda Williams, 7 Year Bitch, Hole, L7, Babes in Toyland, Bratmobile, The Shirelles, Dinah Washington, Tom Waits, Neil Young, Freedy Johnston, Louis Armstrong, Patsy Cline, Diamanda Galas, REM, Valentine Smith, Leonard Cohen, Elvis Costello, Del Shannon, the Ramones, and Richard and Linda Thompson.

 In Chapter 1, the Internet usage statistics were originally published by James E. Pitkow and Margaret M. Recker (1994), results from the First World Wide Web User Survey, in Proceedings of the First International World Wide Web Conference, Amsterdam. Elsevier.

About the Author

Angela Gunn is a journalist specializing in the Internet and online communications. She is a contributing editor at *Home Office Computing* and a frequent contributor to publications such as *PC Magazine, Computer Shopper,* and *Internet World*. She also writes about women's issues and comic books on a semi-regular basis, and has worked as a political writer, a staff editor at *PC Magazine*, and a cyber-salon event coordinator. She's been logging on and off since 1987.

Introduction

First there was all that talk about the Internet. The Internet is full of amazing stuff, they said. You can find anything on the Internet, they said. One day soon everybody will be on the Internet, and we'll all be there, but there's no there, it's all here—at least that's what the little girl in the commercial said. And for over a year, more than a million people each month have been rushing onto the Internet to see what the fuss is about.

Problem is, one look at the Internet and you'd think all the hype was some awful plot for ultimate revenge of the nerds. The Internet has been around for a long time—decades—and it certainly does have a lot of great things to see and do and get. But the Internet was (and is) constructed in bits and pieces, so it's incredibly disorganized. And to use the Internet, you needed to know a strange and cranky computer language called UNIX. UNIX makes DOS, the system most PCs use, read like Shakespeare. Anyone who knows UNIX well enough to really get around on the Internet will snap to attention if you yell "Geek!" in a crowded room. It's a badge of honor. Honest.

Thank heavens, time marches on. New and powerful software can help the average computer user (one who doesn't want to learn UNIX) get onto the Internet and find the wonderful information, pictures, sounds, and people it has on it. You too can get mail from friends halfway around the world, find information on interests from cooking to dilithium crystals to pet care, and see nearly live video of the California surf or of a coffeepot in Great Britain.

The newest and most powerful piece of software is called Mosaic. Mosaic doesn't stand for anything—it isn't an acronym—but it sums up exactly what the Internet is all about.

So What Is It Exactly?

Mosaic lets you hop from interesting place to interesting place on the Internet. You don't need to know strange commands. You don't even need to know much about where the information is that you're seeking. You just need your own curiosity, your computer, and a mouse (or trackball). With Mosaic you can move around the "big picture" that is the Internet, one spot at a time, in any order you like. Best of all, it's nice to look at; instead of reading boring lines of type on a screen, you'll see pictures, hear sounds, and even play videos.

If you have experience with computers, you're probably used to working in one or more applications. Word processors, spreadsheets, and games are all examples of applications. Each lets you accomplish something with your computer (write a letter, figure out your taxes, kill a few hours blasting alien lifeforms). A well-constructed application lets you do that without worrying too much about how it actually does its job, and without fussing too much with the interface (the menus and buttons and other gizmos on the screen that make it work).

As I mentioned, UNIX takes a lot of worry and fuss. The Mosaic application is important because it doesn't—it lets you use the Internet almost as easily as you use your word processor or your games. As we move through the book, you'll find that it won't take long for you to understand how Mosaic works. That means you'll quickly be able to explore what it does, which is to make the amazing and far-flung pieces of the Internet easy to reach and easy to use.

Mosaic does its thing by making it all look familiar, much like something you might see in a regular book (yes, one of those paper things). Instead of presenting you with ugly lines of computer-looking text, Mosaic does a little redecorating and gives you an attractive screen with easy-to-read type. Instead of dumping a bunch of file names onto the screen and letting you figure out what's what, Mosaic shows you pictures, plays sounds, and presents movies. Best of all, Mosaic doesn't expect you to tell it how to do these things—just point it in the right direction and it does all the work.

Some people call Mosaic a "killer app." Translated from the geek-ese, this means that the people who think about such things expect Mosaic to be the piece of software that finally makes the ever-so-cool Internet easy to use for normal people (the ones who don't deal with UNIX). If that sounds like you, you're in the right place.

Who Should Read This Book

Since you've picked up this book, you probably have a computer, and you feel comfortable switching it on and off (especially off). You've come to the computer section of the bookstore because you're curious. You're interested in all this talk about the Internet and the "information superhighway," and you hear that Mosaic makes it easy and fun—but you're not quite sure how to go about getting and using it. You may even have experimented with getting online with a computer bulletin board or on one of the online services such as CompuServe or America Online, but you're not quite satisfied with what they have to offer. And you're wondering about the broader picture—what exactly makes the Internet worth your time and money.

I'm assuming you have access to either a Macintosh or a PC that uses Windows. Beyond that, you don't need anything but a healthy sense of curiosity. My goal is to explain Mosaic and the Internet in terms that don't make you wish you'd taken a course in computer science. I'd much rather you come away from this book talking about how much fun you're having online than about how much you've learned about the arcane workings of the Internet.

How To Read This Book

I hate computer books. They have no plot, the characters bore me, the pictures aren't (usually) pretty, they have a bad beat, and you can't dance to them. Ideally, this book will get through the computer-ese portions of using Mosaic with such ease that you won't notice how good you're getting at "surfing the Net."

Note: A *Net surfer* is someone who enjoys spending time on the Internet. Most of them like to explore interesting new places online. Mosaic is well-suited for Net surfing, since it's easy to move from place to place.

This book gives you the information you need to get started on the Internet with Mosaic. You probably won't read it cover-to-cover; like the Internet, you'll find yourself browsing, hopping around, and picking up the information you need as you need it. Mosaic gives the Internet a good-looking face, and this book will give you plenty of examples that show just how understandable it is. I'm assuming you have a computer and either a modem or a network connection (if you're at work or school—if you're not sure, the answer is probably "no"). I'm also assuming you've heard of the Internet. You may even have an account online already, or you may have at least decided to get one.

If not, don't worry; Chapter 3 is for you—by the time you're done you'll know enough to get an Internet account of your very own, and you'll have some idea of what you'll find up there. If you know about the Internet but need to figure out where Mosaic fits into it, start reading at Chapter 4, where I explain what Mosaic does (and doesn't) do and unveil the World Wide Web—the Web to its friends—in all its glory.

Part II, "Setting Up," gets you online—onto the Internet. Getting onto the Internet involves wading (ankle-deep only) into some strange waters—Chapter 5 will tell you the nine things you'll need to know to get any computer online. Readers calling in from home will read Chapter 6, which tells you how to get online over a regular computer with a regular modem. If you're lucky enough to hook up to the Internet at work or school (why lucky? I'll explain later), read Chapter 7 for instructions on setting up Mosaic on your computer there.

Part III, "And Awaaaay We Go!" leaves the computer-ese behind, and we start exploring the Internet for real. Charity and Mosaic both begin at home, and in Chapter 8 we'll start by looking at a "home page," a place from which to launch your Web travels. In that chapter you'll learn all the skills you need to start moving around on the Net with Mosaic. Chapter 9 gives you more details, including information on what those funky addresses mean and how to find stuff. I'll even give you a peek behind the scenes to show you how it all works. And in Chapter 10, we'll surf the Internet together, exploring three of the best and most intriguing places in this strange new world step-by-step.

Once you're hooked on Net surfing, Part IV, "Be All You Can Be," tells you how you travel even further. Chapter 11 gives you information on other kinds of software you might use to move from place to place; Macintosh users should check this chapter for info on how to get their own copies of Mosaic. (Windows users can just flip to the back of the book, where you'll find two disks with Super Mosaic ready to install on your PC. These disks give you everything you need to get connected.) Chapter 12 has tips for getting at the really cool stuff—pictures and sound, fresh from the Web to you. And if you've ever wanted to be famous, Chapter 13 will help you make your very own home page—put it on the Internet and you have an instant audience of well over 20 million people.

Finally, I've added more technical information in back (for that little geek in all of us). The appendixes include a gallery of some of the best (or at least the most interesting) home pages I've seen in my own Internet travels, with instructions on where to find them and notes on what makes them great. And here's where to turn for more information on building a home page, dealing with the fine points of your chosen software, and finding a place to get online.

Conventions Used in This Book

Occasionally I'll give you something to type. Mainly you'll use the keyboard while you're installing; however, from time to time you'll need to tell Mosaic to go to a specific place on the Internet. When that happens:

`Text like this` shows text that you'll type in exactly as shown, such as the address of a place on the Internet. Any text you would see on the screen appears in a `computer` typeface.

Italics mean that you'll need to type in something else (for instance, when you're installing Mosaic you'll need to type in *`your name`* and *`your computer's address`*). *Italics* also highlight technical terms when they first appear in the text and are sometimes used to emphasize important points.

Throughout the book you'll see boxes of text set apart from the rest of the reading. These boxes give you hints, background, or special information that you can read separately from whatever's going on in the main part of the book. We've marked these boxes with icons (small pictures) so you can tell at a glance what kind of information they hold.

Note: Note boxes give you tips on understanding something in the nearby text. As you've already seen, Note boxes often give background information on whatever's being discussed at the time.

Tech Tip: A Tech Tip will give you hints on how to work with the computer while you use Mosaic. If something is particularly tricky, a Tech Tip might refer you to a different section in the book, where I explain in depth what's going on. Tech Tips also give insight on how the program's doing its stuff and what's happening behind the scenes.

Warning: —Oops! Sometimes it's possible to go astray. A Warning box will let you know what pitfalls you need to avoid (and how).

NCSA Mosaic: An item following the Mosaic icon will help clarify larger concepts, explaining how Mosaic fits into the bigger picture that is the Internet.

PART I

WELCOME TO THE WEB

The first section of this book will give you an overview of Mosaic, of the Internet, and of the world beyond. At the end of these chapters, you'll know what you can expect to find online, and you'll have a sense of how Mosaic fits into the larger world of the Internet (and beyond).

Chapter 1 begins, oddly enough, at the beginning. Here's a quick overview of what's available on the Internet and how Mosaic makes it easily available to you. We'll also get our first glimpse of Mosaic in action; I'll point out some of the features to which you'll soon become accustomed. By the end of the chapter, you'll have a sense of the buzzing hive of activity that is the average day on the Internet.

Chapter 2 focuses on that buzzing hive, watching four Internet users going about their day online. Our Net surfers have varied interests and do different things while online, but all of them find plenty of food for thought on the Internet. We'll figure which of these users can make the best use of Mosaic in their future Internet travels.

Chapter 3 focuses even more closely on two of those users, looking over their shoulder as they go online with Mosaic in pursuit of business and pleasure. By the end of the chapter, you'll have a good idea how you might spend time using Mosaic on the Internet.

In Chapter 4 we'll figure out how it all fits together, moving from the tiny snapshots of our Mosaic users to the big picture of the Internet as a whole. We'll see how Mosaic takes the place of many of the most powerful and sophisticated tools previously available for using the Internet. We'll also pause a moment to consider the why of it all—why the Internet is important, and why it's important that you're on it.

CHAPTER 1

WHY MOSAIC?

"Link by link, making the connection ... that is the state of the art."

—Stephen Sondheim

Now that I've waxed enthusiastic about Mosaic, let's take a closer look at it and at the Internet. This chapter will explain exactly why Mosaic fits so well with the Internet, and what it does to make navigating so easy. (We'll get our first glimpse of the software itself, too.) After that we'll take a broader look at what you can do on the Internet and how it (in turn) all fits into the grand scheme of things.

As I mentioned, Mosaic is software. It sits in your computer's hard drive and translates between your computer's internal language and the various languages used by the Internet.

It also works with another piece of software (called a TCP/IP stack) to take care of whatever piece of computer equipment you're using to get to the Internet—that might be a modem, or it might be a smaller computer network of which your computer is a part. (In that sense, Mosaic is distantly related to modem communications software such as Procomm or MicroPhone.) Mosaic is what's known as "browser" or "client" software. All this means to you is that Mosaic is designed to bring you information that's located somewhere other than your own hard drive. In computer-speak the opposite of "client" is "server"; out on the Internet there are plenty of machines with the server software that works with Mosaic. Those machines hold the information you'll see when you go onto the Internet.

By itself, Mosaic isn't much to look at. If you try to use it without a connection to the Internet, you'll find it almost useless. But on the Internet, Mosaic is a jack-of-all-trades, able to handle almost anything out there. Best of all, it makes the Internet easy to look at, understand and use. That's a big bonus when you're navigating a system with thousands upon thousands of computers and literally millions of files.

What Are You Getting Yourself Into?

Before you decide to load Mosaic onto your computer and dive into the Internet, you should have an idea of what's there and what's not. The Internet is not one computer; it doesn't exist at a particular place, and there's no one person or group in charge of taking care of every single part of it. Chaos, anarchy, madness? Well, yes. But it works out pretty well.

The Internet is a collection of computers all around the world. They're constantly hooked together over telephone-type connections (much more powerful, however, than the connection in the average home!). As shown in Figure 1.1, each computer has one or several "keepers," called system administrators. The administrators make sure the computers and the connections are working, and they help people hook up to the Internet by giving them an account that provides access to that particular computer.

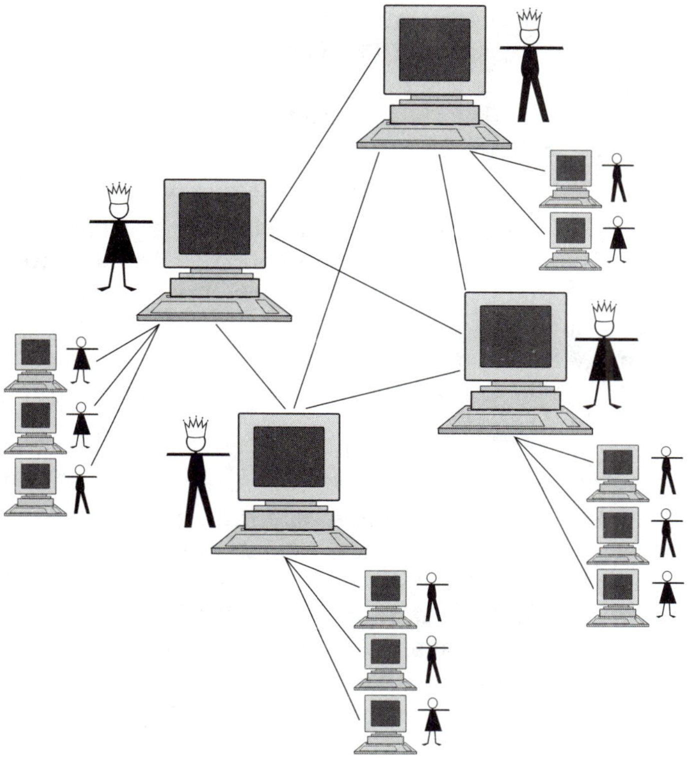

Figure 1.1. Most people on the Internet have an account on a computer run by a system administrator. The system administrator's computer is directly connected to the other computers that make up the Internet.

A user with an account on a computer connected to the Internet is usually free to roam around the entire Internet, using Mosaic (or a motley collection of other programs) to hop from computer to computer. It doesn't matter whether the computer is next door or halfway around the world; the telephone-type connection doesn't rack up long-distance bills in quite the way that regular phone lines do. Once you're connected to one Internet computer, you can go to any other Internet computer. It might as well be on the desk beside you.

Note: Though English is overwhelmingly the predominant language on the Internet, the Internet is very much an international phenomenon. In fact, the technology that makes Mosaic possible was developed primarily at the CERN labs in Switzerland.

Each administrator decides how much access that both "local" users (those that have an account on that computer) and other members of the Internet will have to their computer. Fortunately, the administrators of the world have historically been generous, open-minded people, providing as much access to the outside world as they could without endangering their computers' security. This is why so much is available on the Internet: generosity and open-mindedness.

The individual Internet users, too, have shared in that spirit of generosity. Most of the things you'll find on the Internet were put there by individual users. This means that you may find things that are strange, things that offend you, things that bore you, or things that you think are just plain inaccurate or wrong. However, those things were important to someone who wanted to share them with others—and with 20 million-plus people on the Internet, there are probably at least a few people out there who agree.

> **Note:** Since no one is in charge of the Internet, there is no official set of standards for either behavior or information content. We'll discuss the unofficial standards later. Meanwhile, you should begin by treating the Internet as a strange neighborhood. Proceed with caution, and don't let small children wander off unattended.

What Will You Find?

With all those people on the Internet, you'll find pretty much anything you set your mind to. As you read this, people are typing messages to each other that are delivered instantly, across thousands of miles, from one screen to another. They answer back and forth, and soon they're having a chat through their keyboards. A group of people interested in a single topic—bridge, perhaps, or the latest Quentin Tarantino movie—are chatting together, and the messages appear on the screen like the transcript of some classroom discussion or cocktail party.

Elsewhere, someone is looking for a file that will play a tune when he starts his computer. He finds it and downloads it, moving the file from the Internet to his own computer's hard drive. He notices that his sound card doesn't seem to have the most up-to-date software, so he finds a copy of the latest driver on the manufacturer's Internet computer.

Somewhere else, another person has written a file that explains her doctoral dissertation, and she's putting it on the Internet for other people to read and comment on. Someone who saw an earlier draft of the dissertation is sending her e-mail (electronic mail) to tell her about a book she should read, and where it can be found (or ordered) on—of course—the Internet.

Hundreds of people are online reading the hour's top news headlines. One of them wants more information and moves to an area where people write messages about politics; he sees a heated discussion of health-care plans from several days before and pauses to write a public message adding his opinions. He sends the message, reads a bit more, and decides to ask a question about the upcoming elections. A few minutes later, he checks back and finds that someone has answered it. Happy, he looks up the text of his senator's latest health-care proposal and plans his next message.

Someone—some writer up late, perhaps—is gathering information on a particular company. After checking out the corporate background information the company has published online, she looks through several databases for information about any lawsuits in the company's past.

Scientists are transmitting research data from a lab in Europe to a lab in the United States.

People are playing games that involve pretending to be small furry animals.

Someone is trying to find pictures of Winona Ryder. Wait—he just did.

Someone is sharing her best recipe for banana muffins.

Busy place, the Internet.

What Mosaic Can Do

How does Mosaic fit in? As we said, Mosaic is designed to make the Internet easy to use. It's designed to be an unobtrusive tool, easy to use and flexible, providing benefits for both you (and other users) and for the people responsible for taking care of the Internet.

Mosaic Makes the Internet Easier to Navigate

As I mentioned, you used to need to know UNIX—things like `nn -x -s"mosaic" -n"angela gunn"`—to get from your computer to all those things. No wonder that the Internet used to be the province mainly of academics, scientists, students, and defense-department workers.

A Brief History Lesson

The Internet was started a quarter-century ago as a project of the U.S. Defense Department. It began in 1969 as a network called ARPAnet, and it was designed to make sure that their computers could connect to each other, and that they could keep the connection even if something happened to the network connecting them. They developed the decentralized structure of the future Internet, and created a system ("protocol") for ensuring that messages could get through, even if they had to be sliced into chunks and sent across several different paths to reach their destination.

The first people on the Internet were, of course, people involved with the U.S. defense effort. This included not only government officials but scientists and academics at various universities and research institutions. It didn't take long for them to start using their connected computers to exchange information, mail, and general gossip.

For years the Internet (still in its ARPAnet incarnation) grew very slowly. Meanwhile, other organizations—other universities, businesses, and even a few private individuals—started building their own networks using the same protocol (called Internet Protocol, or IP) as ARPAnet. In the mid-to-late eighties, government funding from the National Science Foundation, NASA and the Department of Energy (as well as a relaxation of certain aspects of ARPAnet bureaucracy) made it possible for these IP-based networks to interconnect and merge into what we now think of as the Internet.

In the past few years, the federal funding for the telephone-line "backbone" of the Internet has been supplanted by non-government money. This means more commercial users on the Internet, and partly explains its phenomenal growth. Additionally, many non-IP networks now hook into the Internet via "gateways." Just as ARPAnet and the other IP networks that merged into the Internet were eventually absorbed by it, it's probable that one day other networks, such as the online services (CompuServe, America Online, Prodigy, etc.) and even networks in offices, will be just another part of the Internet. In some parts of the country, even televisions can have Internet-type connections.

Mosaic spares you knowing what UNIX commands to type to get around on the Internet. Everything appears on a screen that looks very much like a page from a book—in fact, they're often called "home pages." "Home page" has become a generic term for almost any Mosaic screen. A home page is actually a document you go to when you start up Mosaic and get onto the Internet. Many documents on the Internet make excellent home pages. The page might have only words, or it might show a combination of words and pictures (and video and sound). Still, it all looks very normal, something like a file made by a sophisticated word-processing program.

Not only does Mosaic make the Internet look refreshingly normal, it allows you to do some pretty extraordinary acrobatics without breaking a sweat. The World Wide Web—the system Mosaic uses to navigate the Internet—allows you to hop from place to place via little "doorways" called hyperlinks, or links for short. A person creating a particular home page decides to add a link to their page. The link, if you click on it, tells Mosaic where on the Internet to look for a particular piece of information.

Note: The World Wide Web—also called "WWW" or "the Web" or "W3"—is not separate from the Internet. It is a service and a set of tools that make the Internet easier to navigate.

For instance, someone writing a page about President Clinton might want to make a biography of Socks available to the readers. Rather than including that information in the page, the writer can include a link that, when the reader clicks on it, jumps to another file altogether (with the bio of Socks, the Clintons' cat). Another link might lead to a photo of President Clinton and Socks together. The page, the bio and the photo might be on three different continents. That's not your problem; as long as the person writing the page added the links properly, you'll never need to know or care where the information is actually stored. It just comes to you and that's it.

Macintosh users have known about a version of this system for years. It's called hypertext. Hypertext connects separate documents together and lets users chart their own path through the information. By choosing a particular word in a document, the user can see other information on a topic related to that word. Users who didn't want more information on that word, of course, didn't have to look at the information.

Since users can easily hop around to get information, hypertext makes it easier and more practical to keep information in many small files instead of one big file. In much the same way, the Internet is many (relatively) small computers, instead of one big mega-computer. The World Wide Web is based on the concept of hypertext. Mosaic goes one better: It's based on the hypermedia concept, which means that it can "do hypertext" not only from word to word but from word to photo, or photo to sound bite.

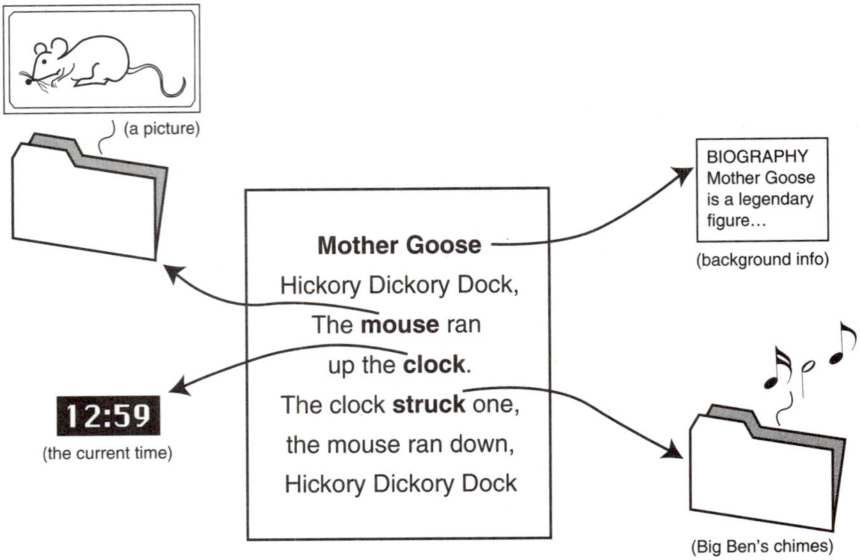

Figure 1.2. A hypertext or hypermedia document is actually many smaller files connected together. When you move around in a hypertext or hypermedia document, you're actually moving from file to file according to instructions the writer added to the document. Such documents can hold all kinds of surprises.

> **Note:** Hypermedia is an expanded form of hypertext. Hypertext only allows you to hop from one piece of text to another. Hypermedia allows you to hop from any kind of information to any other. A hypermedia link might play a video or sound sample, open a text file, or even start a program. The illustration shows a hypermedia document.

Mosaic is a visual environment, and how better to explain a visual environment than with an illustration?

Figure 1.3 shows a typical Mosaic session in action. At the top of the screen, you see the menus and buttons you'll use to move from place to place. The two most important buttons are the arrow buttons in the upper left. These will let you retrace your steps easily; if you follow a link but want to get back to where you were before, you can use these two buttons.

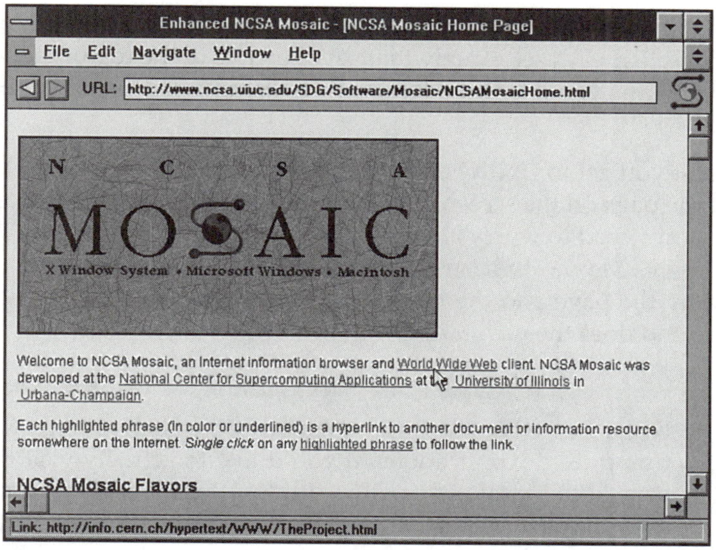

Figure 1.3. Mosaic in action.

The main event is taking place in the large white window below. This is a page for the National Center for Supercomputing Applications, the research group that developed Mosaic. You see a Mosaic logo in the upper-left corner of the page.

You see that certain words are underlined. Those words have links attached; clicking on them takes you to a related document. For example, clicking on the words "World Wide Web" (in the first line) takes you to a computer in Switzerland that has information about the Web that makes Mosaic possible. Clicking on the words "National Center for Supercomputing Applications," meanwhile, gets you information about the NCSA and about the University of Illinois, where the center is located.

> **Note:** You'll always recognize links by either an underline or, in the case of graphics, a thick border. Also, if Figure 1.1 were in color, you'd see that the underlined words are brightly colored.

Mosaic Makes Users More Comfortable with the Internet

As you see from our sample, there aren't many buttons and menus in Mosaic itself. All the strictly Mosaic stuff is along the top of the screen. For now, the important thing to know is that that's all there is. That's the entire Mosaic interface. You will always see exactly that set of menus at the top of the screen—and most of the time you'll just use two or three commands (usually the arrow buttons).

The closest you get to UNIX is that line of text next to the arrows. That's the address of the page on the screen, and later on I'll explain how to make sense of it, but you don't need to worry about it to get from place to place. But it's useful to remember that Mosaic itself isn't in charge of knowing all those connections; that's handled by the page and the links imbedded within it. Mosaic just knows the language and does the navigation.

Note: Our example is the home page for the National Center for Computing Applications. If you'd like to actually visit this home page with Mosaic, its "URL" address is `http://www.ncsa.uiuc.edu/SDG/Software/Mosaic/NCSAMosaicHome.html`. We'll explain exactly how to do this in Chapter 9, once we've got you safely onto the Internet.

That simple, unchanging menu bar makes Mosaic unobtrusive and simple to use. You only have a few basic actions to learn, mainly involving the concepts of moving forward and backing up. Mosaic allows you to concentrate on what's on the Internet instead of what's on your computer, whether you're getting files, looking at pictures, answering a questionnaire or searching through page after page of data.

Mosaic takes the place of several different UNIX commands and programs; in one screen it might act as a file-transfer package, in another it can guide you through someone's self-published Internet "newspaper."

Note: When you click on a link—an underlined word, for instance—you tell the system that you want to hop from the page you're on to the page it's offering to show you. (Nevermind that the place may be halfway around the world; the Internet doesn't care.)

That's all. The pages you see are on their own computers, not on yours. You cannot accidentally damage or erase them. You cannot break the Internet, or even your computer, by clicking. Run the mouse around and click all you want. You can't hurt a thing.

Once you feel comfortable hopping halfway across the planet in a single bound, you'll find that there are plenty of things to do with Mosaic—tricks that will help you navigate even more easily and even capture some of the wonderful things you see online. Again, you can't do much damage doing any of these things. The Internet was originally designed and built to withstand a nuclear war. You aren't going to make much of a dent.

Mosaic brings you the Internet in multimedia form, meaning that it's not just text you'll see in your travels. Multimedia means sounds, pictures, and even animation.

If the salesperson told you that your computer is multimedia, it probably means that you have a CD-ROM drive or some other piece of hardware that allows you to have multimedia. You don't need special hardware to take advantage of Mosaic, though if you have a top-notch video system or a sound card, you'll be able to use them to play the sounds and see the pictures.

Note: If you're not sure about these multimedia things, we'll cover the issues in depth in Chapter 12.

Finally, Mosaic not only helps you find new things, it helps you re-find old things. It's very easy to waft from spot to spot, looking over the latest Dilbert cartoon here, playing a game there, picking up a file over yonder. However, you're very likely to find sites on the Internet that you'll want to revisit. For instance, there are a number of Internet "magazines" making their way online. Checking in regularly is the equivalent of subscribing in many cases. Also, you may find that a particular site carries a collection of files on a particular topic, or perhaps it has an excellent set of games or information on your hobbies or business.

When that happens, you'll want to find your way back. Mosaic is designed to remember the last few "hops" you made (the last few links you chose). If you want to back up, you can retrace your steps easily. In addition, the software lets you store a list (or lists) of your favorite places, so you can find them again next time you log on to the Internet.

Mosaic Offers Flexible but Relatively Secure Connectivity for Internet Administrators

That's a mouthful. For the average Mosaic user, it simply means that the administrator can allow you to get at interesting files without letting you accidentally stray into the rest of the system and possibly cause damage. That's why so many people in charge like Mosaic and the World Wide Web, and why the Web is growing so very quickly (even faster than the Internet itself!).

It's possible to do almost anything on the Internet via Mosaic. However, some aspects of the Internet make better use of Mosaic's ability to hop from place to place (its hypertext support) and its graphical interface than do others. As the Web grows in popularity, more and more sites will be geared toward using its special features. It's fortunate that Mosaic's so easy to use; more and more, the people putting the good stuff onto the Internet assume that a Web browser like Mosaic is what you're using.

CHAPTER 2

WHAT YOU'RE GETTING YOURSELF INTO

"And you may ask yourself, Well, how did I get here?"

—David Byrne

So, why do you want to be on the Net? (Enough, by the way, with the formalities. From here on out, you're familiar enough to call it the Net.) You've seen Mosaic, and it looks good, But telling you that you can do almost anything on the Net doesn't really help you know what you might want to do. In this chapter we'll look at how a few ordinary people use the Net's resources, and how Mosaic fits into the picture. You'll see people using it for business and for pleasure, to meet new people and to keep in touch with people they already know.

So again—why *do* you want to be on the Net? You probably won't give the same answer as the next person—and you might not give the same answer twice. Compare these Net surfers:

Sophy is a Net surfer purely for fun. She got started in college when the computer center offered free Net access to anyone who wanted it. She logged on and was immediately hooked. She e-mailed professors at other universities to discuss her papers and their books; she followed discussions on everything from conspiracy theories to women's issues; she gathered data for projects from places around the world, she worked, she procrastinated, she learned (old, obnoxious) UNIX. These days she corresponds with friends she's met either at college or strictly over the Net—some of those, in fact, she's never seen except in photos online. In the past year or so she's watched the Net overflow with people, many of whom (she feels) don't respect the friendly, open culture online—or worse, only want to take advantage of it.

> **Note:** You can keep photos on your computer (and by extension) online, by using a scanner to make a computer image file. You'll occasionally see these images, called "GIFs or JPEGs," after one of the file formats commonly used for storing them.

She probably wouldn't care for Robert, who sees the Net purely as a business opportunity. The fabric company for which Robert works has little interest in computers, but Robert knows a marketing opportunity when he sees one, and about a year ago Robert went online.

He's in charge of making his company a "presence" on the Internet, reaching both current and potential customers. When Robert posts to one of the public discussions groups (called newsgroups, or more properly usegroups), it's probably not one of Sophy's social areas. Instead, he watches for messages in groups relating to his business and posts notes describing the fabrics his company offers.

Robert doesn't feel he's doing any harm or taking advantage of anyone—he's just providing information to interested people in an inexpensive, effective manner. Lately he's been hard at work developing a Web site for getting product information and pictures of the fabrics to anyone who wants it. He thinks that perhaps he should open his own company to help other businesses that want to do the same thing.

> **Note:** There are well over 6,000 newsgroups on the Net, and more are added monthly. Topics range from the arcane features of various computers, to weddings, to almost every hobby you can imagine, to politics, to education, to music, to the finer points of insulting your fellow Internet denizens.

Emily might be interested in that information. The Net is a business venture for her, too, but her business IS the Net. Emily is a professional researcher, and the Net is a major weapon in her arsenal. She never knows what she'll be called upon to discover, so she's familiar with places on the Net neither Sophy nor Robert are likely to know, including the tango information center, resources for students at theological seminaries, and the price lists for various computer companies. If you need to know the history of adult-education courses, want information on clothing styles shown in Rembrandt's paintings, or want a few recipes for baklava, Emily knows where to look and who to ask. She gets results quickly, too—most of her questions get answered within hours or even minutes, since the Net never sleeps.

Neither does Joshua, since he got his Internet connection. He's worried that he might miss something. When he first logged on he just wanted the free stuff he'd heard about—files, games, pictures of women in various states of undress. But once Josh started exploring the newsgroups and mailing lists, he was hooked. Of course, now that Josh has a better, faster, stronger Net connection, he's checking out some of the Rembrandt clothing styles himself—of course, he's jumping via computer to Amsterdam to look at them....

These examples give you a sense of how various people use the Net. However, we can make it simpler and divide almost all possible Net usage into four basic food groups:

- Info-harvesting
- File transfer
- E-mail
- Chat

I'll explain all four, but in this book we'll focus mainly on info-harvesting and file transfer, for reasons you'll soon understand.

Info-Harvesting: The Main Event

Info-harvesting is a very broad category. It covers almost everything that Emily does, Josh's Amsterdam missions, all those people looking at Robert's Web site, and Sophy's project research. If you're info-harvesting you might be reading a newsgroup, checking out an online art gallery or museum, or catching up on the news. Info-harvesting is a category that includes almost everything on the Internet, since the Internet is made up of information.

If you're truly interested in being on the Internet, you want that information, for whatever reason. Since there's information about literally everything, it's beside the point for me to ask you what information you want. (I'll give you some suggestions later, though.) It's out there somewhere—tips on planning a wedding, song lyrics, a list of 100 ways to annoy a roommate, gardening advice, on and on.

Much of the information on the Internet is put there by individual users. It started with research scientists making their papers publicly available for comment and collaboration, but almost immediately non-scientific interests crept in. Thus began the explosion. Since even the earliest Net users had interests outside the purely academic, they began to type in things that amused them for the express purpose of sharing with others. Most of the files of song lyrics, for instance, were laboriously typed in by one fan of a particular artist or band—with varying degrees of accuracy.

It became more organized. Small groups of people began to systematically put information on the Net. Since the Net was still based mainly in academia at this point, a lot of the information was of a scholastic bent. But with groups of people dedicated to making their information complete and comprehensive, the quality of information began to improve. In particular, a lot of the "fun" files became more accurate and organized.

One of the most fascinating early endeavors is Project Gutenberg, dedicated to making great works of literature freely available on the Internet. Since a lot of the great works of literature are in the public domain (meaning that no copyright laws apply to them), volunteers could freely type them in and put the files on the Net.

Project Gutenberg currently has versions of hundreds of masterworks, including *Beowulf, Alice In Wonderland,* and the Sherlock Holmes mysteries of Sir Arthur Conan Doyle. Other databases came online, with information on history, the media, science and the arts; universities with particularly strong departments in one area or another committed themselves to publishing their archives for public use.

Note: I keep mentioning all this cool stuff on the Net. In later chapters—once I've explained how to get online—I'll be sure to give you instructions for getting to these great places. You'll also find a list of every Net place I mention in Appendix D.

It's possible for a researcher to make full use of files at universities around the world. Soon libraries began to automate their card catalogs. For instance, now anyone in the world can check to see not only if the New York Public Library system owns a particular book, but which branch has it. Many reference books, such as Webster's Dictionary, also became available via the Net.

Note: Although much of the information available on the Internet is no longer protected by copyright laws, some is. And some information is on the Internet in violation of copyright law; that is, it has been put there without permission from or payment to the publisher or author. Copyright law is changing rapidly because of the Internet.

As the Internet continued to grow, the sophistication of the information increased as well. Many museums have begun to make themselves available online; by photographing their holdings and scanning the photos, they can give any Net surfer the opportunity to view their collections.

And commercial enterprises are putting their information online too. Some businesses charge for access to their information; for instance, Lexis/Nexis, a database of articles from most major American magazines and newspapers, is available by relatively expensive subscription and is mainly used by journalists and politicians. Other companies sell subscriptions to the outfit that provides you with your Internet account, and you have access to the information as part of your account fee.

Currently many businesses are scrambling to jump onto the Internet bandwagon, seeing the Net as a good way to reach a large audience.

Many businesses, such as Robert's fabric firm, put information about their products online so interested parties can look at it; if they're interested, they can send e-mail or phone the company.

Other businesses, such as newspapers, use the Net to supplement their regular product. An online newspaper might add notes and information that the reporter was unable to work into a particular story; some TV networks give biographical information about their stars and keep an up-to-date schedule of their programming.

Of course, the earlier systems haven't ceased; plenty of Net citizens still create files of song lyrics, and free non-commercial use of the Net continues to increase.

Note: A few companies are very aggressive about advertising on the Internet. It's considered extremely rude, however, for companies to send advertising to people who haven't specifically asked for it—it's almost like forcing people to pay for junk mail. There's a term—spamming—for folks who post or advertise indiscriminately on the Net. Our Robert does *not* spam.

Mosaic is designed primarily as an information harvester; it helps you easily find it and helps you easily collect it. And a good Web page is also designed, to the best of the designer's ability, to guide you to other places that have information related to the page you see in front of you.

File Transfer: Bring It On Home

File transfer is in some ways a subset of info-harvesting. However, it's a much simpler thing: The Internet has files, you take copies of the files off the Internet. When Josh went looking for games and women, he found the files on the Net and transferred them to his own computer by a process called FTP (File Transfer Protocol).

File transfer became popular a microsecond after the first user posted the first file to the Net. As one person posted a file (say, the research paper or song lyrics mentioned above), other users could download the files if they knew where to look, either by hearing about it on one of the newsgroups, or searching for files with the name of the band in question, for instance.

File transfer was made possible through the benevolence of the system administrators, as I mentioned in the introduction. It was helped along by the benevolence of programmers, who wrote small utility programs for searching out files across the Net, and by the intelligence of all the users who named their files in such a way that the utilities could identify them as search targets. (You might use a quirky, individual naming system for files on your own computer, but on the Net a file of information about sea otters is very likely to have a name with the words "sea" and "otter" in it. This is one of the benefits of using UNIX, which allows longer file names than DOS does.)

> **Note:** There's really no estimating how many files actually exist online; there may be millions, or even billions by now.

With file transfer came the rise of shareware—computer programs available online. If you need a shareware program you download it; if you like it and use it, you send the programmer money. Another system, freeware, also came into being—same idea, but the software was free. (You weren't allowed to resell it for a profit, and the programmers sometimes asked you to drop them a friendly e-mail if you liked the program, but otherwise there were no strings attached.)

This sounds too good to be true, relying on the honesty of strangers and what-not, but in fact it's worked out fairly well. Shareware and freeware survive and flourish to this day. Mosaic, in fact, began life in this fashion, written under the auspices of the National Center For Supercomputing Applications and distributed Netwide.

File transfer is also one of Mosaic's strengths; it's not much more complex than using Windows' File Manager. With Mosaic you'll transfer files to your computer; you cannot yet transfer files via Mosaic to the Internet.

E-mail and Chat: The Great Beyond

E-mail and chat are a lot of what Sophy's doing these days, keeping in touch with friends either by sending a letter (to be read at the recipient's convenience) or getting together in an area where they can type instantly to one another. Both chat and e-mail are more or less beyond the scope of today's Mosaic. At the moment you can't send or receive e-mail via Mosaic, but that will change in the future. Chat is possible through a process called telnet; Mosaic doesn't do telnet, but you can use Mosaic to run a telnet program. (Confused? Don't be. We'll talk about telnet and other Mosaic accessories in Chapter 12.)

E-mail includes both person-to-person mail and mailing lists, which broadcast mail on a particular topic to anyone who's signed up to receive it. A chat is what you have when you join a group of people all typing into their computers in an online area called a MUD (Multi-User Dungeon), a MOO (an object-oriented MUD), or the like. Chats happen in real time, which means that you see what each participant has typed no more than a second or two after they've typed it.

> **Note:** Mailing lists resemble the newsgroups, but they're not as easily accessible to the casual user; you have to know where to find the discussion group and send mail to subscribe to it.

Both e-mail and chat are very popular, for different reasons. Much of the person-to-person communication on the Net happens in e-mail. For instance, Emily may send e-mail to a useful contact if she has specific questions about a topic, or Robert might ask anyone interested in his products to send him e-mail if they have questions.

The chats are also popular, especially among the crowd that enjoy role-playing games and general socializing (and don't mind the expense of being online for large amounts of time). The MUDs and MOOs are an intense environment, and many people become quite absorbed by them, making friends to which they're as close as anyone in the "real" world. However, chat and e-mail aren't available through Mosaic, and so we will leave them here.

So Who Are These People?

Who is the "normal" Internet user—Sophy or Robert, Emily or Josh? With millions of people using the Net, there's no simple answer to this question. However, information collected from a group of Web users by James E. Pitkow, a researcher at Georgia Tech, is enlightening:

- Fifty-six percent of the people currently on the Internet and using the Web are 21-30 years old; 36 percent are 31-50 years old; 2 percent are over 50, 6 percent are under 21.
- Ninety-five percent of the Web's users are male, which reflects the gender disparity of the Internet as a whole. Guess that lets Sophy and Emily out—but those numbers are changing as the Internet and the Web become more well-known and accessible beyond the scientific community.
- Sixty-eight percent of the Web's users are in North America, and 28 percent are in Europe. However, the Internet reaches every continent—even Antarctica has researchers logging in.
- Academic types—students and faculty—make up 44 percent of the Web's population, which again reflects the origins and strongholds of the Internet. That's almost equal to the users calling themselves professionals—45 percent. And about 3 percent describe themselves as business users. That total will grow as the Net opens up to commercial use, and as people like Robert begin to add information to it.

- Everyone answering the poll uses their computer at least 6 hours each week. About three-fifths are on between 21 and 50 hours per week; the hard-core users logging over 50 hours each week make up around 27 percent.
- And 97 percent of Web users use Mosaic.

All those numbers, of course, have very little bearing as far as your decision to get on the Net. And as it expands it becomes increasingly difficult to define what's normal online, since everyone who logs in wants something different. Some users are just curious, some don't have a clear idea about what they want to do once they're there, and an increasing number have no abiding interest in computers. Old-timers like Sophy may get cranky about them, but those users are the future of the Internet.

So Why Are You Here?

You have a sense now of how some people use the Internet, and who's out there. What I haven't explained is how they got there, and how you will get there.

Cynically speaking, there are two kinds of Internet connections: the kind you pay for yourself, and the kind you get someone else to pay for. Being an essentially cynical person, I've reserved two chapters (6 and 7) for in-depth description of each kind of connection. For now, though, let's analyze where connections come from.

If you don't currently have Internet access, you're probably considering getting online through a public access provider. These companies have large computers running UNIX and are connected to the Internet; for a subscription fee (usually billed in monthly increments and often including either a limited number of hours of access or a per-hour fee above the subscription) they will set up an account for you on their computers. You use your computer, modem, and communications software to call their system; you'll log in with your user name and a password.

> **Note:** If someone finds out your passwords and knows your username, they can log in and, effectively, be *you* on the Net. Some people do this for fun, some for more nefarious purposes. You should guard your password carefully and change it frequently.

What happens next varies. Some systems (known as *UUCP connections*) merely provide a drop-off point for e-mail; these are extremely basic (and they don't handle Mosaic), but some users like them.

Some systems are set up to allow you only to pick up your e-mail, check newsgroups, and make simple hops from one Internet site to another, usually via the aforementioned nasty UNIX interface. This kind of connection is known as a *dial-up* (or *shell*) account, and it can be useful (and may in fact include basic Web access), but again it doesn't allow for Mosaic and its sophisticated navigation. (It also does little annoying things like download your files to the access provider's computer instead of your own; you'll have to move it from there yourself.) When you have a dial-up account, you're aren't really "on the Internet;" your computer is connected to a computer that's on the Internet. It sounds like a semantic difference, but it's crucial. All you need to use a dialup account is regular terminal-emulation software such as Procomm or Microphone—you can even use the simple programs included with your operating system, such as Terminal.

To use Mosaic via modem, you'll need a special kind of connection called a *SLIP* (serial line Internet protocol) or *PPP* (point-to-point protocol) account. It doesn't take anything special—just the computer, networking software known as TCP/IP, and a fast (9,600 bps or better) modem—but it connects to the Net very differently.

> **Note:** SLIP is the older version of PPP; if you can choose, get the PPP service.

You won't see the difference at first; you'll dial a number and type your username and password. But once you're online, you're *really* online—your computer becomes a full member of the Internet. Think of it this way: If a dial-up account connects you to a computer that's connected to the Net, a SLIP or PPP connection plugs your directly into that computer's phone line. Mosaic needs a SLIP or PPP connection to function, unless you happen to use a network (perhaps at work or school) that can make the necessary connections for you.

Why? Because Mosaic works with a set of technical protocols called TCP/IP (terminal control protocol/Internet protocol). TCP/IP is the real language of the Internet, in the sense that it handles the tiny packets of information that you're asking for. A dial-up account relies on the access provider's TCP/IP connection to do the actual work of talking to the Internet computers; all your computer can do is talk to the access provider's computer, with UNIX.

> **Note:** Sometimes both SLIP/PPP and dial-up connections are both called dial-in connections. In that case, they can be referred to respectively as dial-in direct and dial-in terminal connections.

Where does TCP/IP come from? In the future—probably by mid-1995—TCP/IP will be handled by your operating system (if you upgrade to Windows 95, OS/2 Warp, or System 7.5.) For now, TCP/IP stacks, as they're called, are usually purchased from vendors such as FTP Software or Novell. We've included a disk with TCP/IP software (and a copy of Mosaic, of course) in the back of the book. A few kind public access providers will help you get the TCP/IP stacks, too. Prices vary.

Some users don't need to worry; they're already using a system that provides TCP/IP. These are the users getting online through a networked computer—either hooked to a larger computer (such as a university mainframe) or to a local area network of computers, usually at work. If you use a computer that allows you to store files somewhere other than a hard drive on your own desk, you're probably hooked to a network, and it's very likely that the network has access to the Internet through a *permanent connection*. You won't even need a modem on your computer. In that case, you'll go to the person in charge of taking care of the system, tell them that you'd like to use Mosaic, and ask them to give you certain information for setting up your system. (Ask nicely; these people have a tough and thankless job, and a little kindness pays off.) Again, we'll cover this thoroughly a bit later, in Chapter 7.

> **Note:** Anyone can have a permanent connection; however, the price is out of reach for almost everyone but medium-to-large businesses. Yearly costs are in the five-figure range, as opposed to three figures for the average SLIP, PPP, or dial-up connection.

A number of people now connect to the Internet through accounts with one of the online services. These include CompuServe, Prodigy, America Online, GEnie, and Delphi. Online services have a lot to offer: most have their own file areas, their own chats, and their own newsgroups in addition to Net access.

However, even the largest online services have no more than 2 million members, and all but CompuServe are more or less limited to the United States. This is a sizable group of people, of course, but the variety that characterizes the Internet isn't there. Also, the online services are privately held, and can thus regulate what you do and say on them. That may or may not be a problem for you, but you should be aware that the freewheeling nature of the Internet doesn't necessarily apply.

If you choose to get access through an online service, you'll find that your level of access varies. Two services, Delphi and America Online (AOL), provide fairly full Internet access, nearly equivalent to that of a dial-up account. You'll get e-mail, news, and some forms of info-harvesting with both; Delphi also offers FTP transfers and telnet, which is the ability to login on another computer on the Internet remotely (that is, from your own computer).

CompuServe and Prodigy are further behind, offering mainly e-mail and newsgroup access, but they're working to offer other options in the near future. The rest offer simple e-mail through gateways—their own non-permanent Internet connections, which dial up the Internet periodically to exchange e-mail. You'll find that if you ever send mail to and from an online service, it'll take as long as a couple of hours, as opposed to a couple of seconds with a standard SLIP/PPP or dial-up connection.

A Few Paragraph's Worth of The Hard Sell

Which is right for you? If you've read this far, odds are you've decided against the simple UUCP e-mail connection. Sure it's inexpensive, but you won't get the best parts of the Internet—the files, the games, the information that's there for the harvesting.

That leaves—well, a lot of people. This book is geared, of course, toward Mosaic, and so I'm assuming that you'll choose to get a SLIP/PPP connection or hook up through a smaller network to take advantage of it.

Of our friends above, only Sophy doesn't really need Mosaic; Josh thinks it's fun, Emily finds that it speeds up her searches and leads her to sources she might not have found otherwise, and Robert depends on it to present the materials he's putting online. And many of the newest sites and services on the Internet assume that you're running a graphical Web browser like Mosaic, that lets you see images and video and so forth—if you don't have the connection, you'll miss out.

Now that you have an idea of what you'll find on the Internet, how people use it, and how you can connect to it, the next chapter will describe how you can use Mosaic to bring it all together. We'll leave Sophy behind—she's got a lot of e-mail to catch up on—and we'll sit in on Josh and Emily as they go about their business. (We'll deal with Robert in Chapter 13, if you decide you'd like to add something of your own to the Internet.)

CHAPTER 3

ENTER THE WEB

"We always did feel the same, we just saw it from a different point of view."

—Bob Dylan

It can be difficult to imagine yourself on the Internet using Mosaic if you don't have a clear idea what it's like to pilot it, and what you might find when you do. So let's follow Emily (our ever-so-serious researcher) and Josh (our ever-so-whimsical Net surfer) through part of their online days.

Efficiency, Thy Name Is...Emily

We'll start with Emily, since her mission today is pretty well-defined. Emily is looking for a particular piece of information for one of the magazines for which she does research: Are there any romantic movies that feature jugglers?

Emily shakes her head—from this she makes a living?—and fires up the computer. She uses the modem to dial her access provider and types in her username and password; she is connected. She clicks the icon and Mosaic begins to do its thing.

Every Mosaic user chooses a place on the Net from which to start explorations. When you start the software it includes the address of such a place, just to get you going. For instance, the shareware version of the NCSA Mosaic software is configured to start on the page for the NCSA Mosaic server at the University of Illinois Urbana-Champaign campus. (That's where they keep the National Center for Supercomputing Applications.)

Note: The page on which you start all your Mosaic sessions is called your *home page*. (You'll often hear any Web page called a home page, but once again that's incorrect.) The Mosaic software allows you to choose any home page you like.

The site Emily has chosen as her home page has a software search tool called the WebCrawler. It allows her to search most of the Net by a key word or phrase. Such tools are occasionally referred to as worms or web-crawlers ("spiders" didn't sound quite right) since they scurry out across the Web and look for such things.

Note: You may have heard of another kind of worm, related to computer viruses and other electronic nastiness. Search tools such as the WWW Worm are a different animal altogether—they're not viruses, and they do no harm to the computers they touch.

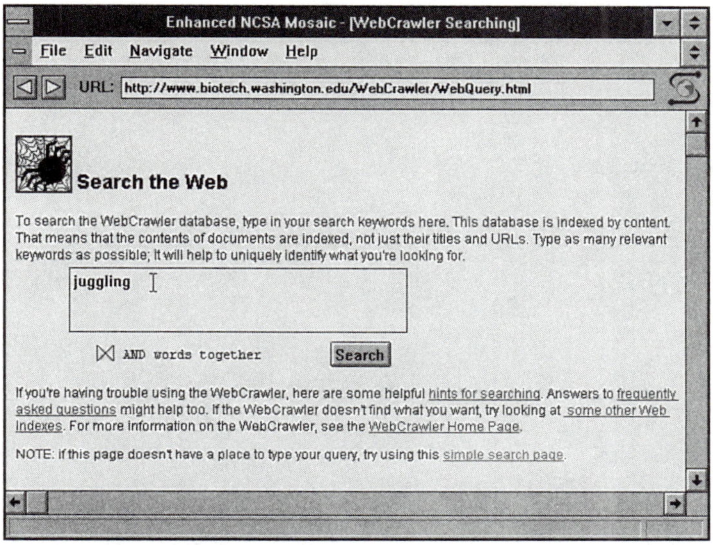

Figure 3.1. The WebCrawler page, located on the Internet at `http:www.biotech.washington.edu/WebCrawler/WebQuery.html`. Once we do a bit of Net surfing, you'll be able to use this URL address to go there on your own.

Figure 3.1 shows the Web page Emily uses as her home page. As you see, it has a blank to fill in the information she's looking for. The WebCrawler does a very simple search. Other search programs are more sophisticated, and if the Web search doesn't pan out she'll use one of those.

She decides that a juggling page would probably have the word "juggling" in its title, so she uses the mouse to scroll down to the blank. She clicks once on the field and enters `juggling`.

Eventually—a few minutes later—the computer returns with a screen with links to Web pages that include the word "juggling," as we see in Figure 3.2. All Emily has to do is click on one of the listings and she's on her way there.

Tech Tip: Throughout the book, I'll give you URL addresses for the pages we see in our travels. These addresses point Mosaic to the exact location of the page you want. You should type the URL address exactly as I've shown it. However, you will often see URLs that look a bit different at the beginning; I'll explain how to handle those later.

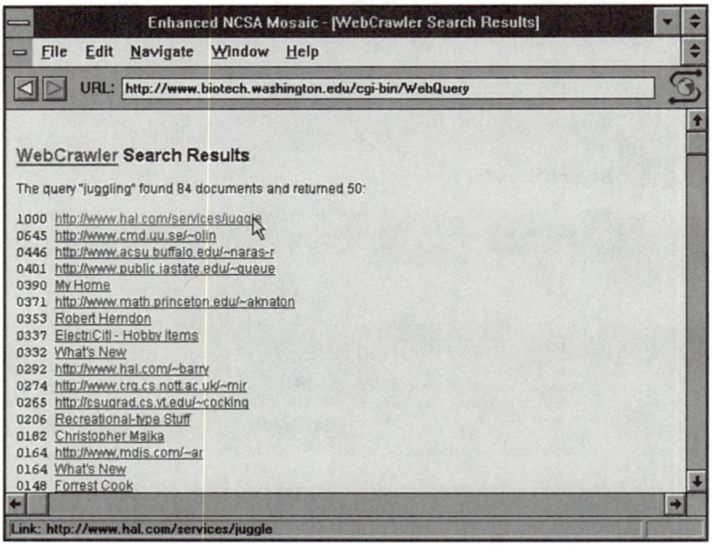

Figure 3.2. The results of Emily's search.

Gracious, she thinks (and rolls her eyes at her own play on words). Somebody's put a lot of work into this one. Figure 3.3 shows what Emily sees; this page even has a sound clip attached (represented by the speaker in the upper-left-hand corner).

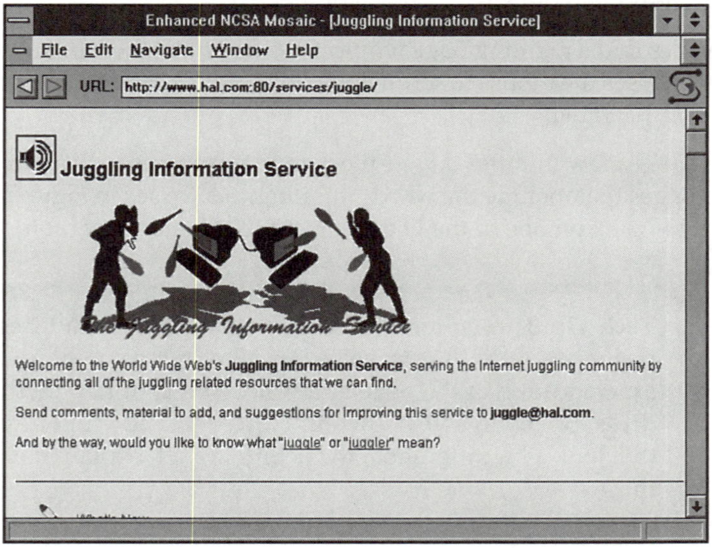

Figure 3.3. The beginning of the Juggling Information Service page, located at `http://www.hal.com:80/services/juggle`.

She's certainly interested in finding out what "juggle" really means—she suspects that sooner or later the magazine will ask her to check—but for now she wants to get the title of a romantic movie with jugglers, and quickly. She scrolls through the page until she finds a link that looks useful: "Juggling in the Media." As is her habit, she looks at the bottom of the page (shown in Figure 3.4) and makes a note of the Internet address of the person in charge before clicking on the media link.

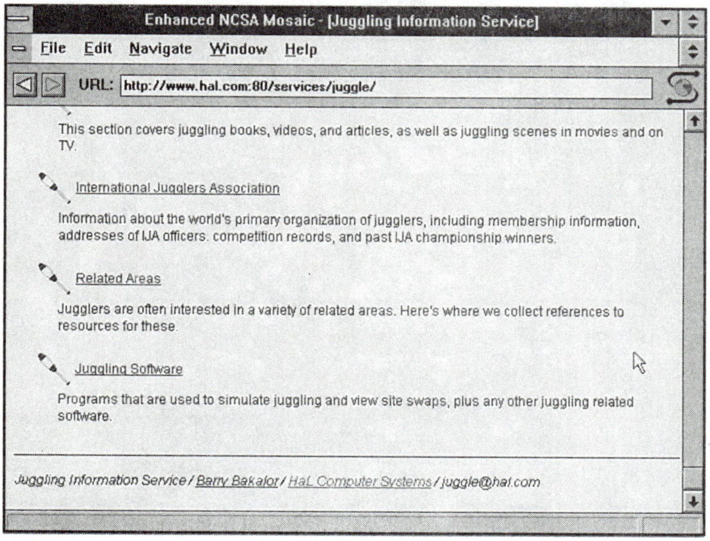

Figure 3.4. The bottom of the same page, at the same place on the Net.

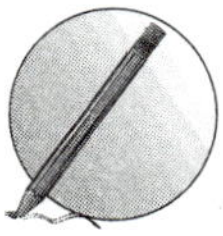

Note: At the bottom of many Web pages, you'll see an e-mail address for the person or group in charge of maintaining that page. You'll often see a copyright © notice as well.

The "Juggling in the Media" page looks intriguing, as we can see in Figure 3.5—books, tapes, even mathematical treatises. This site is wonderful, she thinks, and breathes a thank-you to the dedicated soul that put it together and takes care of it. She also adds the address of the site to her hotlist. A hotlist is like a bookmark for places you find in your Web travels. All she'll have to do to get back to this juggling page is to open the hotlist menu and click once to get back here from anywhere on the Internet.

She spots the link to the movie section and clicks on it. The movies page is an ordinary text file; there are no links here. But that's OK, because she's now exactly where she needs to be. She notes the date at the top; the information's a bit old, but since she doesn't need particularly recent movies this information will work just fine. Six minutes after she started her day's work, she calls her editor to recommend that the article include references to *Benny and Joon* and *The Princess Bride*.

Let's leave Emily here—her editor has something else for her to do, and as ever Emily's in a hurry—and pick up with Josh, whose session is already underway. (I told you he never sleeps.)

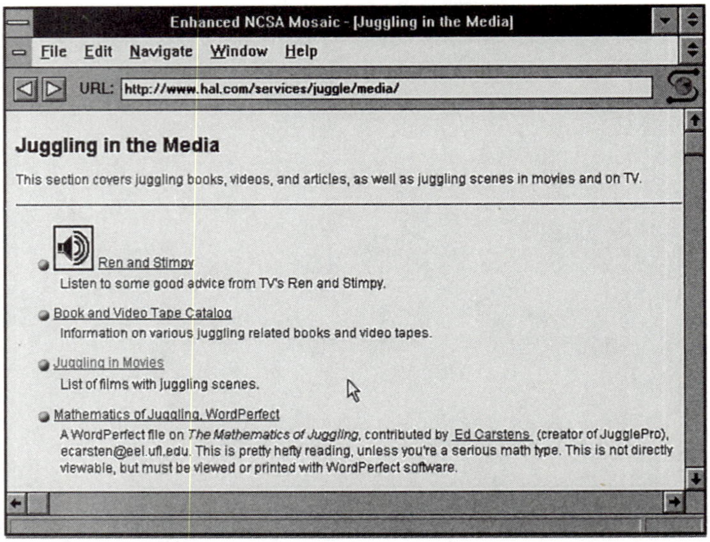

Figure 3.5. The "Juggling in the Media" page.

Joshua, Netsurf God

Josh can do what Emily just did—when he's looking for information on something that interests him he's like Sherlock Holmes with a keyboard. However, Josh isn't looking for anything in particular today. He's having fun, netsurfing, with no particular place to go.

Josh doesn't bother loading a home page. Instead, he starts the day by randomly checking a number of favorite hangouts, which he keeps in a hotlist much like the list Emily used to make note of the juggling page she liked.

Today he's hoping to get some concert information for the Gin Blossoms; he's also hoping to find a few games to play, and he thinks he might check out a UFO-related site a friend told him about. He starts his day by going to The Metaverse, Adam Curry's Web site for all things hip and happening. (This is a great and famous place on the Web; we'll talk about it more in Chapter 5.) They keep a pretty extensive list of these things, he figures. It must be there. He clicks on the

Navigate menu item and selects "The Metaverse" from his hotlist. Mosaic has the URL address, and it sends the commands over the Net to fetch the page.

By the way, I haven't really shown you a full Web page yet. The screens I've shown you are just that: one screen from various pages. A page can be of any length, though most are under eight screens. The Metaverse index page Josh is heading for is four screens long. I've scrolled down the page and taken four pictures—Figures 3.6, 3.7, 3.8, and 3.9. Together they should give you a good idea of how these things look.

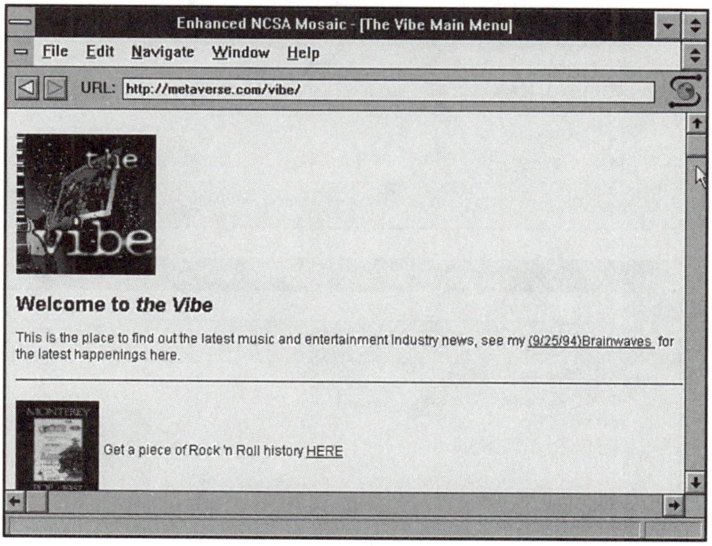

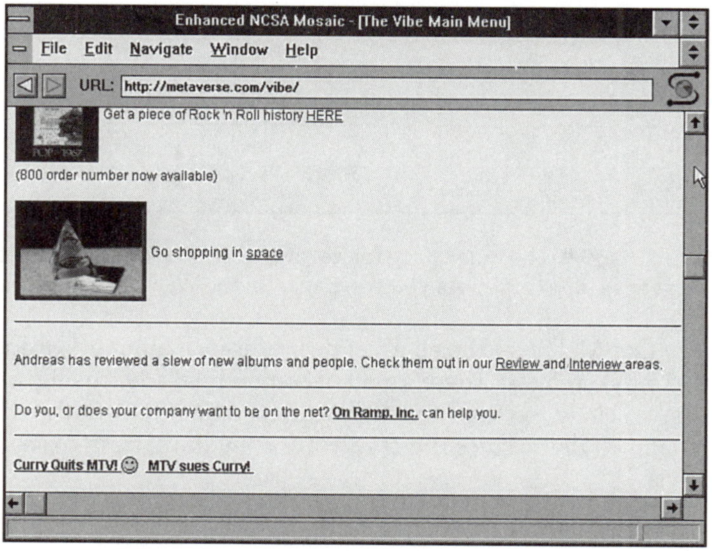

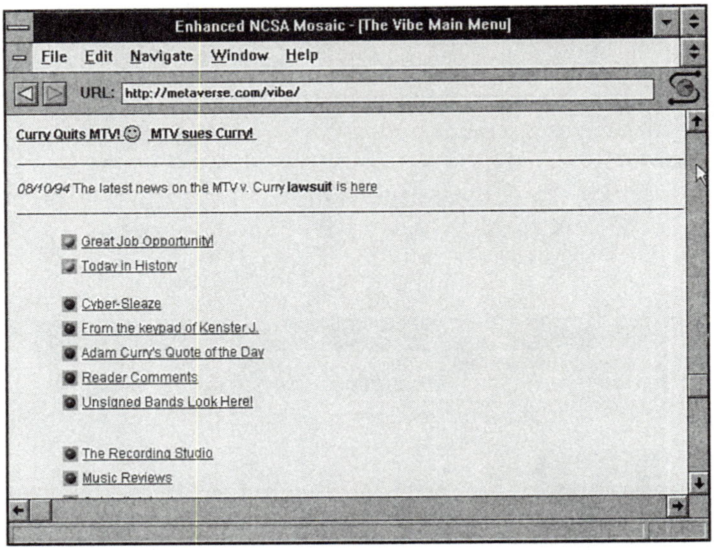

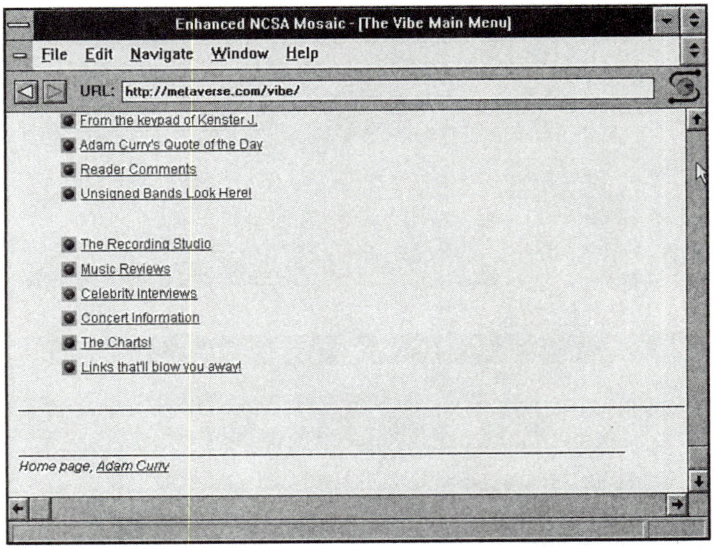

Figures 3.6, 3.7, 3.8, 3.9. The index page for `metaverse.com` (or, more properly, `http://metaverse.com/vibe`). As you see, pages on the Web can be quite lengthy.

You can see that Metaverse has a great deal of information on various subjects. Most of it is music-related. There's a bit of commercial advertising, and the folks in charge have several sections that they update daily. (Josh finds himself checking in here almost daily, since there's always something fresh to see.)

> **Note:** Like many other places on the Net these days, Metaverse is run by a company—you'll remember that Robert was doing the same thing in the preceding chapter. It's one of the nice aspects of the current state of the Net that it's economically feasible for so many companies to offer interesting spots to the Web, free for the accessing. Let's hope it stays that way as long as possible.

The "Concerts" link is near the bottom of the page. Josh clicks and gets an index of concerts, thoughtfully arranged in alphabetical order as shown in Figure 3.10. You'll see the Gin Blossoms in the "G" section. Josh clicks and checks the dates for concerts nearby. It's a page of text much like the page of movie juggling references Emily found, so we'll let him read it on his own.

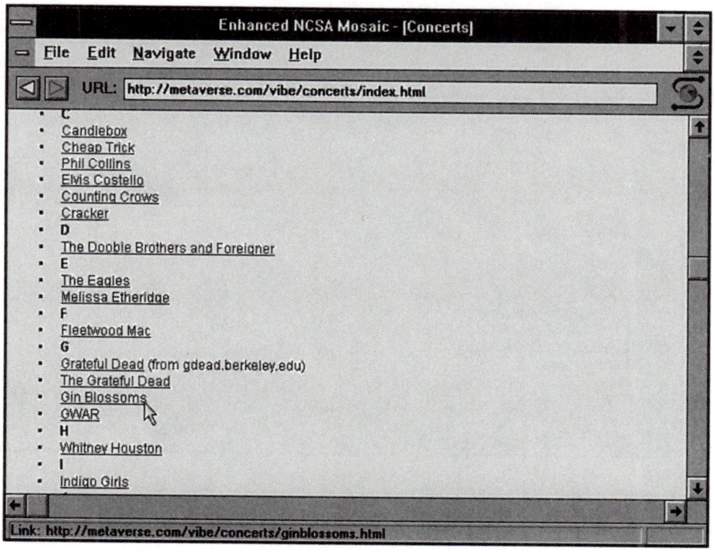

Figure 3.10. Concert listings on a Metaverse page.

Josh backs up a few screens to read the daily music gossip and browse through a few album reviews. After a while he decides to leave Metaverse for the day. Since he's still in a mood for music, he looks at his hotlist for other suggestions. He decides to check in at another favorite site, bianca's Music Listening Room. He's already seen the site, of course, but biancaTroll (the proprietor) has great taste in music and adds music-related links to her page whenever she finds something good during her own Netsurfing.

Note: biancaTroll is an entity—not a person, exactly—but she could easily be one person. Plenty of people create Web pages for their own pleasure and the pleasure of those who find the page. bianca's place is a particularly baroque and lovely example of this generosity—full of many great pages, of which this is just one. We'll spend some quality time at biancaTroll's place in Chapter 10.

Josh hasn't stopped in for a while, and the screen in Figure 3.11 has a link—"WNUR's Rock Info Base"—that he hasn't seen before. He clicks to check it out.

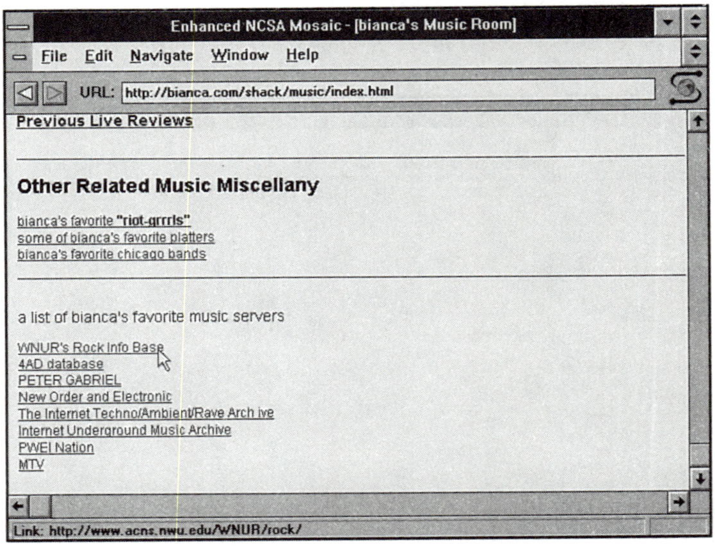

Figure 3.11. Visiting biancaTroll's music page at `http://bianca.com/btp/`.

The page is new—a Chicago radio station has decided to start putting music information online. For now they have an interesting list of alternative-press music magazines and an amusing "name-droppers' list" with brief biographies of various musicians. Josh thinks it looks promising and adds it to his hotlist; he'll want to check in again later.

He looks over the magazine info, and grumbles a bit because none of the magazines listed seem to have any site staked out on the Net. He's hoping that the magazine list will eventually have links to all these publications; someday, he thinks, he'll be able to skip paper magazines altogether and just pick them up online.

Note: Even though the magazines listed don't have their own Internet sites, many do. In Appendix D, "Things To See, Places To Do," I'll list several that you might enjoy. I'll also give you instructions on how to reach all the sites I mention in the course of the book.

He looks around the WNUR pages a little longer. He doesn't find any new links, so he decides to hop to a sure-fire site: the "Cool Site of the Day" page on `infi.net`. He moves again to his trusty hotlist and clicks on the menu entry he made when he found the site.

Glenn Davis is a friend to Netsurfers everywhere. On this page, he keeps a list of interesting (attractive, useful, unique) sites and posts a new one each day—as the screen in Figure 3.12 says, you never know where you are going until you get there. Josh has followed his recommendations many times.

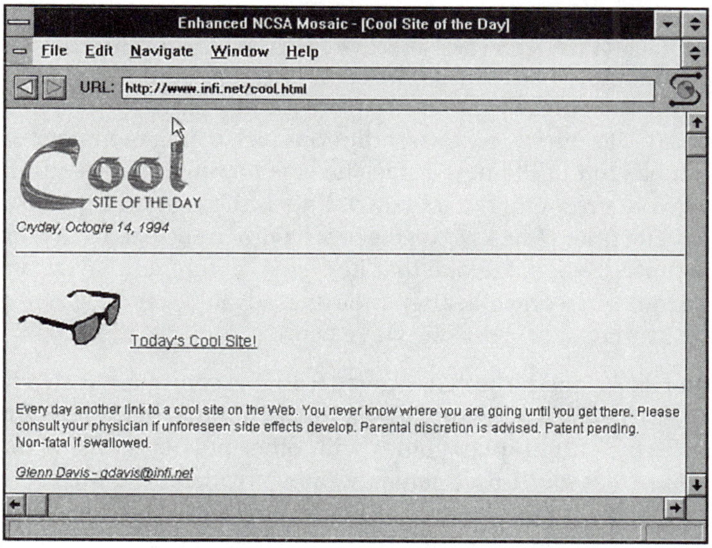

Figure 3.12. Glenn Davis' Cool Site of the Day, at `http://www.infi.net/cool.html`.

Josh has become fairly wise about figuring out what might be found in a new site; he rolls the mouse cursor onto the "Today's Cool Site" link and glances at the bottom of the screen to see what the link's URL address might be. The word "Games" is a good sign. Maybe Josh will get his wish for something new to play, maybe even one of the new Web games. (Otherwise, he thinks he'll try his luck at the latest Internet scavenger hunt.) At any rate, he doesn't remember ever having visited the `www.bu.edu` site. He clicks with great interest and gets... Figure 3.13.

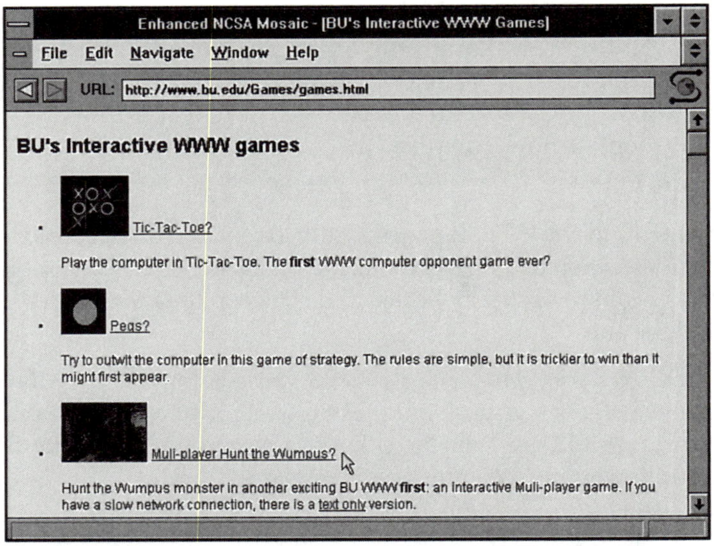

Figure 3.13. Voila! A collection of interactive games at Boston University. This cool page can be found at `http://www.bu.edu/Games/games.html`.

What can I say? It's one of those serendipitous Netsurfing moments; without even trying, Josh has found the new games he was hoping for. Serendipity—finding something wonderful without looking for it—is the heart of the Netsurfing experience. Regular surfers (the kind on the beach with the boards) talk with awe about riding the perfect wave, the one that just goes on forever. Netsurfers have that experience too, when one link after another leads to fascinating new places. Josh senses that he may have a serious wave here.

Lest disaster strike and he be called away from the computer, Josh adds this page to the hotlist. Tic-Tac-Toe is fine; Pegs is vexing but fun. Hunt the Wumpus looks great—it's always fun to play games with other people on the Net, and Josh is psyched to see that multi-user games are now available via Mosaic—but he can always come back. This Net wave feels right, and he's sure he hasn't checked this place out before. He rolls up to the URL: window, deletes everything after "edu," and hits return to get to the "top" of the computer that has this wonderful page. He's sure there's other great stuff here, and perhaps the top page will give him some ideas.

Hey, neat. Josh is at Boston University. He's directed to check out another page, which acts as an introduction to BU. He's never been to Boston, but this looks like a pretty great guide: restaurants, the BU campus, even a subway map (yes, they call it the T, but he doesn't know that). But wait—there's a link that says "Web puzzles and games." Puzzles *and* games? This bears closer investigation.

But wait again—he's been thinking about making his own Web page, and the previous page had a link to an introduction to writing Web/HTML documents. HTML is the set of codes that makes things in Mosaic look and work the way they do. Josh knows that it's easy to learn, but he hasn't bothered trying it yet. This Netsurfing session is obviously charmed; maybe there's something here that could be useful.... He backs up to the previous page and clicks, and he's looking at a list of files like we see in Figure 3.14.

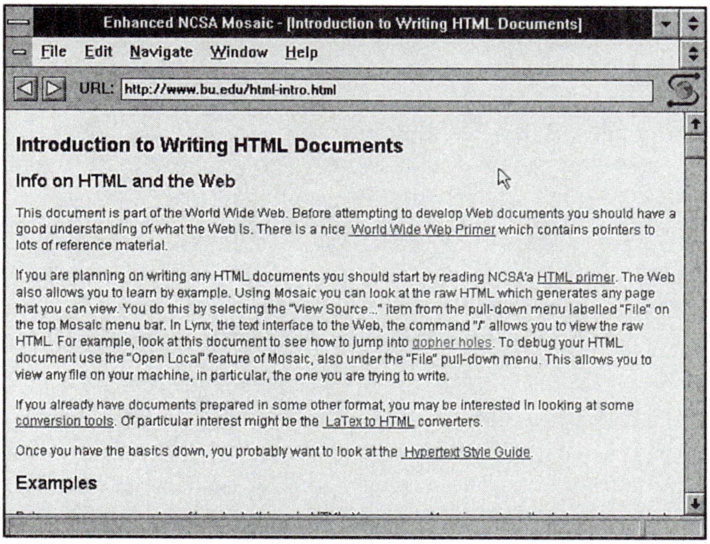

Figure 3.14. Instructions for creating Web pages, kept at `http://www.bu.edu/html-intro.html`.

He clicks a few times to figure out what's what, and with a couple more clicks downloads copies of the appropriate files to his hard drive. OK, that's a good day's work accomplished; he'll read those later. Now, about those puzzles *and* games....

One click, and he's off and running again.

And The Rest?

Meanwhile, Robert is designing a page not unlike some of the pages Emily and Josh saw in their respective travels; he could probably tell Josh everything that's in those files he collected. He's spending the day looking at the screen of his word processor. And he'd be the first to tell you that what they saw may have looked pretty straightforward (and it wasn't really that difficult to create once you know how), but the links they followed took them all over the place.

Emily may have been sitting in New York, but her day started on a computer in Switzerland, which in turn directed her to a spot stateside. (Her editor's next assignment involves finding out about snakes; she'll find a good site in the United Kingdom.) Josh started his travels on a computer in New Jersey, skipped off to Chicago, moved back cross-country to North Carolina to find out what the Cool Site of the Day might be, and hopped to Boston to check it. If he ever remembers to check out the UFO information his friend told him about, he may or may not notice that it's in Switzerland.

Robert's busy creating some of the pages they may see in their travels one day. The latest page is looking great, and pretty soon it'll be part of the Web, ready and waiting for anyone looking for information on his company (like Emily) or just wandering around (like Josh). Robert's no Net expert; all he really knows are the URL addresses of the places he wants people to link to on the Net from his own home page.

As you see, none of our three Mosaic users are experts about the inner workings of the Net. Emily uses it as a fast, efficient research tool; Josh uses it for entertainment; Robert uses it as a place to distribute information on his business. They all use Mosaic to do these things, in large part so they don't have to think about how to do them.

To put all this in context, almost everything you saw in this chapter was in fact one type or another of info-harvesting, which we described in the previous chapter. After this chapter you should have a good sense of what a normal day is like online with Mosaic.

In the next chapter I'll show you Mosaic's other tricks—what you can and can't expect it to do. The chapter gives you a quick overview of all the many tools that have been developed for hanging out and digging into the wealth of information and files on the Net. It should give you a good idea of the other possibilities for traveling around, finding things, and generally amusing yourself. After that, we'll close this section of the book by talking about what the Net can do and how Mosaic fits into it all.

CHAPTER 4

THE CAMERA, THE STAGE DIRECTIONS, AND THE MOVIE

"It's time to stop talking about the camera and start focusing on the movie."

—Michael Swaine, quoted in the second issue of *Wired*.

You've gotten a first glance at Mosaic—enough to say you've seen it, at least—and taken a look at a couple of real Mosaic users doing normal things. We'll take a step back to get an overview of what the Internet can do, one last look before you dive in for yourself.

I've talked about the four Internet food groups: info-harvesting, file transfer, chat, and e-mail. Of course, it's too much to ask that those activities use simple names like that on the Internet—that would be too simple, and the Internet is the home of difficult things like UNIX, after all. By the end of this chapter, I promise you won't be inundated with sticky technical stuff (let's try and keep that confined to the Mosaic setup chapters in Part II), but you will have a grasp on a few of the terms, concepts, and ideas you'll need to have under your belt. There are plenty of before-and-after pictures too—once you see the alternative, Mosaic will be looking better than ever.

I mentioned before that Mosaic can't quite do everything—for instance, the things Sophy does can't be accomplished (yet) with Mosaic. That's liable to change rapidly as more programmers get interested in adding to Mosaic's capabilities and as the various companies that sell commercial versions of the software race to outdo each other with attractive new features and capabilities. (In the time it's taken to write my way from Chapter 1 to Chapter 4, in fact, several advances have been made on that front.) And Mosaic is definitely the most flexible tool yet for exploring the Net; its shortcomings are real, but compared to the rest of the pack they're minor.

Meanwhile, shall we fling around a few tech terms—telnet, FTP, Gopher? As we go through the first part of this chapter, I'll be sure to tell you which of these strange and inscrutable words you can pretty much ignore once you have Mosaic, and which you'll have to deal with (usually with the help of a utility thoughtfully provided by whoever's supplying your Internet account). After that, we can think even bigger thoughts about what it all means for you, me and the rest of society.

The Internet in All Its Glory (Piece by Piece)

In the past, using Internet tools meant understanding the ins and outs of each tool's interface—and remember, these things were written separately, by different people at different times. Some tools, such as Gopher, are fairly sophisticated and flexible in their own right. (It's not coincidence that Gopher was created fairly recently, when the need for simple and powerful Net interfaces was becoming apparent.) Others, such as the various readers available for reading the thousands of Usenet newsgroups, are distinctly unfriendly to the average user.

Mosaic not only puts a pretty face on the Internet, it puts a consistent face on all these tools. This means that you usually won't need to worry about exactly what sort of tool you're using; you're using Mosaic, and Mosaic is in charge of working with the tool. (Don't you love delegating these responsibilities?) Still, it's good to know what to expect, since some of these tools will look slightly different to you, and you'll have Mosaic do different things with them.

I'll explain the various tools of the Internet in terms of the four Internet food groups. However, even the pre-Mosaic Internet tools were often flexible enough to do more than one thing, so I'll occasionally mention a tool more than once.

Info-Harvesting: WWW, WAIS, Gopher, Newsgroups, Telnet

Since Mosaic relies on the World Wide Web (WWW) to do its thing, I'll give pride of place to it and the other search and navigation tools. There are several, all designed to make Net travels easier and more organized. The newsgroups are not a tool but a resource, but you'll harvest information from them, too. And telnet is a tool of sorts, but it doesn't do any thing specific—or, rather, it can do almost anything.

World Wide Web

WWW, as I've mentioned, uses hypertext to navigate among documents that are linked together. The writers of the various documents are in charge of linking them; WWW browsers simply read the link information to move around. It's possible to use WWW without Mosaic (with, for instance, a piece of software called Lynx); the files appear onscreen as text, and the links are numbered. To hop across a link, you type in its number. In Mosaic, you don't see any numbers; you just click on the link as we saw in the introduction. (Of course, with Lynx you don't see any graphics or other neat stuff either, but that's why you've chosen to use Mosaic, right?)

Figure 4.1 shows "raw Web," as it were—this is how the Web appears when Mosaic's not there to translate it into beautiful screens.

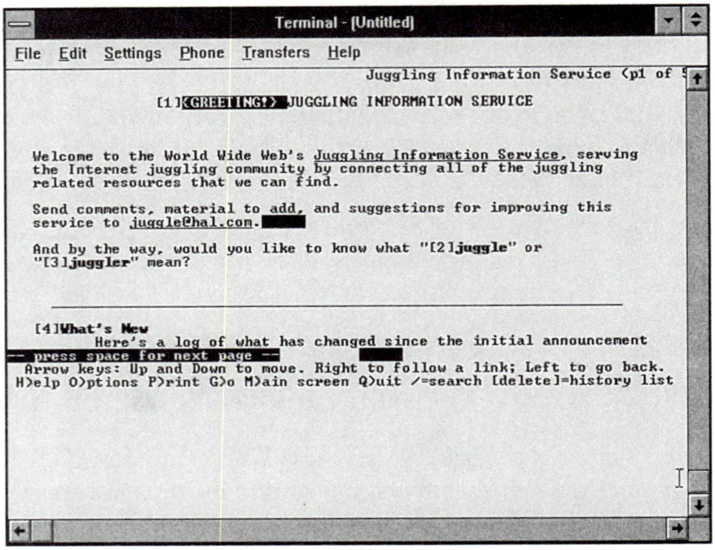

Figure 4.1. The unadorned Web. This is the juggling page we saw in the previous chapter—`http://www.hal.com:80/services/juggle`.

Figure 4.2 shows the same page once Mosaic does its thing. Graphics are the most obvious advantage of using a browser like Mosaic.

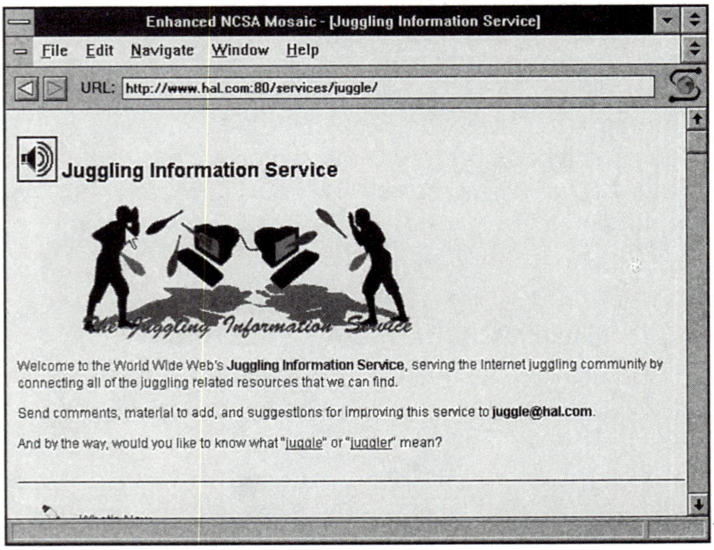

Figure 4.2. The Web as viewed through Mosaic.

WAIS

WAIS (Wide Area Information Service) is another popular info-harvesting utility. WAIS lets you search through articles and other files for specific words. This is useful if, for instance, you'd like to find files on a particular topic.

If you're not using Mosaic and you're looking for information about juggling and movies, for instance, you can do a WAIS search and it will bring back a list of all the files it knows about that have the words "juggling" and "movies" (or "cinema" or "film"—the art of using these things is knowing how to ask for information, as Emily will be glad to tell you). WAIS does this by using sets of indices created by the owners of the documents; it scans through them for keywords and reports back on its findings. There are a number of other WAIS-type tools available for searching, and we'll list those in Appendix D. Let's compare a WAIS search for "juggling" with the search Emily did in the previous chapter. In Figure 4.3 we see a basic WAIS search.

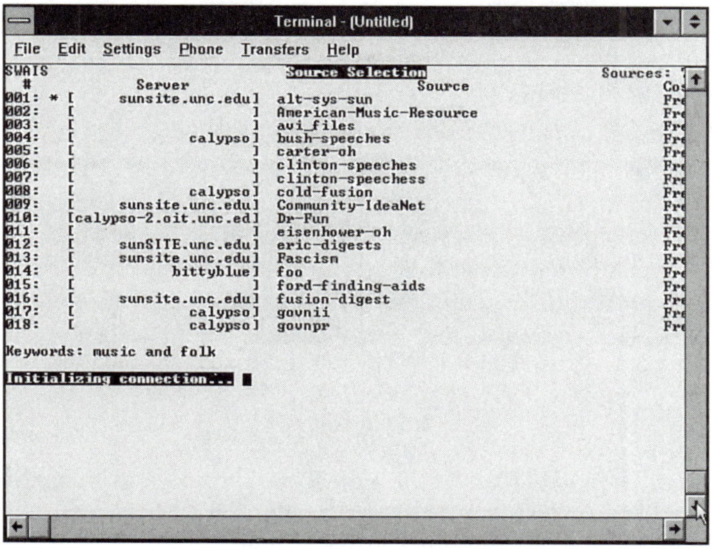

Figure 4.3. A text-based WAIS search.

Figure 4.4 shows the same search via the Web. This is the World Wide Web Worm, another one of the many search tools in Emily's arsenal.

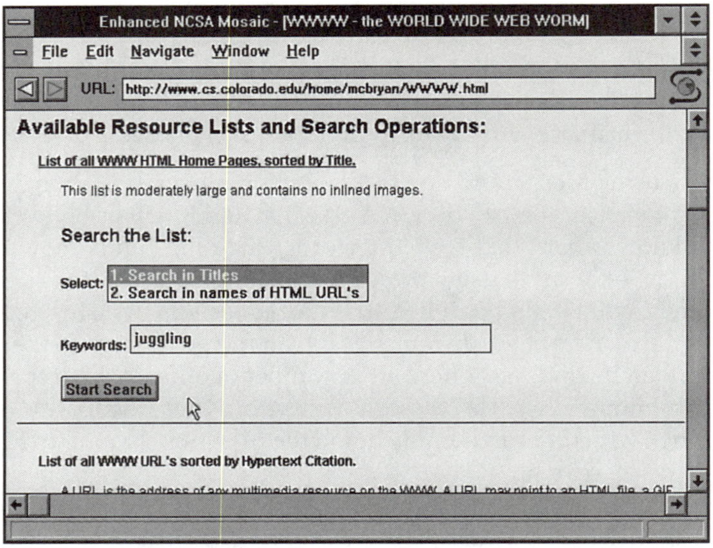

Figure 4.4. WWWW in action. The Worm lives at `http://www.cs.colorado.edu/home/mcbryan/WWWW.html`.

> **Note:** It's possible to do WAIS searches via the Web, if you find a WAIS site in your travels. You'll type "find" followed by the term for which you want to search. However, in most cases you'll get better results by using the Web-specific tools available.

Gopher

Gopher is another kind of search tool; it's fast and flexible, and before Mosaic came along it was the simplest way of using the Net. Like Mosaic, Gopher smooths things out by showing all the things it finds, no matter where or what format. It doesn't expect you to know how it works behind the scenes. However, it doesn't have hypertext links to other places; it simply gives you lists of information and tells you a little about what format the information might be in. Figure 4.5 shows you Gopher in text form.

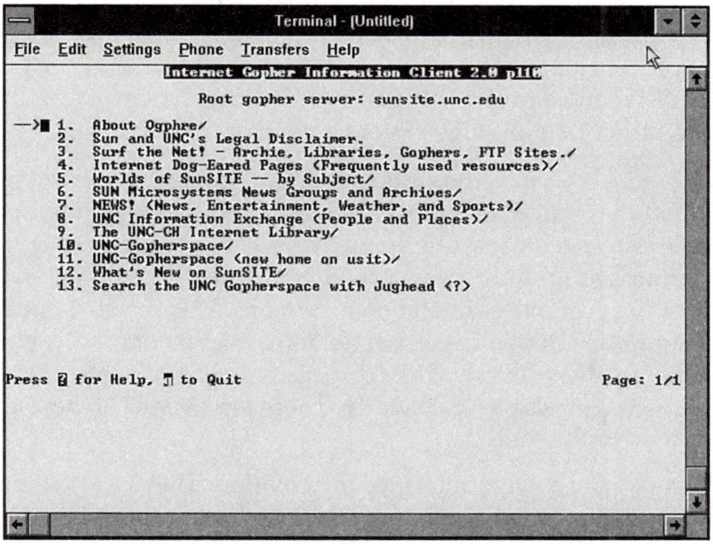

Figure 4.5. Gopher, the best precursor to Mosaic.

In Mosaic, Gopher sessions look a little like File Manager screens (as you see in Figure 4.6), with lists of what's available next to icons representing the format in which you'll find the file.To get at the information, click on the name of the file.

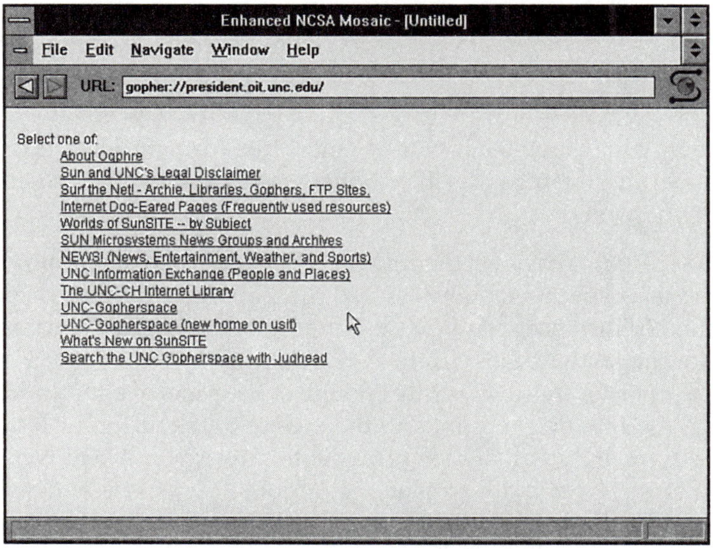

Figure 4.6. Mosaic checking into the same Gopher site.

Usenet

All these tools are geared toward finding information that has been placed on the Net. Some of the tools in the info-harvest category, however, tend to generate information rather than provide easier access to it.

First among these is Usenet, the system of discussion groups (called newsgroups or usegroups) that ranges across thousands of topics—some fascinating, some obscure, some strange, many utterly unconnected to computers or the Internet. The newsgroups are public areas to which people with similar interests send messages for the group to read and comment on. (This is called "posting a message.") Newsgroups can be sweet, contentious, informative, silly, obnoxious, or dull, but they're always fresh. They're all in a perpetual state of change, since people are posting messages constantly. There are over 6,000 newsgroups, and more are added each month.

The newsgroups are a great source of information. They're also a great way to find out what other users are thinking and doing. Your Internet provider will offer you access to the newsgroups; you will look over the titles (usually they have names such as `rec.skiing` or `alt.music.alternative.female`, both of which give you a good idea about what the topic of discussion is) and choose what interests you. Mosaic is able to look at newsgroups and let you read the messages in them. However, it can't yet help you post messages; like e-mail (see below), Mosaic support for news isn't quite available yet. Still, if you're looking for current information and discussion on any number of topics, Mosaic is a useful way of checking out the sprawling newsgroup system.

Telnet

Finally, there's telnet, which is both the most free-form info-harvester (read: rotten interface) and the most flexible. Telnet allows you to log onto another computer anywhere on the Net.

Wait, you say—isn't that what the entire Net does, log onto other computers? Well, yes. But telnet is special; it allows you to run particular programs kept on those computers. For instance, many of the computers that gather news and weather information make their most up-to-date information available via telnet. (And telnet is glorious for those of us silly enough to keep lots of e-mail addresses; you can always log into one account and then telnet to the rest to pick up the mail.) Telnet is a noun, but it's also been turned into a verb; you'll hear Net surfers talk about telnetting from place to place. In Figure 4.7, we see a telnet session in progress, as I use my local Internet connection to connect to a computer that would normally be a long-distance call away.

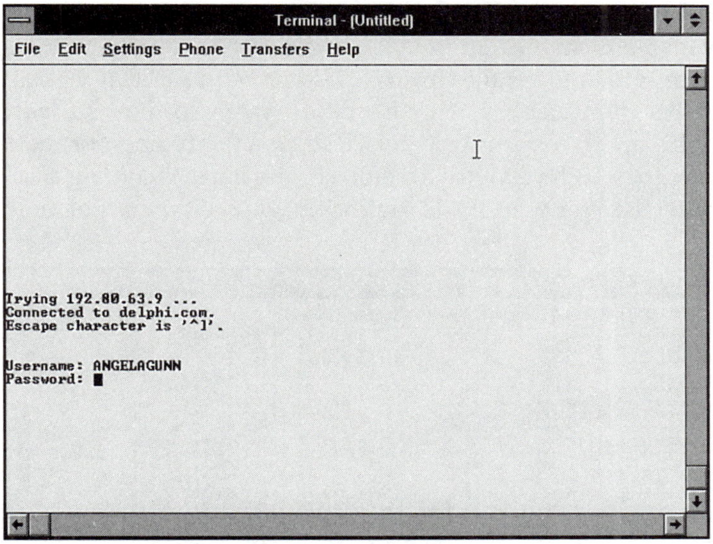

Figure 4.7. A telnet session in progress.

As I said, telnet is free-form; how you use it will depend on what you intend to do. Of course, Mosaic doesn't ask you questions like that. If you happen across something on the Net that's available by telnet, Mosaic is happy to hook you up—if you give it a telnet program to use. The interface isn't hypermedia; in fact, you're technically off the Web entirely. However, Mosaic will go back onto the Web when the telnet session ends. Makes sense—since there's no telling what you'll find in a telnet session, Mosaic very wisely stays out of your way while you're busy with that, returning as soon as you're ready. In Chapter 12, I'll go online with you to get a telnet program to use with Mosaic. (And since it will look like the telnet screen we saw above, we won't look at it again here.)

File Transfer: FTP, Gopher

File transfer, as I've mentioned, is a special kind of info-harvesting, in which you actually go onto the Internet, get a file, and make a copy onto your own computer. Mosaic does a great job of file transfer, much better than the older FTP utility.

FTP stands for file transfer protocol, and the term has also been turned into a verb, referring to the action of transferring files between Internet computers. Also, the term "FTP site" refers to a computer or directory that holds files available for FTP. And "anonymous FTP" is the process of logging into a distant computer and retrieving files.

It's not really anonymous. It's much better. A file available through anonymous FTP is available to anyone on the Net. You don't have to have an account on a particular computer to get files from it via anonymous FTP, if the system administrator of that computer has set up her or his system to allow such access. Under the old UNIX interface, you start an FTP session (by typing **ftp** and the name of the computer to which you wish to connect), and log in by typing **anonymous** when the computer asks for your ID. In Figure 4.8 you see the start of an FTP session.

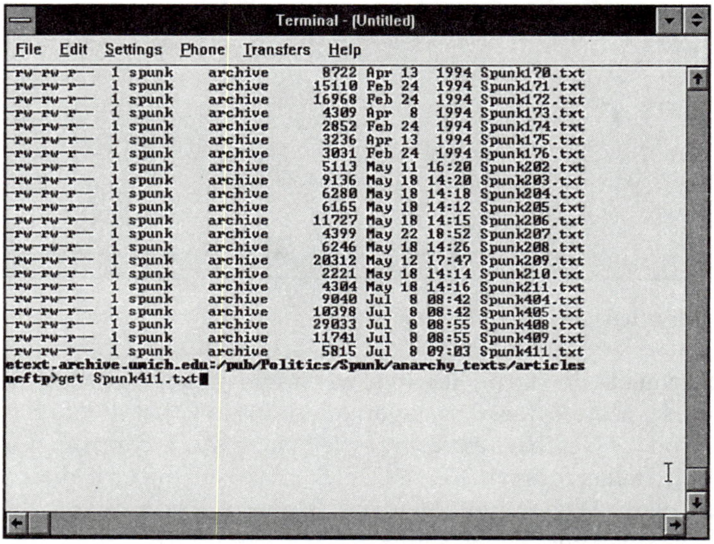

Figure 4.8. A plain-text FTP session.

Notice that it's asking for a password. It's considered good form to enter your Internet address as your "password" for the FTP session; it's mainly a matter of politeness ("netiquette"), but it does help system administrators figure out who's been visiting their site.

Mosaic makes all this moot. It's designed to do all the login legwork for you—making the connection, sending the word `anonymous` and your Internet address, and getting you information about the files available to you. Under UNIX you saw a list of files and a bit of information (file size and type) about each. Mosaic shows you the same thing, but in a list much like that used in a file-management program (as you see in Figure 4.9).

Each file is represented by its name; an icon showing whether it's a text file, one of the various kinds of binaries (programs, video, sound clips), a search index or a telnet link; and the size of each file. To transfer a file to your machine, just click on it.

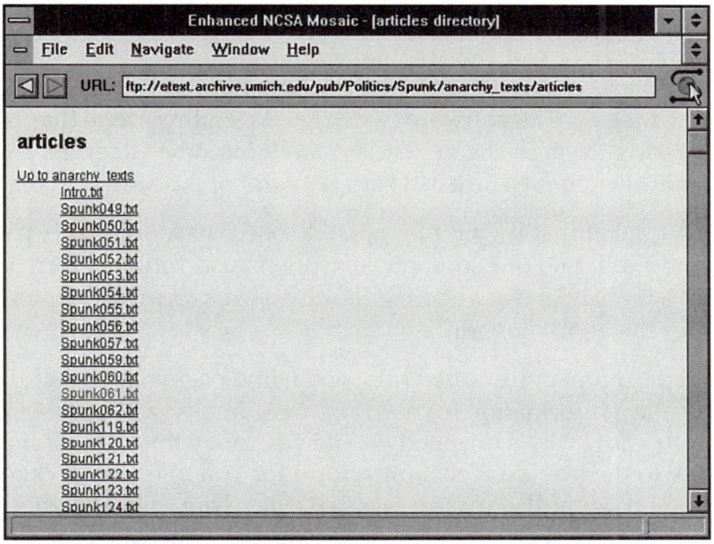

Figure 4.9. Mosaic at the same FTP site.

> **Note:** Text files are made mostly of normal letters, numbers, and punctuation. You can open an ASCII file in a regular word processor or in a simple editor such as Notepad and read it. A binary file is made of code—if you open it in a word processor you'll just see garbage. Programs, graphics files, sound clips, and videos are all binary files.

Mosaic makes file transfer much easier. Many of the sites you'll find in your Web sessions lead to FTP sites where you can pick up both text and binary files. However, with Mosaic you can currently only retrieve files; you cannot put them on the Net.

> **Tech Tip:** Mosaic is designed to automatically start an anonymous FTP session by sending the proper commands. However, some FTP sites don't do a "standard" (UNIX) version of anonymous login. Such sites give Mosaic a bit of trouble; fortunately, they're rare.

You can also transfer files via Gopher, as I described above. You'll notice no difference between transferring files via FTP and transferring them via Gopher; Mosaic uses the same interface for both. If you're not paying attention to the URL address of the place from which you're transferring, you might not realize the difference between one kind of session and another.

E-Mail: A World of Its Own

E-mail is the most-used function of the Internet. It's also by and large still beyond the reach of Mosaic. The software is designed as a browser—that is, it looks at things and sorts through them. Sending anything other than the commands to browse or retrieve files (which as I said is a kind of browsing) is very difficult.

That doesn't mean that it won't be possible one day soon. When you go online with Mosaic you'll find one solution currently in use: forms. A form is, of course, something with blanks that you fill in. Emily used a form in Chapter 3 when she searched for the word "juggling."

On some of the more sophisticated sites, you'll find pages that include forms. Often the forms collect information for a sort of guest book—whoever set up the page is so eager to know who's dropped by and what they think of the site that she or he has gone to the trouble of making a form for you to fill out. When you do so, the information is bundled up and sent to the page site, and from there it's moved into a special utility that sends the owner of the form your typed information. Some forms are capable of sending the information to their owners via e-mail. Others dump it into a database for further analysis, or just for storage.

But what about real person-to-person e-mail? Not yet. This is definitely Mosaic's greatest shortcoming. However, there are a lot of people who want to solve the problem almost as much as the users want it solved; expect to hear about mail capabilities in later versions of Mosaic.

For now you'll use one of the programs provided by whomever's supplying your Internet connection. One of the most popular Internet e-mail programs is called Pine. Also, if you happen to connect to the Net through a computer network at work or school you may use a mail program that has connections (called "gateways") to the Internet. A few of the most popular programs are cc:Mail, Microsoft Mail, and daVinci Mail.

Chat: Telnet

Chat—where people gather together in "cyberspace," type messages that appear on one another's screens a second or two later, and occasionally pretend to be small furry animals—is another popular pastime on the Net. It's particularly popular with people who don't need to worry about the clock ticking away—people connecting through a free account at college or on a work-sponsored network connection.

That's good, because chat eats up your time in a frightening fashion. Hours pass. Then more hours pass. All the while you're hanging out, chatting with whoever drops by, exchanging stories, and making friends. What, you say you're just waiting for the party to wind down? Get real. It has no reason to wind down. It's rumored that some of the chats in the largest and most highly trafficked areas (called MOOs or MUDs) have gone on for years. *Years.* A friend of mine once spent an entire day in a chat area, napping occasionally. No one minded; they just assumed she was being quiet. Reputable sources tell tales of friends who flunked out of college because they spent every day—16 hours each day—logged into the MUDs.

What could these people be talking about? After all, they don't know each other—do they?

Most chat habitués will argue that they do know each other. The psychology of chat is fascinating; many regulars speak of the bonds they form with friends and foes they've met in cyberspace. And these are not casual bonds, to be taken lightly or less seriously than interactions in the flesh. There's something very intimate about chat—you're usually sitting in a calm and comfortable space (often at home in your pajamas, as far as that goes), typing messages to other people in similarly relaxed circumstances. There's no pressure to dress or look a certain way, you have plenty of time to choose your words and digest the words of others, and bores (and usually boors) can simply be ignored. The sociology of chat groups is mainly uncharted and unexamined terrain, but there's definitely several hundred doctoral dissertations there—the group reality created strictly through words in the chat realms is fascinating.

Closely related to the chats are the multi-user games, where people meet to play various games of skill, adventure, or luck. A lot of these games are of the role-playing type, like *Dungeons and Dragons.*

> **Note:** The online services—America Online, Prodigy, and CompuServe in particular—also have large sections devoted to chat. The chats are currently only open to the members of the various services. One of the smaller online services, The Imagination Network, is almost wholly geared to chat and multi-user games.

Since telnet is possible in Mosaic (with a little extra software), chat is possible in Mosaic. However, you're not actually on the Web when you enter a chat group through Mosaic; as I mentioned, when you begin a telnet session in Mosaic you drop out of the Web. Mosaic offers no particular advantages for Internet chatting. Web-based multi-user games are, however, starting to appear (as Josh discovered in Chapter 3). They're interesting, but if you're calling the Net through a modem you won't be able to take advantage of the graphics due to the relative slowness of the connection.

It's Automagic!

Really, you don't need to know how any of it works—the file transfers, the searches, the links from place to place. But knowing what's going on back there will help you understand what you can do on the Net. It will help you understand what Mosaic is doing and working with. Also, you're likely to run into some of these terms in your travels; if you spend a few minutes with them now, they won't perplex you later.

A lot of the Internet works "automagically"—meaning that someone, somewhere wrote a program that does whatever it's doing, but almost no one but the programmer really knows the processes it's using. Serious gearheads use the term to refer to truly arcane mechanisms and pieces of code, but the term is too wonderful not to use for all the strange smaller programs that go into making Net navigation more or less smooth.

But What About the Movie?

So now you've seen a couple of Internet users in action with Mosaic, and have some idea of what it does (and doesn't). (You understand, of course, that no two, twenty, or 2,000 examples would encompass everything that's happening out there on an ordinary day.) Interesting, sure, but neither the Internet nor Mosaic would be worth this much fuss if it were just a matter of people essentially flipping channels to find something they like. Net surfing, channel surfing—there's got to be a difference, or there really is no point to all of this and I should be writing about something useful. Breakfast cereal. Felt-tip pens. The Gap. Something.

Here's the difference: Not only are you running the remote control when you're on the Net, you also have an opportunity to run the camera and plan the programming. The exciting thing about Mosaic and the Internet is that it makes it very easy not only to find things on the Internet but to put them up there yourself. If you don't choose to do that, fine—lots of people don't. But lots of people do, and it makes for an extremely vibrant, diverse, elegant cacophony of voices, opinions and information.

Personally (she wrote, clambering onto her soapbox) I think this makes the Internet and Mosaic worth the process of installing it, setting it up, and learning how to use it. Twenty-five million people on the Internet? You may get some argument about that figure, but no one will deny that growth over the past year or two has been phenomenal. A lot of people are getting online. A lot of businesses are getting online. And—perhaps most significantly—the various branches of government beyond the military are getting online.

That sounds like a great convenience for those people, moving files about and sending e-mail and so forth—but it also means that the Internet has the attention of a lot of folk who have power in your life. Time was when the town crier was the main source of such information, and democracy happened in town meetings and other small, personal gatherings. Then more people learned to read (and moved to the big cities), and newspapers became the place where we kept an eye on the workings of government and culture. Journalists and writers had a great deal of power—but there were fewer of them, and they were harder to actually meet and talk with. Then radio came along, and television, and the pundits and commentators (along with the odd camera-friendly politician) shaped the information you got and how you thought about these issues.

That's where we are today. Unfortunately, the odds are very good that you don't own a television station or host a radio show, nor do you have a lot of ability to talk directly with those who do. Whether you like it or not, you find yourself relying on people you don't know and can't reach to find things out and tell you about them. You depend on them to give you the best possible information on all the things you're interested in. That's a tall order. You'll almost certainly be disappointed in the results.

On the Internet, though, everyone has the potential to be a broadcaster of information, and has the potential to seek out information. Granted, the information is only going to be as good as the people and organizations providing it—but that's true with any medium. With 25 million people out there potentially telling truths, lies, and rumors, you're going to find that you have to think about the information you get to evaluate whether it sounds true, accurate, or reasonable. (But shouldn't you be doing that anyway?) The Internet, by giving you the ability to get more information on practically anything, can help you make decisions about the things in society and life that are important to you.

Up to this point the Net has been the home of a fairly homogenous group of well-educated souls who held in common a certain way of analyzing the world, if not always the same views (far from it!). As business and the government become more directly active, their opinions and voices will be added to the mix. And others are joining in; not a week goes by lately but another celebrity of some sort turns up online to hobnob with adoring fans and others. But each one is, after all, just another person logged into a computer, thinking onscreen. If you go online, you have access to them and to their ideas; if you put something of your own online, your voice is equally loud in the ears of the other 25 million. Sounds an awful lot like that old idea of democracy—but first you have to be there.

(She clambers off her soapbox.)

Of course, it's fun too.

Ready? There's a bit of work in your near future: The next section tells you how to get the software set up and ready to roll. I'm hoping our little chat has inspired you to put up with the inconvenience. After it's ready, we'll start checking out what's already on the Net for your enjoyment and edification. Later we'll plan how we'll change the world with it.

PART II

SETTING UP

The next three chapters are designed to go through the not-too-laborious process of getting onto the Net via Mosaic. We'll first cover the nine pieces of information you should gather before you start off—it may look like gibberish, but it's not that hard to understand (and once you type it in you'll never need to think about most of it again).

After that, it's time to think about how you intend to get on the Net. As I said before, there are two kinds of connections: those you pay for and those you don't. In Chapter 6 we'll take a look at the kind you pay for and use via modem—that is, the SLIP/PPP connection. In Chapter 7 we'll move on to the kind you don't pay for and don't need a modem to use—connections through a workplace LAN (local area network) or another large networked system, such as a university computer. You need only read the chapter that applies to your particular situation; once you've finished, you can move along to Chapter 8, where we'll start exploring the Net in earnest.

CHAPTER 5

WHAT YOU NEED

"If you don't eat your meat, you can't have any pudding. How can you have any pudding if you don't eat your meat?"

—Pink Floyd

No matter which type of connection you choose, there's a certain amount of information you'll need to set up your software. This information tells the software who you are on the Net, what access provider you use, how the Net recognizes it, and several other important addresses.

Once you set up Mosaic with this information, you don't need to remember it anymore; however, you should keep a copy on hand just in case. I've left spaces in this book for you to jot down the information; this way you know where to find it. (Nothing like losing that all-important Post-It Note, right?)

You'll get this information from whomever's in charge of your Internet connection. If you have a SLIP/PPP account, the public access provider will give you this information when you set up your account. If you use an existing network to connect, the administrator will have the necessary information—it may even be set up and ready for you, as I explain in Chapter 7, "Network Hookups."

Note: The software that's included on this book's disks—Enhanced Mosaic from Luckman Interactive—is designed to be as simple to install as possible. If you're just interested in getting online with Mosaic as quickly as possible, see the page facing the disks in the back of the book for a "quick start" installation. If you manage to successfully install the software, and if you want to continue to use Portal as your Internet access provider, you probably don't need to read this, or the following two chapters—you can skip directly to Chapter 8, "Basic Mosaic Skills."

If, on the other hand, you would like to use a different Internet access provider (see Appendix A for a list), or if you're just curious about the technical inner workings of the Internet, read on.

Getting Ready: Nine Pieces of Vital Information

Different TCP/IP software asks for different information about who you are and how your little corner of the Net is set up. Your package may not request all of these things (or it may ask for them by a different name). This chapter will help you understand what's needed.

The pieces of information you need are:

- Your IP address
- Domain address
- Gateway (or domain) name

- Domain name server address
- News server
- Subnet mask value (maybe)
- Username
- Password
- Miscellany (maybe)

DON'T PANIC! I promised that we were only going ankle-deep into the weirdness. Trust me on this one; by the time we're through this you'll understand very clearly what these things are—and you'll know exactly enough not to worry about them again.

Let's look at each piece of information separately. First, though, I think we've been bandying the term "TCP/IP" long enough. Let me explain. It'll make everything else that much clearer.

TCP/IP: How It Works

As I mentioned in the previous chapter, TCP/IP is the real language of the Internet. It's how the computers connect to each other and send the information back and forth.

TCP/IP is even more unlike English than UNIX is. In fact, it's technically not a language but a protocol—in other words, a set of rules for communicating, rather than the language itself. Think of it as grammar: proper grammar lets the computers on the Internet communicate without misunderstanding, just as proper English grammar helps me get my message across to you.

How does it work? As you may have guessed, there are two components working together: TCP (Transmission Control Protocol) and IP (Internet Protocol).

IP—Internet protocol—helps the computers on the Internet figure out what to do with every piece of information roaming around the wires. For instance, when you click on a Mosaic link, your software translates that into a command to go to a particular place. The software turns that command into a request to the computer at the place you want to go, asking that it allow you to connect to that computer. IP puts a note on each request with your address and the address of the place you want to go, and flings your request onto the nearest computer on the Net—that is, the computer you connected to with your own, your gateway to the Net.

Every Net computer knows about other computers. The computer gets your request, looks at the address of the site to which you wish to connect and asks itself if it knows where it might find that site. If it's acquainted with that site, it sends the request directly to it by whatever route has the few packets on it at that instant.

If the computer doesn't recognize the site, it asks another computer to take the request and see if it can't find the site you want. This process is repeated until the request gets to the site you want—a process that takes just a fraction of a second. I'll describe how this actually works a few pages from now.

Note: The piece of computer equipment in charge of checking the addresses and moving the packets is called a *router*. A router looks like a medium-sized box with a lot of phone jacks and cable ports in it. You will never need to own or even see a router. It's your network administrator's problem.

But let's say your request is split into several pieces (as it will usually be; the pieces of information that IP can handle are actually quite tiny, no more than 1,500 characters long). What happens if the second piece gets there before the first? After all, there's nothing that says they'll all follow each other along the same path; since the Internet is designed to use whichever path is most efficient at a particular instant, one chunk of your request might go through Atlanta on its way to Chicago, while another detours through Los Angeles before it hits the Windy City. If the computer looks at the pieces out of order, it won't make any sense. (Or, to put ourselves in that position: out of order it won't If the computer looks at make any sense the pieces. You see why grammar is important in these situations.)

TCP—transmission control protocol—is in charge of breaking up your request and numbering each piece. When the piece gets to wherever it's going, TCP on the other end looks at it, collects the pieces, and puts them in their proper order. If something happens to one of the pieces—if it gets lost or if something mangles it in transmission—TCP on the other end sends a message back to your computer to re-send the missing chunk.

Now that you know how the Internet does its work, you'll see that the information you need to get simply provides your vital statistics so the Net knows how to find your computer (and to explain to other computers who you are).

Your IP Address: Baby, It's You

Every computer on the Internet has its own address, of course; otherwise, you'd never be sure of getting the information you asked for. Since your computer is on the Internet, the first piece of information you should find out is the address IP will use for sending and receiving your packets. (Remember the description of dial-up connections? Those computers aren't directly connected to the Internet, so they don't have their own IP addresses. The Internet sends their packets to the access provider's host computer, and it takes responsibility for getting the information to the right account.)

Your IP address will be one long number—actually, four smaller numbers (each 254 or less) connected by dots (that is, periods—on the Internet, though, you'll call them dots. Heaven knows why). No spaces between numbers. For instance, here's my current IP address:

```
198.80.32.250
```

Not much to look at. However, it's the only one like it in the world. No one else has my IP address. And obviously it's no big secret—not like my password, for instance.

How do I know that my IP address is unique? All IP addresses are regulated by the Internet Assigned Numbers Authority, which relies on a smaller organization called the Internet Registry to do the day-to-day legwork of assigning groups of them to access providers, who in turn assign them to people like us.

In practice, it's your access provider that makes sure your personal IP address is unique. When she or he went into business, they obtained rights to a certain number of IP addresses. They are free to distribute them as they will.

When you get your IP address, ask your access provider or network administrator which IP addressing scheme your Internet site uses (don't worry if you don't know what you're saying; the administrator will). The usual answer will be "IP," which just means that your IP address is yours, all yours.

However, some systems are designed to give out IP addresses on a case-by-case, login-by-login basis; when you sign off, somebody else on the network gets to use your IP address. The systems that allow this are called BOOTP and RARP; if your site uses these, you'll need to make sure your TCP/IP software can handle it. Your network administrator or access provider can give you the details—however, both systems are fairly uncommon, and when in doubt you can assume that you're using good old IP.

Let's get interactive: Write your IP address here for safekeeping.

My IP address:

____

Gateway Address: Home Sweet Home

Your computer has an IP address, and it is indeed a real live computer on the Net. However, you still need your access provider's host computer to get through; that's where your account information is kept, after all. Your access provider's computer acts as a gateway between you and the Internet. You'll need to know your host's IP address—called a gateway address or domain address—in addition to your own.

Like your IP address, the gateway address is a unique set of four numbers (under 223) connected by dots and without any spaces. The IP address of the domain `pipeline.com` (my Internet access provider) is:

```
198.80.32.2
```

Again, no big secret. In fact, you can go onto the Internet and look up such things. And that's the job of the next piece of our puzzle. For now, though, write your gateway address here.

My gateway address:

____

Your gateway address is also known as your domain address—you may see it referred to as such in some TCP/IP installation manuals. Don't let it throw you.

Domain Name: What Are Words For?

By now, you can see that the numbers that make up your IP and gateway addresses aren't entirely random; they have a definite structure. (You may have noticed that they have a pattern, too, and I'll explain that in a bit.) However, it can be very difficult to remember even the few numbers it takes to set up your own Internet connection—much less the IP addresses for every single place you might want to go on the Net!

That's why most places on the Net have unique names in addition to their unique numbers. Like the addresses themselves, domain names are handled by the Internet Registry.

Domain names, like IP addresses, have a well-regulated structure—and you can even learn something from a domain name. Let's look at a few. For instance, here's the domain name of my Internet provider:

```
pipeline.com
```

This domain name has two parts: the name of the service itself (`pipeline`) and a top-level domain (`com`). They're separated by—you guessed it—a dot and no spaces. The name of the service was chosen by its owners; `com` indicates that this is a commercial Internet site.

Many Internet providers use a system of top-level domains that indicate whether the provider is a commercial site (a public access provider or even a business with its own domain, an academic institution, part of the government, or so forth. Knowing these can tell you a bit about the organization behind the address. Let's try another one:

```
oregon.uoregon.edu
```

This address has a subdomain—`oregon`. The `uoregon.edu` site is rather large—it's a big university—and so the administrator subdivides access among several computers. `uoregon` is the domain, and `edu` is the top-level domain; in this case, an educational institution. (By the way, this is a very straightforward domain name as these things go. Many subdomains are blessed with names that reflect the interests of the administrator. If you start reading domain names you'll see plenty of references to *Star Trek*, the *Lord of the Rings* trilogy, *Hitchhiker's Guide to the Galaxy*, and other passions of the individuals in charge of the various sites.)

> **Note:** The most common top-level domains are `com` (for commercial providers and businesses), `edu` (for educational institutions), `gov` (for entities that are part of the U.S. government), `int` (for certain international organizations), `mil` (for U.S. military installations), `net` (for various networks and certain administrative parts of the Net), and `org` (for research outfits, non-profits, and other unclassifiable creatures).

Of course, it would be too much to hope that this system applied to every site on the Net. Here's one to confuse you:

```
well.sf.ca.us
```

This name looks different; it uses a top-level domain based on geography. This site is based in San Francisco (`sf`), which is in California (`ca`), which is in the United States (`us`). The site itself is called the WELL (short for Whole Earth 'Lectronic Link). The two-letter geographic domain names are used internationally, and every country has its own two-letter code. Some of these are obvious, such as the United States' `us` domain; others, such as `eh` for Western Sahara, may not spring immediately to mind.

In any case, you'll become quite familiar with domain names; you'll see them again when we look at URLs, the addresses for finding resources via Mosaic. Also, your domain name is part of your Internet address, for instance:

```
agunn@pipeline.com
```

Your username goes to the left of the "at" (@) sign, and the domain name goes to the right. We'll deal with your username later; for now, write your domain name here.

My domain name:

____

The Internet Registry in the Soup

Once upon a time—two or three years ago—the Internet Registry had a comparatively easy time of it. It was clear that there was growing interest in the Internet, but things were progressing smoothly and by and large everyone was very gracious about choosing a suitable domain name and not making a fuss about it. The Registry, which is handled by the InterNIC Registration Service (which is in turn managed by a company in Reston, Virginia called Network Solutions Inc.), had an important but relatively simple task, and all was well.

Those were the days. With the explosion of Internet providers, particularly in the commercial area, the Registry has found itself in the middle of several controversies. Imagine playing Solomon to a few of these:

Adam Curry vs. MTV. Adam Curry, at the time a VJ on MTV, decided to set up a site on the Internet to give fans access to various bits of music information and trivia. He chose the domain name `mtv.com`. `mtv.com` proved to be quite popular, and as time went on Curry's interest in maintaining and improving it grew, while his interest in VJ'ing waned. One day he announced his resignation—on the air—and declared that he would be devoting his energies full-time to `mtv.com` and to OnRamp, the company he formed to help others get onto the Net.

MTV wasn't necessarily interested in Curry's Net site, but they had by no means ruled out creating a Net site of their own—and they'd prefer to call it `mtv.com`, or at least they'd prefer that Curry not confuse the issue by using that name for his site. They sued Curry, and Curry sued MTV, and no one knows quite yet what will happen. As of midsummer, Curry's site was using the name `metaverse.com` during the litigation.

Stanley Kaplan vs. The Princeton Review. Students preparing for the SATs and GREs will recognize both of these names as major test-prep centers. However, anyone checking into `kaplan.com` for information on Stanley Kaplan courses will be somewhat surprised that they're connected to the Princeton Review site. The Princeton Review folks, thinking very quickly, snapped up the rights to `kaplan.com`. A court case in the fall of 1994 returned the use of the name to Stanley Kaplan.

Josh Quittner, Hamburglar. Joshua Quittner, one of the leading reporters on the cyberscene, had been covering episodes such as these for some time. He was writing a story about the situation for *Wired* magazine when he discovered that McDonald's (yes, the fast food chain) hadn't reserved the domain name `mcdonalds.com`. And no one at McDonald's seemed particularly interested in it when he called to ask. In the spirit of experimentation, Quittner grabbed the name and announced the acquisition in his article.

The mail began to flow to `mcdonalds.com`. Some people encouraged Quittner to sell the rights to the domain name back to McDonald's for a healthy fee; some suggested that he use the site to lobby the company for changes, such as veggie burgers.

McDonald's, meanwhile, was not amused. At all. And when they made a fuss to the Internet Registry, the Registry attempted to shut down Quittner's `mcdonalds.com` while they sorted the mess out. But the shutdown generated a fuss of its own, and at press time Quittner's still holding rights to `mcdonalds.com`. Much to his own amusement, I understand.

The *Max Headroom* Wars. As I mentioned, many sites are named somewhat whimsically, according to the interests of whomever's in charge. That's fine for subdomain names—which don't need to be unique—but when two providers both decided to take as their domain name `network23`, the name of the TV network that was the setting for the *Max Headroom* TV series (another cult favorite), something had to give.

Unfortunately, both providers felt rather strongly about their choice of name, and the nasty e-mail flew. In the end, the first provider to register the name kept it (`network-23.com`); the second had to be content with the shorter `net23.com`. However, this solution wasn't perfect. At last report, the similar site names were confusing many Net users, who accidentally send mail to the wrong site on a regular basis. Still, neither side will budge; expect such impasses to become even more common as the Net expands.

Domain Name Server Address: Keeping Track of Who's Who

As you might have guessed, domain names are a convenience for users, not an accepted form of IP address. To use a domain name, you must have access to a *domain name server* (DNS). A domain name server (or "name server") translates domain names into domain addresses and vice-versa.

The DNS does its job before you make your connection, as I mentioned earlier in the chapter. When you type in a URL in Mosaic, the application glances over the portion that includes the domain name of the Internet site you're seeking, and it forwards the name to the local DNS. If the DNS recognizes the site and knows its IP address—if, for instance, you're simply moving to a different file on the computer to which you're currently connected—it sends back the IP address and the application proceeds with whatever it was supposed to be doing. (Again, all this takes a fraction of a second.)

If the local DNS doesn't recognize the address, it wrinkles its silicon brow and starts to dissect it. It looks first at the very right-hand end of the name to find out the top-level domain, and then it sends a message to the root server asking where to find the DNS server in charge of keeping track of all domains in that top-level domain. It then contacts that DNS server and asks for the IP address of the desired domain; if there's a subdomain, it contacts the domain to get the subdomain's IP address, and so on. This is all, thankfully, invisible to the user, and it really beats looking up the address yourself.

Life Before DNS

It's possible that your network doesn't use a domain name server; an older system, called a *hosts* file, still survives on some computers. A *hosts* file holds the names of computers with which the system is familiar along with their IP addresses.

Back when the Internet wasn't adding a million-plus users each month and thousands of domains each year, administrators maintained the *hosts* list and periodically sent fresh copies to all the computers on the network. Of course, that's not feasible anymore. There's simply not time—lists would go out of date literally within hours.

Also, the hosts system was most effective back when the Internet was situated mainly in the United States. Now that it's internationally connected, it's much easier to have each country handle its own domain-name requests (remember, there's a top-level domain for almost every country, so there's no danger of duplication of domain names from country to country).

Finally, using DNS rather than hosts allows the process to be decentralized. Instead of making the InterNIC crew directly responsible for all domain names, DNS enables different people to choose different parts of the domain name without fear of duplication. For instance, when Pipeline added a remote-access server, they were free to name it `remote.pipeline.com` without consulting anyone. They had responsibility for the name, since `remote.pipeline.com` is a subdomain of `pipeline.com`.

Domain name servers don't have domain names of their own in every case; at any rate, you won't need to know it yourself. Domain names are, once again, just a convenience for humans, and humans rarely have direct contact with the DNS. So here's another IP address to write down, use, and forget. It looks much the same as all the others. In my case, it's `198.80.32.3` with the usual four numbers, separated by dots, with no spaces. Write your domain name server address below.

My domain name server address:

____

Some installations will ask if you have a secondary domain name server. If you do, your access provider will tell you. Either way, it's nice to have a second, but it's not terribly important either way. The software at the back of this book asks about both a primary server and an alternate (secondary) server.

News Server: All the News That's Fit to IP

To reach the Usenet newsgroups—the vast systems of public discussion areas—you'll need to find a news server and connect to it. Most TCP/IP software will let you choose a news server either by name or by IP address; in most cases, the software even comes with a news server pre-chosen for you.

Ask if your access provider recommends a particular news server. They may have one of their own right on the system. Write in the name or IP address or your chosen news server below. However, unlike most of the other pieces of information you're gathering in this chapter, it's possible that you may decide to switch news servers at some point; if you find one you like better (some carry more newsgroups than others, for instance), you should feel free to switch as long as you can get permission and access from the administration of the new news server.

`My news server address:`

____

Your package may not ask for the name or address of your news server during installation (Enhanced Mosaic, which is included with this book, doesn't). Don't worry; it's still good to know and it will come in handy if you decide you'd like to occasionally read Usenet news with Mosaic.

Subnet Mask Value: Method to the Madness

By now you may have noticed that the addresses on my system follow a pattern: the first three numbers are always the same—`198.80.32`. Only the last number changes—2 for the domain, 3 for the DNS, 250 for my personal address.

The subnet mask helps the network administrator or access provider to keep your little portion of the Net organized. Pipeline's subnet mask looks like this:

```
255.255.255.0
```

255 and 0 are the only two numbers you'll ever see in a subnet mask. Furthermore, there are only three possible subnet masks: `255.0.0.0`, `255.255.0.0`, and `255.255.255.0`. And your administrator or access provider should know exactly which one to use. When they tell you, write it here:

`My subnet mask:`

____

Note: You may never see a subnet mask at all—the software at the back of the book, for instance, fills that information in for you.

Username: Who Are You?

The worst is over. Of course, you actually have to memorize the next two items, so I suppose it depends on your definition of "worst." Your username is who you are, the name you use to present yourself to the world. It's generally a one-word name, and it can be as formal or as cheesy as you like. Mosaic doesn't use your username or password, but of course you'll need them to get connected to your access provider. (If you use a network school at work to access the Internet, you already have your username and password.)

You choose your username when you set up your account with the administrator or the access provider. The only requirement is that it be unique; no one else on your network or provider can have the same name. (Some sites, however, don't allow you to choose a name that could be considered offensive or unsuited for use in polite conversation. We try to be adults online, as much as possible. Really.

You'll find that there are other restrictions on usernames, but those are created by the system itself. For instance, you usually can't use a space in your Internet account name. Internet users often get around that restriction by using the underscore (the character you get when you press the shift and the hyphen keys). Your name would then look like this:

Your_name

There's no single accepted way of mangling your name for Internet use, though. My name could be any of the following: `agunn`, `angela_gunn`, `ag`, `angela_g`, `angelag`, `gunn`, `angela`, `angela-gunn`, `a-gunn`.... You get the idea. If at first you find that someone else is using your name, try, try again. (Perhaps someone should tell that to Stanley Kaplan, mentioned earlier.)

> **Note:** Some Internet access providers, such as America Online, allow you to have spaces in your username. Those spaces will be filled in by the access provider when you sally forth onto the Net.

Of course, if you're feeling creative the sky's the limit. Just try to make it easy to remember; sometimes an unusual word that you happen to be fond of is a great choice. (You might want to avoid using the names of favorite TV or movie characters, though—trust me, there are plenty of `Mr._Spocks` out there. It's been done.) Write it here, and then tell all your friends:

`My username:`

____

Your username is also known as your account name, your login name, or simply your name. In most situations, you'll know exactly what they're asking for.

Password

Your username should be easy to remember. Your password should be impossible to guess.

You'll choose a password when you choose your username. However, unlike your username, you can (and should) change your password often. The password is the key to your Internet account; if someone has it, they can login and pretend to be you. This is bad—bad for security, bad for anyone whom the intruder annoys or offends while disguised as you, and very bad for your monthly bill. Think of it as someone stealing your credit card—only with your Internet account, it's even harder to prove that it wasn't you that ran amuck.

You'll find that the system administrators and access providers use several methods to keep you on your toes about protecting and changing your password. For starters, many software packages will not let you store your password on the computer in the way that you can store the rest of the information I've listed in this chapter. You'll simply have to remember your password. (And don't write it down on or near the computer; if you really must write it at all, jot it on a slip of paper and keep it in your wallet. It's that important.)

Also, many systems will not allow you to use words that can be found in the dictionary. This protects the systems from hackers who might try every word they can think of to break into an account, either by typing in words randomly or using a program that tries every word in the dictionary. This is called the "brute-force" method—as opposed to more elegant ways of deducing or discovering the proper password—but it doesn't take much brute force to test super-obvious words such as "password" or your own name. Also avoid the names of family members, pets, important dates, nicknames—anything that someone might somehow associate with you.

A Word About Hackers

A hacker is a person who investigates other computer systems, usually by "borrowing" the username and password of someone on the other computer. Many hackers are simply very intelligent, very curious people who like exploring, or enjoy testing their computer skills again a Net site's security system. However, some so-called hackers are nasty customers, bent on committing acts of computer vandalism and even theft. Real hackers tend to look down on the vandals and their ilk, not least because it takes more skill to not trash a system than to simply trash it. However, the term "hacker" has, quite unfairly, come into popular use to mean everyone who gains unauthorized access to a computer system. And because a small minority of hackers are nonetheless so dangerous, every Internet user must remain on guard against all hackers.

Use a mixture of upper- and lowercase letters. The system is case-sensitive when it comes to passwords, and the hacker who guesses the phrase `helloworld` might not catch `hEllOworLD`. Also, throw in an item of punctuation—`hEllO!worLD!` is actually a pretty good password. (Not now that it's in a book, of course, but you get the idea.)

And do not give anyone your password unless you know who they are, why they need it, and when they'll be finished—and once they're finished, change your password immediately. (This applies even when you tell your password to a friend.) And never, ever give your password to anyone who phones you. Again, think of this as a credit card, and guard it accordingly.

After that? Don't even think of writing your password here!

Miscellany: Remote Servers, Proxy Servers, and Other Oddities

Certain software packages may ask you for other pieces of information. Odds are that you won't need this information to configure your package, or that the information doesn't apply. Still, a brief explanation can be helpful, just in case.

A *remote host* is a computer to which you plan to connect fairly frequently. If your access provider is using a domain name server, you should not encounter this question, since it's designed to help you set up a hosts file. Ask your access provider what gives. If you really are stuck answering this question, expect to give both a domain name and an IP address for the remote host.

A *proxy server* is a form of protection set up by the system administrator or (less commonly) an access provider. As I mentioned, hackers are a big problem on the Net; as more businesses come online, awareness of the problem increases. And since no business wants to leave itself and its sensitive secrets exposed to possible hackers, several methods have sprung up to provide a "firewall" between users and the Internet. We'll cover firewalls and proxy servers much more thoroughly in Chapter 7.

Some programs ask immediately about your TCP/IP transport. They're asking what TCP/IP software you use. If you dial in, you probably use a transport that's Windows Sockets-compatible. Otherwise, check with your systems administrator for details.

Some software lets you name your PC, if someone hasn't already. If you connect to the net over a local area network, the system administrator may have already named your computer, and you should not rename it. Otherwise, you can call it anything you wish (again, though, try to keep it clean, if only because you never know who will see it and misplace their sense of humor).

Net users connecting by modem will need to know the phone number on which their modem can call the provider.

On Your Mark, Get Set...

We're about to split into groups temporarily. Those of you using a modem to connect to the Internet will move to the next chapter; those of you hooking in through a local area network will skip Chapter 6 and proceed directly to Chapter 7. Onward, ever onward!

CHAPTER 6

DIALUP CONNECTIONS: SLIP AND PPP

"To attempt to be a backwoods homesteader in an electronic technology may be as misguided as attempting to be Hindu when one is Anglo-Saxon."

—Tom Robbins

So you're connecting via modem—if you're not (if you're using a network connection), please skip this chapter and proceed directly to Chapter 7, "Network Hookups." Your next mission is to find an Internet public-access provider that will give you an account and let you use her or his computer to hopscotch onto the Internet. Before we start, though, we need a couple of special items to get your system ready for Internet travel. Also, let's take a second to be sure that your computer is mean and lean enough (or fast and big enough, as it were) to run Mosaic.

In addition to the Mosaic software—more on that in a second—you'll need the following items:

- 9,600 bps (or faster) modem—also known as a V.32, V.32bis, V.fast, or V.34 modem
- Serial port with a 16550 UART chip (or the equivalent)—for PCs with external modems only
- TCP/IP software—which is included with our version of Enhanced Mosaic on the disks in the back of the book
- SLIP or PPP account on a public-access provider (see below for details on an account with Portal).

Also, Mosaic requires a certain amount of computer firepower. PC users will need 4 MB RAM (preferably 8 MB), a hard disk drive, and Windows 3.1 or later running in enhanced mode. It's also best to have a 486, though a 386 will work (albeit very slowly).

What Have I Got Against Modems on the Net, Anyway?

A couple of times in the course of the book I've alluded to the idea that Mosaic users that don't rely on modems are getting off easy. Before we continue, let's clarify why connecting the Internet by modem is sometimes worse, and sometimes better, than connecting through an established network.

As a modem user, the main drawback to your connection is speed, or lack thereof. The Internet is very fast, but on your computer it will be no faster than your modem (and the modem on the access provider's system). Also, it's likely that you're connecting from home, or at least from a place where there's no one but your access provider (and this book) to help you through the process of installing and taking care of your software. It's nothing to be afraid of—once the software is installed, you're pretty much home free—but you'll need to carefully follow the installation instructions. Finally, you (not your employer or college) will probably be paying for your connection.

> **Note:** Many parts of the country are lucky enough to have access to Free-Nets. Free-Nets provide free Internet access (free except for the cost of the phone call, that is). They're not perfect—sometimes they don't offer as much Internet access as the commercial access providers, and that includes access to the Web—but they're a great way of trying out the Net.

But there are advantages too. Since you're running the show, you can choose the software you use once you're on the Net; no one can tell you what to put on your computer. Also, if you're connecting on your own, you are free to do as you will (within the bounds of legality and your access provider's rules). Unless you're signing on under the name of a company or some other institution, you own your own words online. If your Internet connection was owned by the company for which you worked, the law says that they have the right to see anything you write or do online. You'd also have to make it clear when you were and were not speaking as a representative of the company. As you see, getting your own modem-based Internet account has its advantages.

What Do I Need Again?

You're already familiar with modems—that's the tool that connects your computer to the telephone line. You'll need a fast (9,600 bps or better) modem to handle the connection; a slower modem simply can't cope with the demands of the network or the software. Fortunately, such modems are now selling for well under $100.

Windows users, if you have an external modem (one that sits outside the computer and most likely has blinking lights), you need to make sure that the serial port that connects the modem and the computer is up to snuff. What you're checking your machine for is a special chip called the 16550 UART (pronounced you-art). The best way of finding out if you have this chip is to ask the company that sold you the computer. Or you can check for yourself by running a program called MSD, which is included in Windows.

> **Tech Tip:** To check your UART with MSD, go to the DOS prompt and type `MSD`. The program takes a few seconds to look at your system and gives you a screen full of various information. On that screen, there's a box labeled "COM ports." Type `C` to open the COM ports information box. The UART will appear at the bottom of the box. Hit Escape and then F3 to exit MSD.

If you have an earlier UART chip—an 8250 or a 16450—throw a brick at whomever sold you the computer. (There's really no excuse for giving you a substandard serial port.) You'll need to purchase an "enhanced" serial port such as the Hayes ESP to add to your computer's innards. Why? Because serial ports aren't really made for high-speed modems. They panic and lose bits and pieces of whatever your modem is sending and receiving. The 16550 chip helps the serial port cope with all that data rushing around.

Windows users need TCP/IP software. TCP/IP software lets your computer talk to the Net, as we saw in the last chapter. Mosaic talks to the TCP/IP software. The TCP/IP software also keeps track of all those names and numbers we saw in the last chapter. Once you install it, you never have to tangle with this stuff again, except to use the dialer (a very simple kind of communications software that talks to the modem) to connect you to your access provider.

As with Mosaic, you can get the necessary TCP/IP software for free. There are also some excellent commercial packages available; these cost as much as several hundred dollars, but they'll make it much easier to get yourself connected. We'll look at some of the software options below, but it's wise to choose your software only after you've talked it over with the access provider from whom you'll get your SLIP or PPP connection. (They may have a few recommendations, as I do below.)

A SLIP (Serial Line Internet Protocol) or PPP (Point-to-Point Protocol) connection simply means that your computer can talk TCP/IP to the access provider's computer. When your computer calls the provider's computer, they synchronize certain things before the access provider's computer lets your computer sally forth onto the Internet. It doesn't much matter which kind of connection you get; you'll just need to know when you install the TCP/IP software. (If you're offered a choice, though, PPP is the most robust and technically advanced.)

Tech Tip: Bad phone lines are a problem for SLIP and PPP connections. If your phone lines are sub-standard, contact your phone company for advice and recommendations. However, don't expect them to help you with Mosaic or the Internet itself. They probably know less than you do.

Finally, you'll get your SLIP or PPP account from a public-access provider, preferably one that's a local call away. There are many companies in the business of providing Internet connections, but not all of them offer direct SLIP or PPP connections yet. Those that do are currently charging in the neighborhood of $20–$40 a month for the connection, and there's occasionally a per-hour fee on top of that.

If you live in a metropolitan area, you probably have several public-access providers near you. This is an excellent time to comparison shop by calling and asking a few questions about whether they offer SLIP or PPP access (and how much they charge). When you contact your prospective public-access provider, be very clear that you want a SLIP or PPP account on which you can use Mosaic. If the company doesn't offer SLIP or PPP access, ask the provider to recommend a service that does.

Once you've found an access provider with rates you like, you'll want to work closely with them to choose and install your TCP/IP software. Again, when you talk with your public-access provider, ask them for software recommendations. Mosaic works with almost anything; I prefer to use a commercial package (FTP Software's OnNet), but your provider might have other suggestions. Your provider might also have the software ready and waiting for you; many have gone to the trouble of selecting and even configuring software for their users. All you'll have to do is pop in a disk and do the usual installation routine. Give high marks to any potential access provider that does this; it'll save you time and hassle.

Portal Communications: Your Internet Is Ready!

The software at the back of the book includes not only Mosaic and the TCP/IP software but a quick and easy connection to a public access provider, Portal Communications. If you don't have an access provider yet, check these guys out—they're even giving you a free month online (five hours, and they're waiving the signup fee). Such a deal! Even better, this will speed up your installation process greatly.

To install the Enhanced Mosaic software and get a Portal account, just refer to the Quick Start Installation page facing the disks in the back of the book.

NETWORK HOOKUPS

"I do not like work even when someone else does it."

—Mark Twain

If you walk into work or school in the morning and log in to a computer network, your Internet access is very likely already available and waiting for you. Connecting through a network has many advantages, and if you have a choice between a modem connection and a network connection, the network connection is often the way to go.

Note: Modem users, if you're interested in how the other half lives, please read on. Otherwise, you're free to move along to Chapter 8.

Why so lucky? There are a few reasons, the best of which is that you probably have someone to walk you through the process of getting Mosaic up and running (other than this book, of course). You mean besides that?

If you use Mosaic on a network such as Novell NetWare or Microsoft LAN Manager (instead of through a public-access provider), the person in charge of your network can add special software that takes care of most of the fuss of getting connected. You won't need to do all the TCP/IP setting-up that modem users do; your computer simply makes a connection to the server computer on which your normal network account is based. That computer, in turn, has a connection (perhaps through another computer or two) to the Internet. But you don't have to worry about that; getting on the Internet will be just as easy as getting on the network is now.

Using Mosaic on an established network not only makes things easier, but also much, much faster. Generally speaking, the connection your network uses to talk to the Internet is more than an ordinary phone line—it's a big, "high-capacity" line much like the ones that hook all the other Internet computers together. A high-capacity line can move more data more quickly, which means Mosaic will enable you to work a lot faster than one of those folks connecting by modem.

Also, if you connect through a network, you probably work with or near the people running the network. If something goes wrong with the connection, you know who to talk to so things get fixed quickly. If your Mosaic (or the software it needs to run) gives you trouble, the fix-it person is nearby. And, if you decide you'd like to add a little something of your own to the Net, your university or place of business is likely to grant you space for free (or very cheaply).

There are a few drawbacks, though. You should always ask the network administrator (the person in charge of connecting the computers wherever you are) when you add a new piece of software to their system. If they say no, well, you should flip to the previous chapter and connect via modem. Keeping a network running is very hard work under the best of circumstances; if your administrator doesn't want to add your Internet access to her or his responsibilities, it's understandable (if regrettable).

Also—and this applies to your general Internet usage more than it does to your Mosaic travels—if you do log in with an account "sponsored" by your place of business, you'll need to consider how you represent your business online. Most people whose network connection is through their work put a disclaimer on everything they post, along the lines of "The opinions expressed above do not reflect the opinions of Acme Widgets, Inc." Even with a disclaimer, though, your employer may frown on certain kinds of Net usage.

Finally, recent legal opinions have stated that you have no guarantee of privacy when you use a computer at work to send messages. In other words, your employer is entitled to read everything you write online, even if it's private e-mail. Do not, DO NOT send anything you wouldn't mind coming back to haunt you. Several people currently under threat of indictment or multi-million-dollar lawsuits would agree with me on this one. Freedom of the press, as they say, is restricted to those who own one. Same goes for freedom of Internet access.

How To Talk to Network Administrators

Aside from small gifts and a pleasant demeanor, you'll want to approach your network administrator with an explanation of what you'd like to do on the Net, and with any information you have about the computer you're using.

Be prepared to tell your administrator about the computer you're using (PC or UNIX, and the processor speed if you know it), how much memory (RAM) you have, how much space is left on your hard drive, any special video or sound cards you have in the computer, and which software you'd like to run. Your administrator probably knows this, of course, but it's best if you can refresh her or his memory as necessary.

If you're lucky, the network administrator will set up the client software for you, which means you can skip the next section and move directly to the section titled "Installing Mosaic." If you've already installed the version of Enhanced Mosaic included with this book, or if your administrator has chosen one of the TCP/IP stacks that includes a version of Mosaic—Spry AIR Series, NetManage Chameleon, or perhaps one of the others, then you now have a Mosaic icon and you're ready to roll.

> **Note:** If you're the first person at work to ask for an Internet connection, the administrator might be rather reluctant to set this up just for you. It involves a considerable amount of bureaucracy (both with the InterNIC Registry people and, one presumes, with the people at work who approve these expenditures). Be patient, be persistent, and be ready to make a case for your increased productivity and effectiveness (to many people, not just the network administrator).

Nagging Feelings of Insecurity

A few thoughts here about network security. As I mentioned, computers on the Internet are constantly being "hacked" by the curious, the conniving, and the just plain mean. This is of passing interest to the average Net users but of consuming concern to the people responsible for keeping things up and running.

Several of the more popular security systems for smaller commercial networks connecting to the Internet involve "firewalls." Firewalls protect the smaller network from intruders by strictly regulating what kinds of IP packets are allowed to enter and leave over the Internet connection. These are great for networks, and they're becoming quite popular for businesses wanting to put information online without endangering sensitive company networks and documents. (So far, such security measures are found mainly on commercial Net connections, not at universities and so forth.)

If you're behind a firewall, you don't have a truly direct connection to the Internet. This can pose a real problem for certain older versions of Mosaic. By the time you read this, several companies (and the NCSA) will offer security-conscious versions of the software. Also, there's a fix available that enables Mosaic to make an end-run around certain kinds of firewalls by talking to a different server. Called Socks, it's available from the C & C Software Technology Center of NEC Systems Laboratory, at

```
ftp.nec.com/pub/security/socks.cstc
```

A version of Socks is available for PC users at

```
ftp.nec.com/pub/security/socks.cstc/PC_Socks_Pack
```

Note that your network administrator will need to set up the necessary programs.

Installing Mosaic

Now that the hard part's over (and just think, someone else had to do the hard part), the fun part is at hand. First, though, you need to install Mosaic. Most of you will just use the version of Mosaic at the back of the book—Luckman Interactive's Enhanced Mosaic, a direct decedent of the original. Don't worry, though, if you use another version of Mosaic; we look at several variations in Chapter 12.

You'll find two Mosaic disk at the back of the book. Insert the first disk in your 3.5-inch drive and follow the instruction on the installation page facing the disks in the back of the book. Installation will wrap up quickly and a new Windows group will be created for the Enhanced Mosaic icons.

Mosaic is now available whenever you're logged into the network server (as long as the server is connected to the Internet and not experiencing technical difficulties). To start the program, you'll simply click on the Mosaic icon. Now let's skip forward to Chapter 8, where we'll start exploring the Net via Mosaic together.

PART III

And Awaaaay We Go!

We're ready to go on the Net at last! You've successfully prepared for access to the Internet by finding an access provider and choosing the proper software. Now we'll use these tools to explore what's available.

This section will teach you how to use the Mosaic software. We'll start in Chapter 8 with a simple Web session that will introduce you to the main Mosaic tools for navigating. You'll be pleasantly surprised to see that you can do wonderful things with Mosaic by using only a few of its features.

In Chapter 9, we'll explore the rest of the Mosaic interface. We'll look at every option on the menus and see how you can use them to surf the Net even more effectively. I'll also show you how to customize certain parts of Mosaic, making it look and act in the way that best suits your needs.

Chapter 10 lets you practice your Mosaic skills by touring three large Web sites. There's plenty of stuff to do and see, and I'll act as your tour guide just long enough for you to start exploring on your own.

By the time you've finished this section, you'll have an excellent understanding of how to use Mosaic to surf the Net. Afterwards, we'll talk about some of the finer points of the software—but, even if you only finish this section, you'll be more than ready to Net surf with the best of them.

CHAPTER 8

BASIC MOSAIC SKILLS

"You don't need to leave your room. Remain sitting at your table and… the world will freely offer itself to you."

—Franz Kafka

At last! You have your connection (whether via modem or over a network), and you've successfully installed the Mosaic software. This is it: We're about to go online. Please put all trays in the upright, locked positions, and make sure your seat belts are securely fastened....

While I'm in this flight-attendant mode, it's useful to look at the interface one more time before we get started. (It has been a while, after all, and we've done a lot of fairly technical stuff since then. I'd hate to think your enthusiasm was flagging.) Let's take another look at the Mosaic screen shown in Figure 8.1 and review the basic components. As we progress through the next two chapters, we'll look at every menu selection individually. For now, I want to you feel comfortable with the basic tools you'll need to get around.

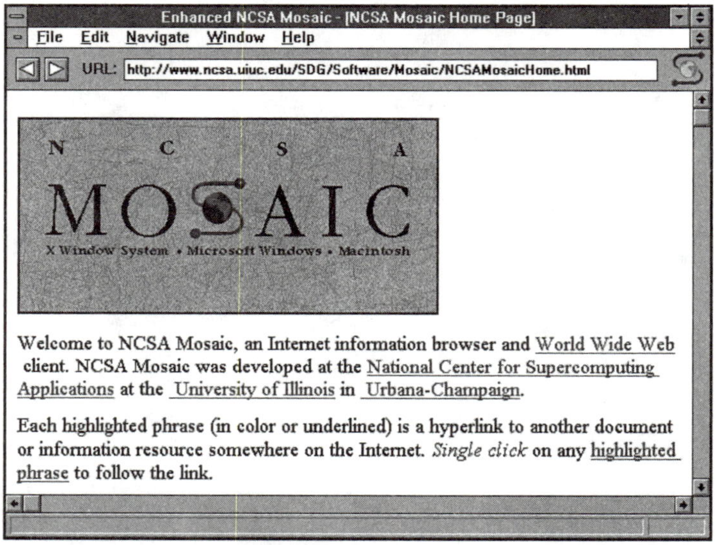

Figure 8.1. The NCSA Mosaic Web page we saw in Chapter 1.

A Quick Basic Review

Once again we're looking at the Mosaic Web page for the National Center for Supercomputing Applications (the NCSA). The large area in the middle of the screen is the page itself. The area around it is the Mosaic interface.

The Mosaic interface is simple, even plain. You see before you a very normal Windows menu bar, with normal Windows areas. Again, we'll investigate these further a bit later in the chapter. Beneath the menu line is a one-line text window and two small buttons. The buttons will help you retrace your steps through any

Mosaic session, backwards and forwards. In the upper-right-hand corner, you see a small globe.

> **Note:** Also, different versions of Mosaic for different types of computers (like the Macintosh) have slightly different menus and buttons. Throughout the next few chapters, I'll occasionally stop to talk about what you might see in other versions of Mosaic.

On the page, we see the NCSA logo and a few paragraphs of text, each of which contains several words that are underlined. (Again, if this picture were in color you could see that the words are also displayed in another color—on my computer, they're blue.)

The colored words are links—the tools that allow you to hop from site to site on the Internet via hypermedia connections. This screen has, proportionally speaking, a reasonable number of links showing. You will occasionally find pages on which almost every item is a link; sometimes a page will have no links at all. Don't worry, they're not dead ends! There's a way out of everything.

Move the mouse arrow so it's on top of one of the colored links, and look at the bottom of the screen. You see a longish line of characters starting with `http`. This is the address of the file that the link will take you to. Later on, we'll tell you what all that means. You will, by the way, only see that line of text when you place the cursor over the link. If you roll away from it, the line of text will disappear. If you roll to another link, the line of text will change to the address of that link.

> **Note:** Some versions of Mosaic change the mouse arrow into a pointing hand-shape when you roll over a link.

For now, though, look up above the logo to the small white window. You'll see another line of characters also beginning with `http`. This is the Internet address of the NCSA Web page you see before you on screen. And on the Windows title bar, you'll see the phrase "Enhanced NCSA Mosaic—[NCSA Mosaic Home Page]." The phrase in [square brackets] is the title of the page in English. "Enhanced NCSA Mosaic" is the name of the software.

To review, we are looking at a Web page with several links. Clicking on the link shown will take us to another page. We know we're looking at a link because the text is a funny color and because moving the cursor to this spot makes text appear at the bottom of the page. If we want to follow a link, we can use the mouse to click on the link.

Yes, I do believe you're ready. We're going online.

The Guided Tour Begins: First Steps

Start your TCP/IP connection according to the instructions at the end of the installation chapter you read (Chapter 6 for modem users, Chapter 7 for the rest of you). Once you're connected, click on the Mosaic icon.

Mosaic starts, and after a few seconds you see before you your home page. We'll take a second to note that some people call every Web page a home page. Technically, your home page is the page at which you start your own particular Mosaic session. Any Web page can be your home page.

At the moment, though, if you've successfully installed the software that's included with this book, your home page is the "Plug-n-Play Mosaic for Windows Home Page." Before we tell you how to access the wealth of Web resources that are on this page, however, we're going to take a short tour, beginning at the place where it all started—the home page for NCSA Mosaic at the University of Illinois Champaign-Urbana.

You can get to the NCSA Mosaic Home Page by doing the following:

1. In the File menu, click Open URL.
2. Then type `http://www.ncsa.uiuc.edu/SDG/Software/Mosaic/NCSAMosaicHome.html` and hit Enter. (I'll explain everything later.)

Let's have a look at the beginning of this page, shown in Figure 8.2, and spend a minute to locate all the links.

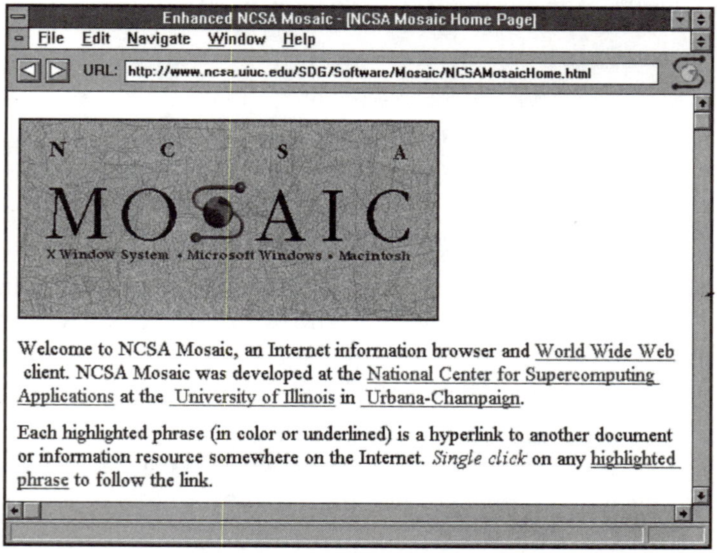

Figure 8.2. The NCSA Mosaic Home Page.

You'll notice that there's a large logo with a thin black band at the top of this page. That's just a graphic; it doesn't do anything if you click on it. How can you tell? The border is very narrow. A graphic with a link attached has a border about four times as wide as this one, and on a color screen you'll see that it's colored. (The normal color is blue; you can change it later if you like.)

Beneath the logo we see several paragraphs of text. In each paragraph you'll note that there are several underlined words (which appear in blue on the color screen). The words "World Wide Web," "National Center for Supercomputing Applications," "University of Illinois," "Urbana-Champaign," and "highlighted phrase" are underlined and colored. These phrases are links to other pages on the Web. This is the heart of what makes Mosaic cool.

So those are the links we can see in Figure 8.2. If you roll the mouse to the elevator bar at the right (the bar with the sliding box in the middle and the arrows on each end; did you know that it had a name?) you can move down the page and see the other links on this page. You see some of these in Figure 8.3. There are a lot, but they're easy to identify—just like the other links we saw, they're underlined (in the case of text) or surrounded by a colored border (in the case of icons and pictures).

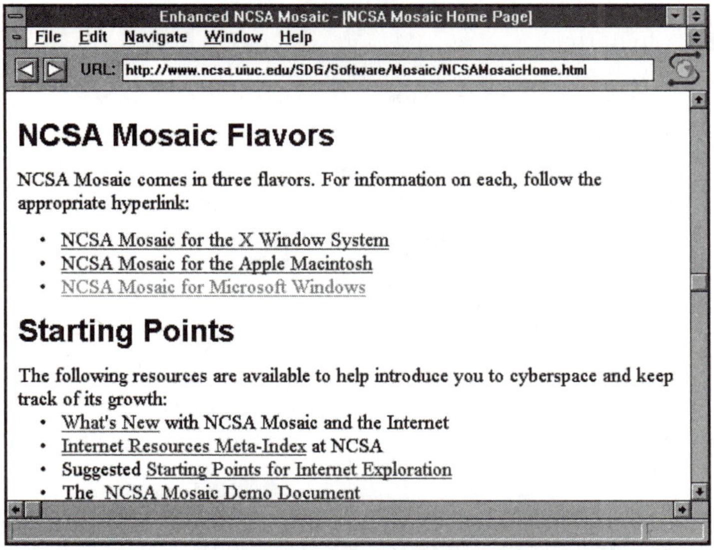

Figure 8.3. More links farther down the page we saw in Figure 8.2.

Let's test a link! Any link will do, but let's stick together on the tour and choose the same one. In the second paragraph at the top of the page, you'll see the words "highlighted phrase," which is a text link. Roll the mouse directly atop the link.

The cursor will turn into a hand shape, and a line of text will appear at the bottom. The line will read

```
http://www.ncsa.uiuc.edu/SDG/Software/Mosaic/SampleLink.html
```

While that line is showing at the bottom of the screen, click once on the underlined link with the left mouse button.

Mosaic clears the screen briefly and the message "reading response" appears briefly at the bottom of the window. The mouse cursor has turned into an hourglass, the globe in the upper-right-hand corner spins, and the tiny lights follow their S-shaped path.

Behind the scenes, Mosaic has translated your click into a request for the linking page, as described in Chapter 5's discussion of TCP/IP. Once it finds the page, it needs to load it into your machine's memory. Since this is a page of text with no graphics, it'll only take a few seconds.

If the person who designed this page had put a large picture (a photograph, for instance) on it, loading would take a lot longer. In a few seconds, the page will be loaded and the cursor will turn back into the familiar arrow. If you don't move the mouse after clicking on the link, it will occasionally return to the hand shape, even though there's no link. It's nothing to worry about; move the mouse and it'll go back to normal.

Tech Tip: Some versions of Mosaic will show a mutant arrow-hourglass combination cursor, which should look familiar to anyone using Windows NT. This cursor indicates that you're free to use certain other program functions while Mosaic is loading this page.

The page is loaded, and we see it on the screen and in Figure 8.4. You'll notice that there are no links on this page; it's all normal black text.

We'll go to a page with more links in a minute, but first let's try navigating with the arrow buttons in the upper-left-hand corner. As I said above, there's a way out of everything, even the dead ends.

You'll notice that the forward arrow (pointing to the right) is grayed out while the back arrow (pointing to the left) is not. This means that you can go back to the previous page, but since you haven't chosen a "next page" yet there's no forward page in this session. Let's return to the first page by clicking the back arrow.

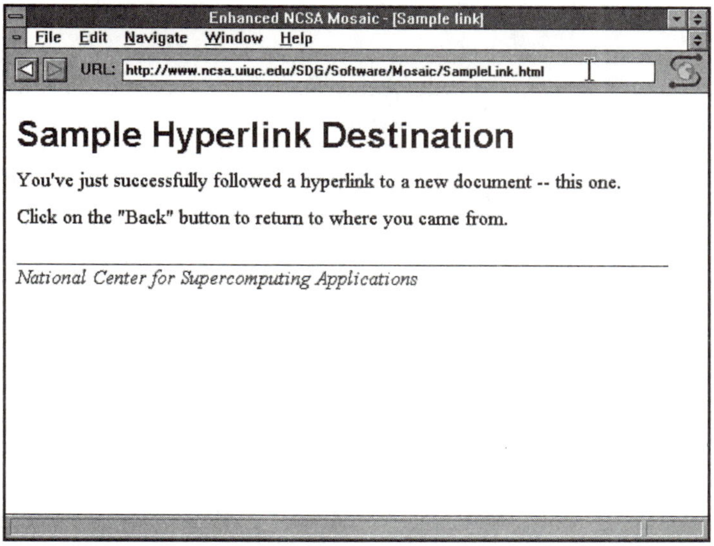

Figure 8.4. The Sample Hyperlink Destination page, to which we jumped by following a link.

You're back where you started! That was very quick, since Mosaic keeps track of the pages you've visited for just such backtracking occasions. You'll notice that the back arrow is now grayed out—we're all the way back to the beginning—and the forward arrow is ready to use. You could click the forward arrow to go to the second page (the page we just left) if you wanted.

Tech Tip: In some versions of Mosaic, you'll notice that the "highlighted text" link upon which you clicked looks different now—it's underlined with a dotted line instead of the straight line it had when you started. The color may also have changed slightly. That tells you that you've visited that link; for the rest of your session, when you return to this page the link will look different. You can see an example of this in Figure 8.3, where the words "NCSA Mosaic for Microsoft Windows" are a different, lighter shade than the other links.

This is very handy on a page with lots of interesting links; you'll know what you've looked at and what you haven't. The link is still the same and clicking on it will get you the same page. The dotted line and color change are just visual aids to keep you from retracing your steps unnecessarily. Some versions of Mosaic only know that you clicked on that particular link on this particular Web page.

> If you happen to find the same link on a different page, it might not be obvious from its appearance that you've used it elsewhere.

You now have the basic skills necessary for Mosaic use: the ability to spot a link and the ability to use the forward and back arrows. But don't kick yourself for spending all that money on this book—even though you could spend the rest of your days on the Net hopping around like this, Mosaic has plenty of tools to make your travels easier and richer.

The Guided Tour Continues: The Home Button

You are now looking at the NCSA Mosaic Web page, marveling at your cleverness for not bringing the Internet to its knees. Let's follow a few more links and see how it goes.

You'll see the University of Illinois link in the first paragraph—this is another text link. Click on it; we're going to campus.

You click; away we go. This page takes a bit longer to get to you than the first link did, but when it gets here you'll see why—there are small graphics scattered through it. You'll find that pages with a lot of graphics load more slowly than all-text pages.

In Figure 8.5 we see the Web page for the University of Illinois at Urbana-Champaign. Very nice, isn't it? The first screen shows a bit of information about the university. The graphic in the upper-left-hand corner is a logo, contained in a file on the computer in Illinois; you'll see that it has the thick, colorful (blue) band that marks a link. In this case, it so happens that clicking on the graphic will get you a better look at the graphic. Farther down the page you'll find more small campus photos and text links that will get you info about the university.

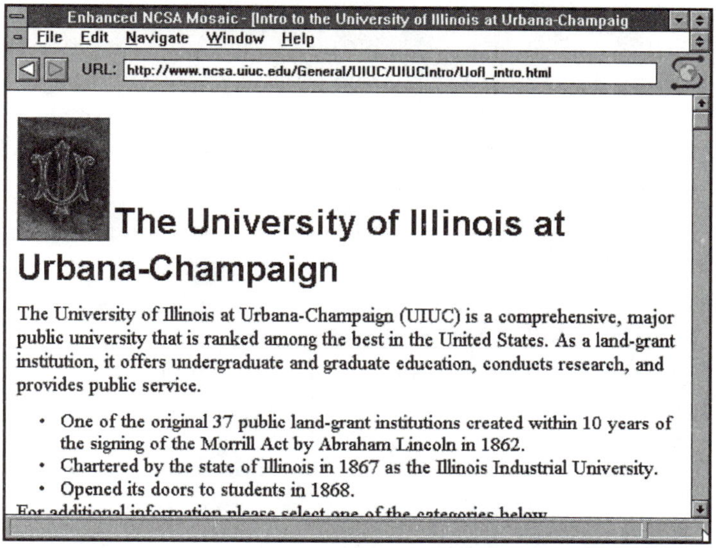

Figure 8.5. The University of Illinois Urbana-Champaign home page.

But for now we have a perverse urge to look at the NCSA Mosaic page again. We could click the back arrow twice and get there, but there's a faster way. If you click on the "navigate" option on the menu bar, you'll see a list of options, one of which is "home." Clicking here takes you immediately to your home page. (For now, of course, it takes you to the NCSA Mosaic page. Later on I'll explain how to change the software to start on any web page you like.) Some Mosaic users have a button-bar icon for returning home; it usually looks like a house.

Setting Off in a New Direction: The Open URL Box

If you like, you could spend the rest of your Mosaic days hopping around the Net. But what if you want to go to a list that's not on the page you're looking at? If you know the URL address of a link, you can type it into Mosaic and go there directly. Go to the File menu and choose Open URL. You get a box labeled "Open URL." Type the following URL in the box, just as it appears below:

```
http://www.ncsa.uiuc.edu/SDG/Experimental/anu-art-history/home.html
```

We're going to the "ANU Art History Exhibit" site. Click once. The menu closes; Mosaic sends your commands barreling across the Net; we're surfing once more. A few minutes later, the page for "Images For Art History At The Australian National University" has loaded onto the screen. Again, since there are lots of images, it takes a little while.

If you like this page, explore the links. Clicking on the photos will bring you files that contain those photos; you probably don't want to do that just now, since it's a very slow process and we haven't told Mosaic what to do with those kinds of files yet. Clicking on the text links, though, gets you a great deal of information on the ANU art project, a tutorial on the history of prints, more photos of sculpture, and an introduction to the professor in charge of this project.

Note: If you scroll to the bottom of the page, you'll find out all about Dr. Greenhalgh by clicking on his name, which appears as a text link. This is a personal Web page, and you'll find a lot of them scattered around the Net. A lot of Web users make their own pages just for fun, personalizing them with photos and links to their favorite places.

Fancy Footwork: The Navigate Menu

The ANU page is great—lots of links, lots of pictures, all very interesting. Now that you've found it, you might want to come back again. Rather than type it in again, you can add this place to a hotlist of favorite spots, kept on your menu bar for easy access.

Roll to the Navigate menu and click; then click on Add current to hotlist. The screen flickers and nothing seems to happen. But if you now click open the Hotlist menu (again, under Navigate), you'll see a new entry at the bottom. Mosaic has made note of where you are and committed the address to memory; whenever you want to return, you can. In some packages you'll find this function referred to as a bookmark, which gets the point across very well. You are putting a bookmark at a favorite spot on the Net.

Let's give this bookmark menu item a distinctive name, though—something you'll recognize immediately. Go back to the Navigate menu, click Hotlist, and click once on the ANU site you just added to the list. Now click the Edit button. A menu opens to Edit title-URL. If you'd like to call this page by some other name, you may type anything you like in the *upper* box. Click OK to return to the hotlist and see the new title.

Warning: Do NOT type or change anything on the lower box. If you do, Mosaic will not be able to find the page again.

Mosaic also automatically keeps a list of the last few places we've been. You can see it if you roll to the Navigate item on the Menu bar and click on the History menu line. A box opens up, as shown in Figure 8.7. This is the history of this session and the last several sessions before. The four items on the top of the list correspond in reverse chronological order to the major jumps we made as we followed the links. You can quickly move to any of these places by clicking on the appropriate line.

Tech Tip: Some Mosaics don't show you the title of the pages you've seen—just the URL address.

You can click once on either of the matching home-page address lines (the second and fourth lines, in this case) and then click on the Go To button (or double-click on the list) to go back to that page. To get rid of this history box click the Close button.

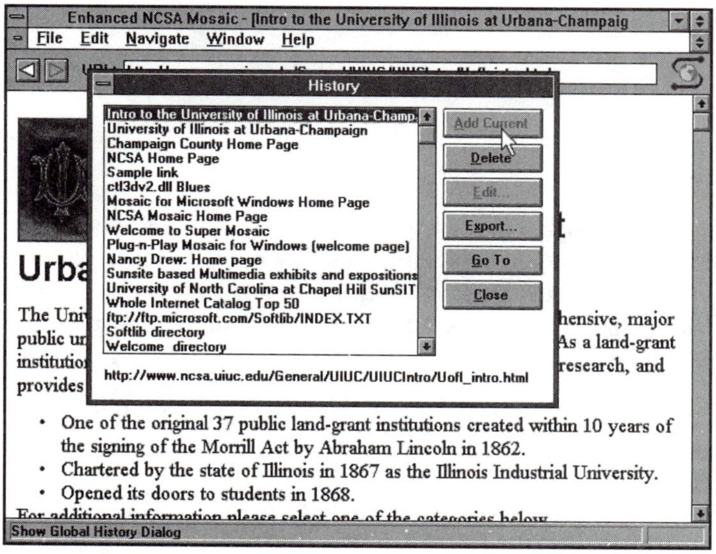

Figure 8.6. The history of our latest Net travels.

We've seen the address lines several times now, typed one in, and even called them by their proper name—URL, or Uniform Resource Locater. Just as you have your own unique address on the Net consisting of your username and the name of your Internet provider (its domain name), every single piece of the net has its own unique address too. In Chapter 9 we'll dissect a few URLs to see what we can learn. Doing so will give you some good background on how it all works, and provide lots of hints for exploring more sites on the Net.

> **Tech Tip:** You'll notice that the History session doesn't list every link we've made. The software doesn't keep track of the moves you make with the left and right arrows.

There are just a few other menu items in the Navigate menu.

- Back and Forward correspond to the left and right arrows respectively; the menu items do exactly the same thing.
- The Home button takes us back to our home page, as we saw.
- The Load missing images option will turn up in the next chapter, when we see how to speed up Mosaic. This option helps you to be selective about just how many graphics Mosaic hauls across the Net for you.
- The Reload button lets you ask Mosaic to get you the same page again.. Every so often a page doesn't make it to the screen intact; this often happens if you use the pull-down menus while the page is loading. If the page doesn't seem to have arrived in its proper condition, try clicking on the Reload button or using the menu item. You'll use Reload again later on when I show you how to speed up your Mosaic sessions.

Closing Up Shop

The next chapter explains the rest of the menu options, and gives you more tools for perfecting your Netsurfing techniques. For now, though, we should practice abandoning ship. It's very simple: the usual exit process takes care of everything. If you're dialing in over the modem, though, you should be sure to go back into your dialer and hang up the phone. SLIP and PPP connections ain't cheap.

Before we go on, though, a word about what to do when something goes wrong. It is unfortunately not uncommon for a link to fail, for pages to load improperly, for Things To Happen. The problem may be with the page you're trying to reach, with the computer on which the page resides, with the Net itself (especially during heavy-traffic periods), with your access provider, or with your machine. Computer networks are annoying that way. And Mosaic itself isn't perfect. Every so often the software simply… faints.

Remember that you can always parachute out of a session that's run amuck by simply closing Mosaic. You can always restart the program; it's rarely necessary to re-dial or reconnect to the network. You will not harm any part of the Net, or your computer, or Mosaic by doing so.

If a particular link is giving you trouble by not loading, you might try reloading the page or backing up a page and starting over. If the software seems fine but you get an error message along the "transfer failed" or "server not responding" lines, the problem lies with the other computer, and you'll simply have to try again later.

You know now how to get on, around, and off the Net with Mosaic. The next chapter will make you an expert. After that, we'll set off on a few practice sessions, in which we'll catch up on some great bands, check the latest news, and hang out with bianca.

CHAPTER 9

Now That You're Comfortable...

"But wait! There's more!"

—Ginsu Knife commercial

At this point you have the software running well, and you've had a few adventures clicking around the Net. You should be able to recognize a link at first sight, and you should feel well-versed in the various methods of navigation.

This chapter will give you the skills to take better advantage of Mosaic, and so to get around better on the Web. I'll guide you through the rest of the Enhanced Mosaic menus; I'll also stop periodically to discuss the original NCSA Mosaic interface with which some of you may be more familiar.

The first section of this chapter explores the rest of the options in the Mosaic menus. You won't use these as often as you'll use the stuff we saw in the last chapter, but you'll find that these tools give you even more power. We'll start by going back onto the Net and bringing some of this great stuff back to your own hard drive. I'll show you how to customize the menu and button bars, and then we'll try our collective hand at writing annotations for some of the pages.

The second section tells you how to change things around, making your Mosaic more personally appealing. Here's where you get to pick your own home page (although you might want to wait until you've had a little more time to explore the Net!).

The third section explains the URLs (Uniform Resource Locators) that you've seen on every screen as you move about. The URL may look like gibberish, but like the configuration information we gave you in Chapter 5 it's actually pretty logical and even informative. Once you understand URLs, you can brag to everyone about exactly how many countries you visited during your latest Mosaic session. Also, understanding URLs can help you "surf smart" and figure out what sites might have hidden riches. Our Netsurfer, Josh, is expert at this.

After that, you'll be about as expert as you can be in Mosaic without having spent much time online. We'll Netsurf in the next chapter; I'll show you around three of my favorite places. By then, you'll know Mosaic's best tricks and tools, and you'll be able to move with ease all around the Internet.

Getting the Goods: The File Menu

Some pages are just too good to leave on the Web. You might find that you'd like to have a copy of a particular page on your own machine—it might have valuable information, or you may want to examine it more closely as you design your own Web pages (which we'll do in Chapter 13).

To save a page, open the File menu and choose Save As. You'll get the Save As box you see in Figure 9.1. The package assumes you'd like to save the file with an `.htm` extension—this is the DOS equivalent to the UNIX `.html` extension you'll see on most Web pages. Saving the file in this format enables you to look at the page with Mosaic and see almost everything you now see, even if you're not online at the time. You'll also be able to open the file in any text editor, such as Notepad.

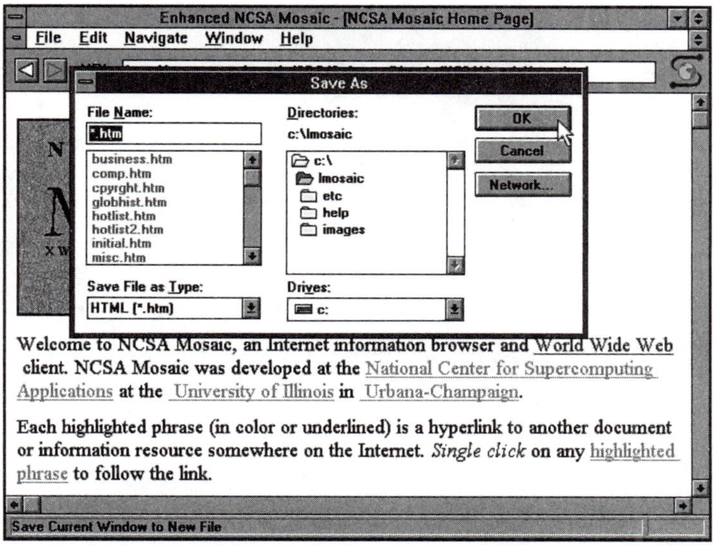

Figure 9.1. The Mosaic Save As screen, found under the File menu.

You'll be pleased to hear that everything else in the File menu works as expected. We used the Open URL option in the previous chapter to leap to the ANU Art page; you can see the option again below, in Figure 9.2. You'll recognize all the Print options (Print, Print Preview, and Print Setup). They're pretty much as you know them from other Windows programs. And you can print out Mosaic pages just the way you see them, as long as you have scalable versions of the fonts Mosaic is using on your screen. (In most cases Mosaic uses Times New Roman and Courier New; those are both very common and you probably have them as TrueType fonts, which are indeed scalable.) The Print option also exists as a button—it's the second from the right in Windows Mosaic.

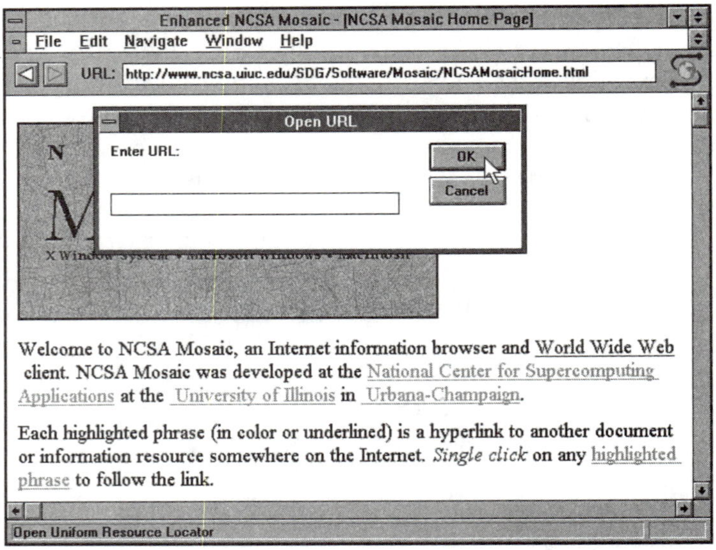

Figure 9.2. The Open URL window.

The final option in the File menu (other than Exit; I think you know what that does) involves the use of multiple windows. You can keep several Mosaic sessions going at once with the New Window option; close windows individually using Close, or close everything at once (in preparation for logging off) by hitting Close All.

This is a good time to make a step to the right and look at the Window menu, which handles the Web sessions you have active. It should seem quite familiar—Tile arranges your active Mosaic windows, Cascade stacks them atop each other, and Arrange Icons put any minimized windows in order. The titles of all pages in all active windows are displayed at the bottom of the Window menu.

The Edit menu doesn't have much that's unusual. You should be familiar with Cut, Copy, Paste, Clear, and Select All from other Windows programs; you'll use these on pages you've stored locally to move bits and pieces of text back and forth from the clipboard. Clicking on View Source gives you a look at the actual page and its coding. Find and Find Again are useful for looking up a particular word on the current page; unfortunately, they work only on whatever page you're looking at.

The Preferences option under the Edit menu is a little more complex than most of the things we've seen so far. This is as scary as the menus get, though, and in exchange for spending a bit of time looking at them you'll find that you can really make the most of Mosaic's options. And really it's not that bad at all in Enhanced Mosaic—users of the original NCSA Mosaic had to find their way through this stuff under the Options menu, where it's scattered around with precious little explanation. In Figure 9.3, we see the Preferences option in the Edit menu.

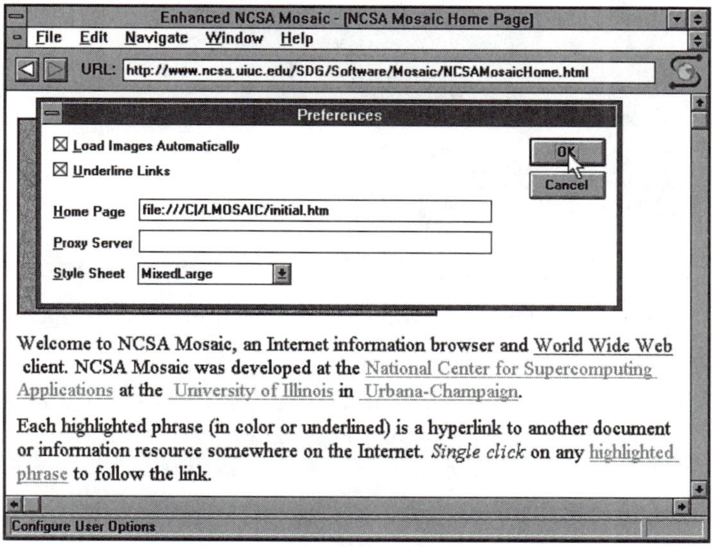

Figure 9.3. The trim and elegant Preferences window.

The window, as you see, has two check-boxes and three windows. Unless you're working on a security-conscious network, you can safely ignore one of the windows, "Proxy Server." (If you need to pay attention to that line, you'll get the necessary information from your network administrator.)

The top box lets you choose whether to load the inline images whenever Mosaic finds them. Images are great, and they make Mosaic look beautiful, but they can take a long time to get to you (especially if you're using a modem). Clicking this button to "off" will speed things up for you. If you decide you want to see the images, just click on the red-x'ed box Mosaic gives you. Figures 9.4 and 9.5 show you the Art History page at the Australian National University, first with "Load Images Automatically" turned on, and next with the option turned off.

Figure 9.4. ANU Art History page with Load Images Automatically option selected.

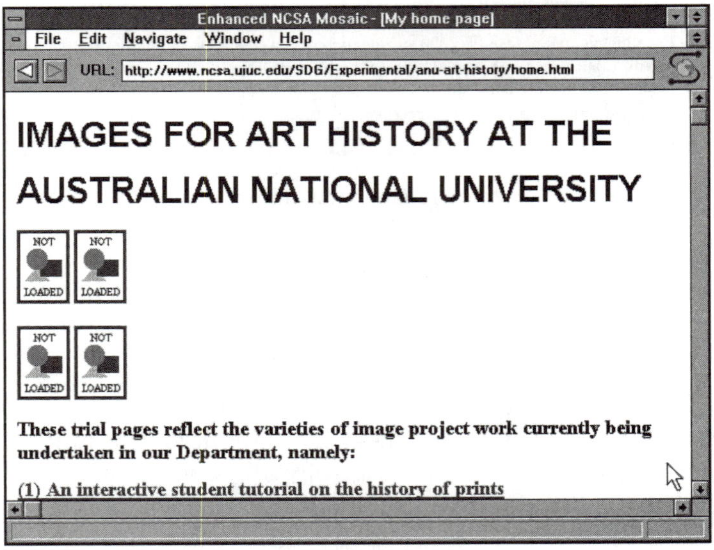

Figure 9.5. ANU Art History page with automatic image loading turned off.

"Underline links" is a question of preference: If you check it, Mosaic underlines every text link. If you switch it off, Mosaic just makes the links blue. The underline function is useful if you're on a monochrome monitor.

The home page option currently loads a page that exists on your own computer. You can type in any Web page URL here—for instance, if you really adore the ANU Art page we saw in the last chapter, you could type in the URL just as you typed it into the Open URL box before.

You'll notice that the home page starts with `file:///`. This indicates that my home page actually exists on my machine. It's much faster to keep your home page on your own machine, so Mosaic needn't drag it in from the Net. Also, note the odd vertical line in the URL, right after the `C`. As you may have guessed, this is actually a colon; if you need to type in a URL for a local file, use the colon as you normally would.

The final item in the window is the Style Sheet collection. The makers of Enhanced Mosaic designed several good-looking style sheets (Figure 9.6) for the various text styles that make up the average Web page. Experiment with the choices until you find one that suits you.

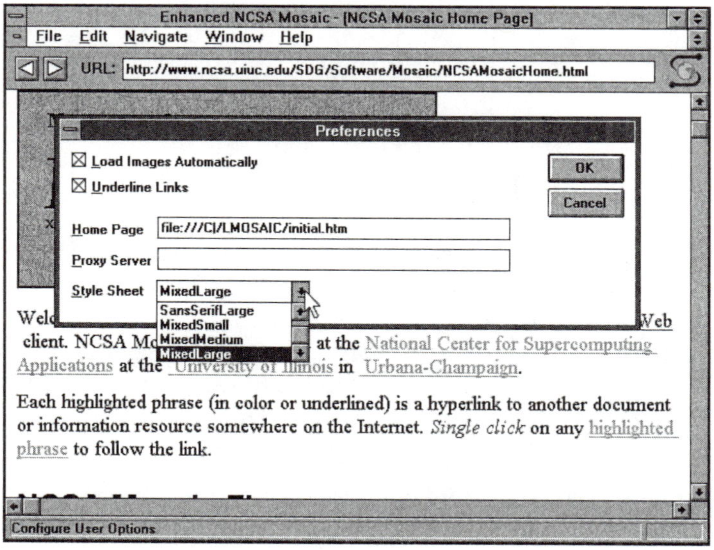

Figure 9.6. Changing the Style Sheet in the Preferences window.

If you're feeling particularly adventurous (or you just despise plain old Times Roman, Courier, and Arial), you can open the `LMOSAIC.INI` file with Notepad and manually edit the fonts that Enhanced Mosaic uses for its style sheets (Figure 9.7).

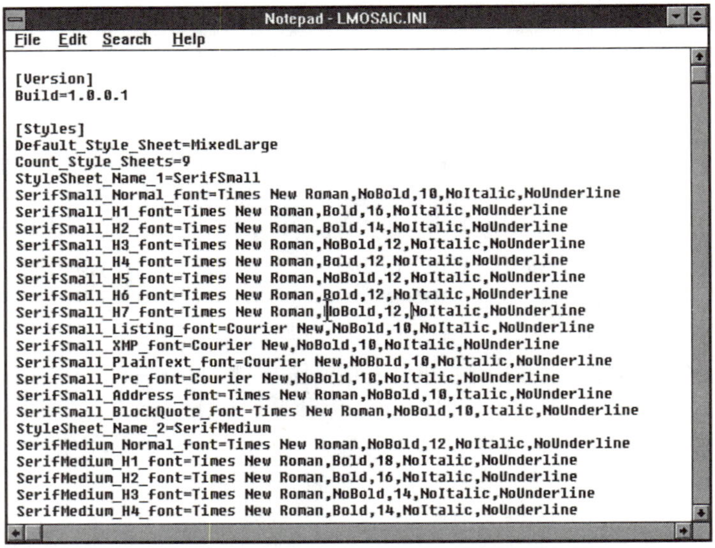


```
[Version]
Build=1.0.0.1

[Styles]
Default_Style_Sheet=MixedLarge
Count_Style_Sheets=9
StyleSheet_Name_1=SerifSmall
SerifSmall_Normal_font=Times New Roman,NoBold,10,NoItalic,NoUnderline
SerifSmall_H1_font=Times New Roman,Bold,16,NoItalic,NoUnderline
SerifSmall_H2_font=Times New Roman,Bold,14,NoItalic,NoUnderline
SerifSmall_H3_font=Times New Roman,NoBold,12,NoItalic,NoUnderline
SerifSmall_H4_font=Times New Roman,Bold,12,NoItalic,NoUnderline
SerifSmall_H5_font=Times New Roman,NoBold,12,NoItalic,NoUnderline
SerifSmall_H6_font=Times New Roman,Bold,12,NoItalic,NoUnderline
SerifSmall_H7_font=Times New Roman,NoBold,12,NoItalic,NoUnderline
SerifSmall_Listing_font=Courier New,NoBold,10,NoItalic,NoUnderline
SerifSmall_XMP_font=Courier New,NoBold,10,NoItalic,NoUnderline
SerifSmall_PlainText_font=Courier New,NoBold,10,NoItalic,NoUnderline
SerifSmall_Pre_font=Courier New,NoBold,10,NoItalic,NoUnderline
SerifSmall_Address_font=Times New Roman,NoBold,10,Italic,NoUnderline
SerifSmall_BlockQuote_font=Times New Roman,NoBold,10,Italic,NoUnderline
StyleSheet_Name_2=SerifMedium
SerifMedium_Normal_font=Times New Roman,NoBold,12,NoItalic,NoUnderline
SerifMedium_H1_font=Times New Roman,Bold,18,NoItalic,NoUnderline
SerifMedium_H2_font=Times New Roman,Bold,16,NoItalic,NoUnderline
SerifMedium_H3_font=Times New Roman,NoBold,14,NoItalic,NoUnderline
SerifMedium_H4_font=Times New Roman,Bold,14,NoItalic,NoUnderline
```

Figure 9.7. Using Notepad to manually edit the default fonts in Enhanced Mosaic.

Getting Around: The Navigate Menu

The Navigate menu should look fairly familiar, especially since it starts with two functions you've already used in their button-bar form. The Back and Forward options correspond with the arrow buttons in the upper-left of the screen. And we used almost all the other options in the previous chapter—History to see where we'd been recently, Add Current To Hotlist to save a page we liked, Hotlist to get back there again. And Reload was explained too.

The remaining option, Load Missing Images, is a bit like Reload. It works with the Load Images Automatically option in the Edit/Preferences window to help you speed up Mosaic operations. As I mentioned, if you do not check the Load Images Automatically box, you'll won't see the inline images. Instead, you'll see a box wherever an image should be. To see just one image, you can click on the box Mosaic gives you. However, you can load all the images on the page simply by clicking the Load Missing Images Option.

They Think of Everything: The Help Menu

Want more info? Scared you won't always have this book handy while you're online? (I can't imagine ever straying more than arm's length away from it, but accidents will happen.) The Help menu in Enhanced Mosaic is actually a small specialized hotlist; clicking on Mosaic Help Page gets you a page with links to several smaller files. (The NCSA Mosaic folks have something similar in the Online Documentation section; however, they need to be online to actually reach those support pages.) The About box gives the usual information about the program; on that screen, the Support button gives further information about your system's configuration, in case a tech-support-type person needs to know.

Getting To Know URL...

Throughout this book I've referred to the URLs (Uniform Resource Locators), the strings of information that act as the address for each site on the Net. Occasionally I've called them "URL addresses," but that was a redundancy and we'll stop now. (I did it that way so you'd know immediately what a URL was without flipping back to the glossary—better a small redundancy than an annoying bit of weird terminology.) Everything you see through Mosaic has a URL; that's how Mosaic tells the Net where you want to go. (It may help to think of it as a kind of e-mail address for Net things, as opposed to Net people.)

If you only ever jump from link to link with the mouse or the buttons, you won't need to pay much attention to the URLs. Mosaic takes care of that for you. However, as you explore the Net you may hear about other interesting places, either from fellow Netsurfers or in this book. (I've made a point of giving the URL for each page we visit, and there are many more listed in the appendixes.) If you don't know of a site that links directly to the site you want, you need to know how to type the URL in to get there directly. We did this in the previous chapter when we used the "Open URL" option, but we're ready now to figure out what exactly we were typing. Let's look at our former home page URL:

```
http://www.ncsa.uiuc.edu/SDG/Software/mosaic/NCSAMosaicHome.html
```

All URLs are composed of three parts. You can pick out which parts are which by looking at the forward slashes. The first part is everything that happens before those two forward slashes. The second part is whatever happens between there and the next slash. The third part is everything after. You say it's Greek to you? Pretend it's Hebrew instead; we'll read it right to left.

The third part of this URL is

```
SDG/Software/Mosaic/NCSAMosaicHome.html
```

This is the name of the file, complete with directories. The filename is `NCSAMosaicHome.html`. It's stored in the `SDG/Software/Mosaic/` directory. Since UNIX allows file names long enough to actually tell you something, we can see that this is a file about NCSA Mosaic; the word `Home` in the name tips us off that it's a possible home page. (This is by no means a standard naming system, unfortunately; the folks at NCSA simply name things very clearly.)

The `.html` on the end means that the file uses HTML, the HyperText Markup Language that makes pages seen in Mosaic look the way they do. We've already looked at a little HTML in the Document Source window, earlier in this chapter, and we'll spend a lot more time with it in Chapter 13. Most of the true Web pages you see will have the .html extension in their filenames. If a page looks unusual to you, check the URL at the bottom of the screen; maybe it's not in `.html` format.

> **Tech Tip:** PC users are accustomed to using backwards slashes (`\`) in directory names. The URL is written with UNIX in mind, and so the slashes are backwards to you. If you ever have trouble getting through to a site for which you typed in the URL, make sure you have the *uphill* (`/`) slashes.

The second section of the name gives the domain name of the computer holding the file. You remember domain names from Chapter 4—they're how the Internet identifies every single computer. The domain name for this computer is

```
www.ncsa.uiuc.edu
```

After what we talked about in Chapter 5, this part should be easy for you. The `edu` in the top-level-domain spot tells us that it's a college or university, and it's probably in the U.S. (since institutions overseas use the country codes as their top-level domain). The `uiuc` makes us take an educated guess—you're likely to deduce that it's a university-of-something, but you might not have known that it was the University of Illinois Urbana-Champaign. Of course, you might have recognized the `ncsa` initials and remembered that the NCSA is at the University of Illinois Urbana-Champaign. And the `www` specifies which of the NCSA's computers this is—this is the World Wide Web server at the NCSA, on the UIUC campus, which is an educational institution.

That leaves the first bit, the

```
http:
```

This prefix tells you that the URL is pointing to a hypertext document—in other words, a Web page. You'll see several kinds of prefixes in your travels, and you'll notice that the URLs vary according to what you're connecting to, as I explained in Chapter 3. Here's a list to help you sort it all out:

FTP	`file://`*`domain.name/complete.file.name`*
Gopher	`gopher://`*`domain.name:port`* (a more complex name usually follows)
Telnet	`telnet://`*`domain.name:port`*
Web pages	`http://`*`domain.name/full/directory/name/and/filename`*`.html`

Now that you know that, what do you do? The more comfortable you are with URLs, the easier you'll find it to navigate even without pre-set links. You'll be able to make educated guesses as you explore the Net, and educated guesses can lead to wonderful discoveries. Remember Josh, back in Chapter 2? He read the URL and figured out that there was probably more good stuff in the immediate vicinity of the page he was on. When we last saw him he was Netsurfing with great glee; he may be online still.

How did Josh figure it out? Let's look at the URL he saw:

```
http://www.bu.edu/Games/games.html
```

Following the rules above, we see that the page Josh found (linked to the Cool Site of the Day) is a hypertext page, on a Web server at some educational facility that goes by `bu.edu`. The page itself is called `games.html`—yes, definitely some kind of Web page with that `.html` extension—and it's kept in a directory called `Games`. The only part we couldn't logically deduct is where exactly `bu.edu` might be.

Josh looked at the WWW part of the domain name and reasoned that there were probably more things he could reach via the Web here—after all, the average computer in use as a Web server can hold a lot of pages! He backed out of the subdirectories to get to the very "top" of the computer, where he found a nice introductory page that told him where `bu.edu` is (Boston).

He backed out by moving the mouse up to the top of the screen, clicking on the URL window, and typing in his best guess at the name of the topmost page of the Web site. He figured that a site with WWW in its name was probably an all-Web kind of place, so he just typed in the first two halves of the previous URL:

```
http://www.bu.edu/
```

and hoped for the best. His ingenuity was rewarded; the whole BU portion of the Web lay before him. Like I said, he may be Netsurfing still.

You can always type in a URL—either one you jotted down while you were offline, or one that you're making up as an educated guess. (For instance, my alma mater's domain name is `oxy.edu`; every so often I check to see if there's a `www.oxy.edu` or its ilk yet. So far nothing.) And once you can do that, you're free to go anywhere on the Net. All you need is a connection and your computer. Could you possibly be any better at this?

Of course, I'd understand if you were a bit nervous. Those first few trips onto the Net are kind of mind-boggling. The next chapter is designed to give you a bit of experience. Instead of a click-by-click guided tour, though, I'd like to show you three of the best sites I've found on the Web. Each of these is terrific in its own way, and all three have lots of great links to explore. I propose to show you a few pages from each one, talk about the kinds of things you might find, and then let you take it from there. Surf's up…

CHAPTER 10

SIGHTSEEING: A FEW DAY TRIPS

"See the pyramids along the Nile, watch the sun rise on a tropic isle...."

—Pasty Cline, and others

"Walking around it's clear that I'm worlds away...."

— The Go-Gos

I've chosen three sites for this chapter, any of which is a worthy starting point for Net exploration. Each site has a number of pages with things to do and see, and each offers a great variety of links to launch you onto the Net for further travels. They're also well-designed. Looking at these pages gives you a sense of how well-built Web sites are designed and structured.

Now that you know how to use the Mosaic interface, I'm not going to focus too heavily on the mechanics of using the pages—in some cases, it's not even important that you see the specific links we'll follow. Instead, I'm going to talk you through a few of them, show you what's available, and then make suggestions for further exploration. By the end of this chapter, you should feel comfortable using Mosaic to navigate and explore, and you should have a good understanding of how to read a Web page. And your explorations are just beginning; in Appendix D, "Things to Do, Places to See," you'll find a list of over 250 excellent Web pages, any one of which will get you started on interesting journeys. I've sorted those by topic (art, sports, food, business, and so on).

Note: Don't panic if I describe a page that looks different to you, or if I recommend trying a link that doesn't seems to be there. The Web changes constantly, and there's no form of publication in existence that could keep up with all the changes. Not even Net-based publications!

The first site, `www.nando.net`, is created and maintained by the Raleigh, North Carolina *News and Observer* (n-and-o—get it?), a newspaper. As such it's representative of the business world's rush to get on the Net. However, this site is no ordinary place to get product information or place an order. The *News and Observer* is making a concerted effort to get online with significantly enhanced content and a variety of information. NandO carries, among other things, several enhanced articles from the *News and Observer*.

In this case, "enhanced" means that not only does NandO carry the actual words and pictures that appeared in the newspaper article, but they've added video clips, sound bites, background information, and cross-references to previous, related articles. The NandO site is connected with the *News and Observer*'s other new-media projects, which include television and audio text information. This is one vision of the future of newspapers, and I think it's an appealing view.

The second site, `sunsite.unc.edu`, is coincidentally also located in the Raleigh-Durham area at the University of North Carolina-Chapel Hill. The UNC site is one of three Sun SITES in the world; the others are kept at Science University in Tokyo and Imperial College, London. It's also the mirror site for the NCSA, which means that anything you might find at the NCSA site is also here. The sites are sponsored by Sun Microsystems, and they have copies of a vast amount of public-domain (that is, free) software, government information, Internet tools, and various other items of interest (including multimedia projects and underground music information).

The site is, in a word, massive—you'll find links for everything, from a rollercoaster page to OTIS (a cooperative literary/art project) to political information, to a truly huge FTP (File Transfer Protocol) site. In a sense, all (or at least many) roads on the Web lead to North Carolina. For example, many of the people involved with NandO got their start at UNC.

The final site is `bianca.com`—bianca's SMUT-shack (Another NetSide Attraction), located somewhere in the heartland (Chicago, to be precise). biancaTroll, the proprietor, is less a person than an entity, and less an entity than a force of nature.

The bianca site isn't part of any organization or commercial concern, although it has links to sites such as local radio stations and carries information on Chicago hot spots. (It's also becoming rather prominent on the Chicago arts scene.) bianca's shack is a supreme example of how individuals can stake out a claim on the Web and go wild. It's nothing short of inspirational.

Without further ado, then, let's start by checking out NandO.

NandO—The Future of Journalism?

Our tour starts at the top of the site. In the URL space at the top of the screen, type

```
http://www.nando.net
```

and hit Enter. You'll find yourself on the page that appears in Figure 10.1. This is the top Web page for the site. We'll examine the page for ideas on what we'll find, and then pursue a few of the links. (Before we start though, many thanks to our gracious hosts at NandO and the *News and Observer* for their kind permission to let us snap a few photos on our sightseeing tour.)

Tech Tip: Many of NandO's pages have lots of inline graphics. They're beautiful, but if you have a slow (i.e., modem) connection you might prefer to switch the Display Inline Images setting (in the Options menu) to Off. Click once on the option to switch it off; click again to switch it back on and load all the graphics automatically, or click on the icons Mosaic presents in place of each image to load that image.

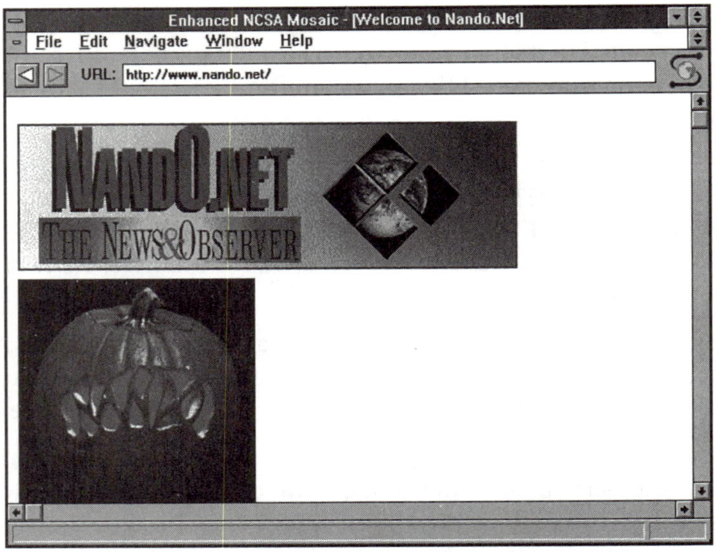

Figure 10.1. The top of the top page of NandO. There are about three more screens' worth of material on this page; you can see them by scrolling down on the screen.

NandO's top page changes fairly frequently, since many of the links are connected to pages with recent articles. The two articles in Figure 10.1 may still be available by the time you read this, but it's possible that the links will have moved lower on the page and replaced by more current articles. Further down the page we see the *News and Observer* sampler and an online "bookstore." NandO contains a number of links both to other NandO material and to points beyond; it's organized along the lines of the various sections of the newspaper.

After that, the page shows another feature article ("Polar Attractions") and then lists several links to other topics less closely related to the newspaper's "paper content." The sites listed in "Coming events," "Commercial organizations," and "Professional organizations" may expand or change, but the departments are likely to remain. Finally, there's a link to get more information about the site itself, and an e-mail address for its proprietor, `zonker@nando.net`.

"Polar Attractions" is a feature story by *News and Observer* reporter Martha Quillen about the North Carolina Zoological Park and its new natural-style habitat. It's a great example of how the Web can be used to publish articles that go far beyond the usual words and pictures. Let's follow the link. I can't predict how you'll see it onscreen by the time you read this—after all, that's like trying to predict next week's headlines—but let's follow the link by its URL:

```
http://www.nando.net/sproject/zoo/zoo1.html
```

The start of the page is shown in Figure 10.2. NandO includes the *News and Observer* logo over links that began as articles in the paper itself.

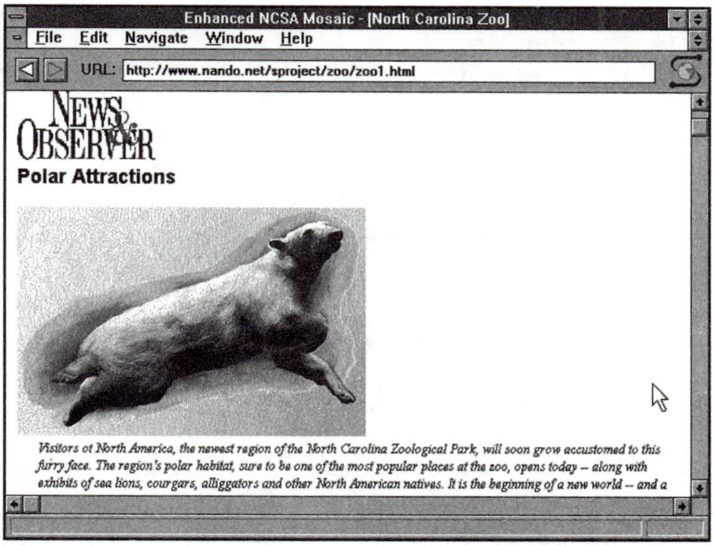

Figure 10.2. Polar bears! The top of a multimedia zoo story on NandO.

The polar bear shown at the top of the page was shown in the original article.

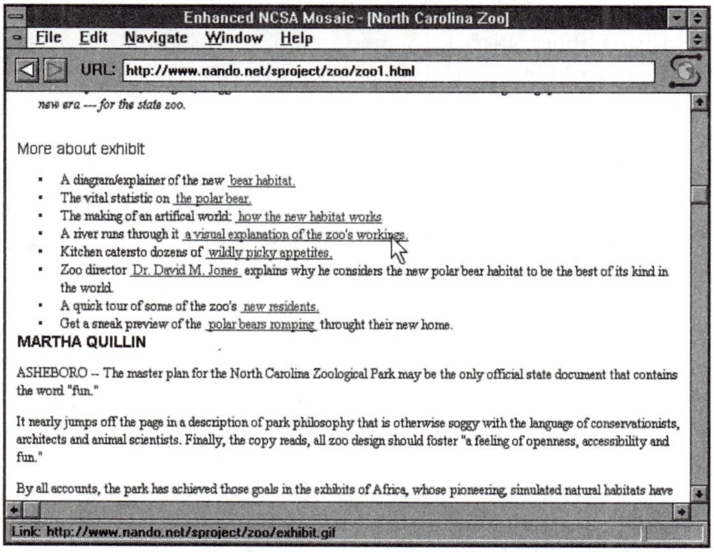

Figure 10.3. There are links to various parts of the polar bear feature listed above the article itself. Lots of good background information is kept here.

There's a section of links, and then the article itself (with no links) starts below that.

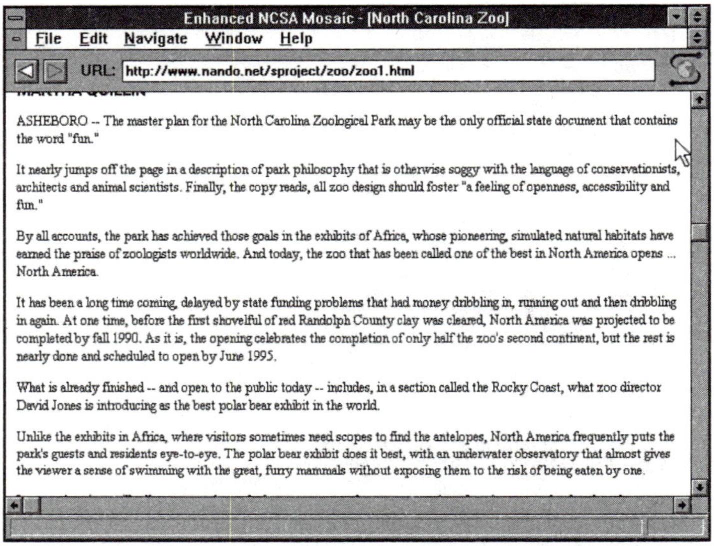

Figure 10.4. The article starts below the other links; of course, you can always scroll back and hop around with Mosaic's navigational tools.

Looking at Figure 10.3 we see the links. Some of the links here—the picky-appetites article, for instance—originally appeared as sidebars to the paper version of the story. Others, such as the new-residents and polar-bears-romping link, are movie clips. And Dr. Jones' discussion of the habitat is a sound file; click here and you'll hear his voice.

> **Note:** The version of Enhanced Mosaic in this book includes utilities (small programs) that can handle sound and video, but not every version of Mosaic does. If your version of Mosaic can't play sound or video on its own, you can get those utilities for free off the Net and add them to your Mosaic. I'll explain how that's done in Chapter 12.

The Discoveries series exploring North Carolina, which ran during the summer of '94, features many of the same kinds of links. The articles are organized in the order in which they appeared; though the link might not appear as we saw it in Figure 10.1, you can still check it out by moving to the URL window on the screen and typing

```
http://www.nando.net/ncd
```

Figure 10.5 shows links on one Discoveries page to a number of other articles in the series. The fishery article also contains such links, but those connect to articles on the same topic that ran weeks or even months earlier. Such links make it easy to see how the newspaper has covered the issue over time. Such links are a great convenience to readers, but it's uncommon to find them done so thoroughly; the necessary research and link maintenance are fairly time-consuming. Many newspapers and magazines haven't started linking their articles by topic yet; however, as sites like NandO set the pace, it's likely that other publications will feel compelled to keep up (fortunately for us readers).

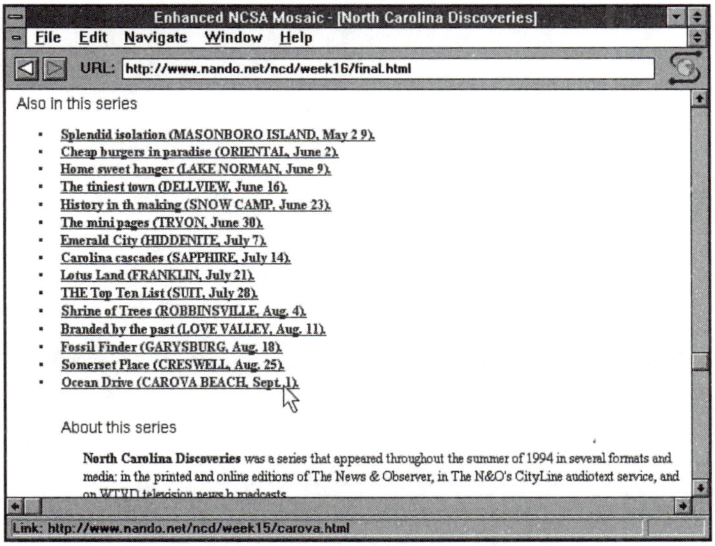

Figure 10.5. The links shown here involve several months' worth of NandO coverage.

As for the newspaper itself, a sampling of today's edition is available. A link at the bottom of the top page leads you to a Gopher menu with news and contact information.

> **Note:** You may have noticed already, but when you use the arrows to back up to previous pages, Mosaic thoughtfully remembers where on the page you were when you left.

The first choice shown on the screen in Figure 10.6 is a file with news from today's edition.

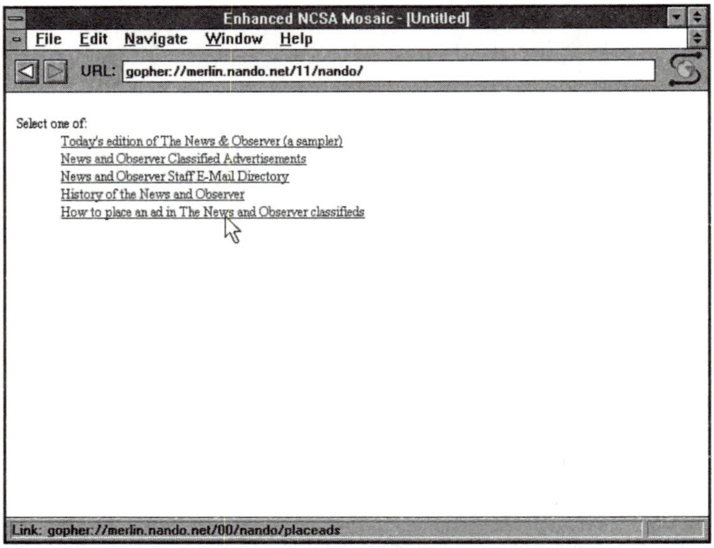

Figure 10.6. Up-to-date with NandO's news.

Clicking on the link opens the menu shown in Figure 10.7. Clicking on one of these links gets you the text of the article.

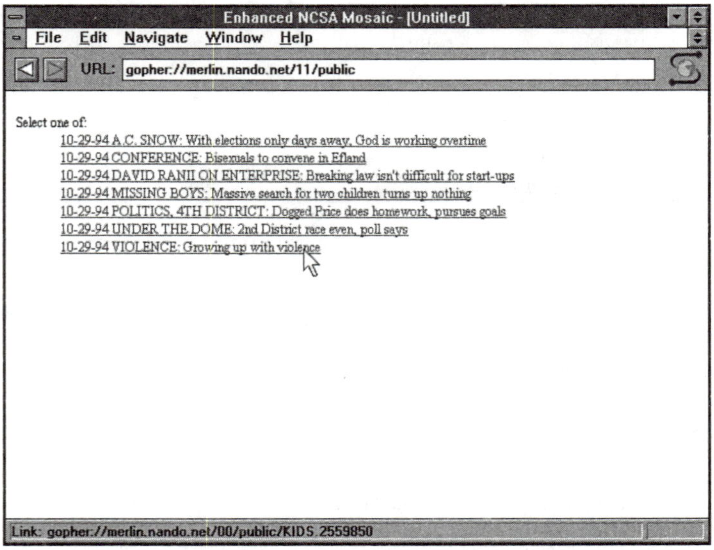

Figure 10.7. Daily editions of NandO News are available on this Gopher screen.

The links in NandO are worth exploring; many of them link to sites other than `www.nando.net`. The proprietors of the sports server state that they'd like this site to be the most complete source on the Net for sports information; they keep up-to-date news and schedules, and during the dark days of the '94 baseball strike they printed a daily simulation of how the games (and therefore the season) might have gone. Figure 10.8 shows those might-have-been box scores. It also shows icons that link the sports server back to the top page and to other sections of the NandO section.

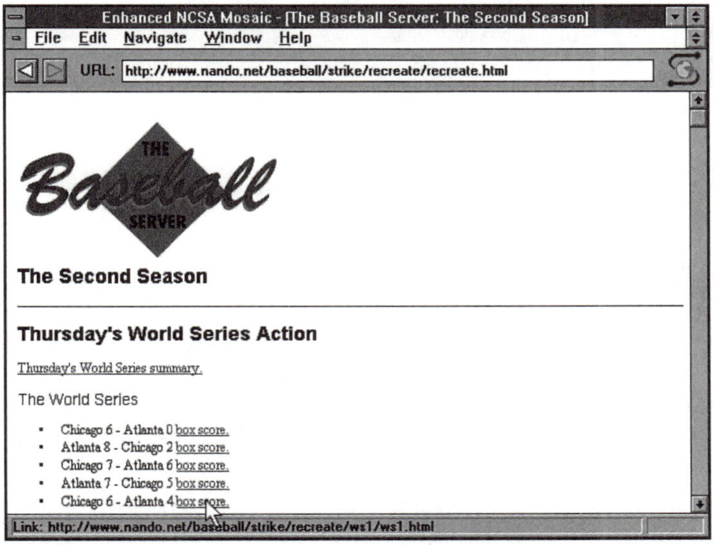

Figure 10.8. Sports server with box scores—a lifeline during this trying summer.

The entertainment section has listings for local events and a number of reviews of movies, restaurants, and music. It also has space for you to list the URL for your own home page, if you like. If you're looking for somewhere fresh to visit, browsing this section (which is arranged by subject as much as possible) is a good start.

The other commercial sites listed on the top page are interesting in their own right; they also show some solutions to certain design problems. Clicking on the Neiman Foundation link on the main page, for instance, leads you to a recent symposium on online journalism. This page is very long, and it starts off with a great deal of background information on the conference. To get directly to the list of links, the writer of the page included a link to another spot on the same page. The `#Contents` line shown in the anchor bar at the bottom of the screen shown in Figure 10.9 (you'll see it if you position the mouse cursor over the word "Contents") points to a spot farther down the page. Clicking will essentially fast-forward you to that section. This is useful when the page is dauntingly long.

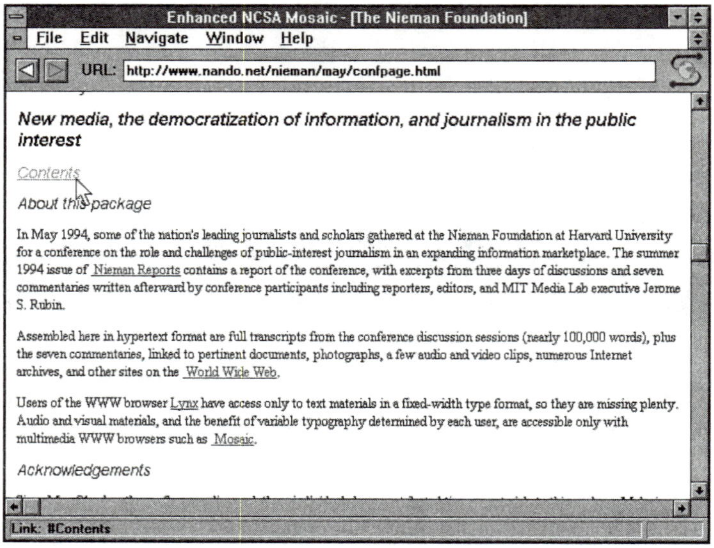

Figure 10.9. The contents intra-page link, shown in the anchor bar.

Plenty of computer functions less glamorous than video and sound have an important place on the Net, especially at a big site like this. For instance, the text of the federal decision about North Carolina's Congressional redistricting plan runs well over a hundred pages; typing that in would have taken a very long time. However, by using a scanner and OCR (Optical Character Recognition) software, the page keepers could scan in the pages and then have the computer translate the scanned image into the actual words. This enabled the *News and Observer* to publish the entire text of the decision within hours of getting their printed copy.

Close the book for a bit and take some time to explore on your own. You should have a good idea of what's here and how to get around. You know that there are movies and sound clips to see and hear in addition to the expected pictures and text. You know how to find current news. And after you've spent some time checking out the beautiful sights of the site, you can check out some of the links to other places in NandO.

In the Music Kitchen, you'll find (among other things) a link to the Internet Underground Music Archives, a site with a collection of information on bands of all descriptions. You'll also find this link as part of the next site we'll visit, `sunsite.unc.edu` at the University of North Carolina-Chapel Hill.

UNC: A Heliocentric Approach

The heliocentric view of the universe tells us that the earth revolves around the sun. The heliocentric view of the Internet tells us that the action revolves around Sun SITES, huge collections of files and archives sponsored by several computer companies and by the universities that take on the day-to-day maintenance of these massive collections. We'll take a long look at the University of North Carolina-Chapel Hill's site, `sunsite.unc.edu`.

As I mentioned, there are three Sun SITES at this writing, with more on the way. You can, of course, connect to any of the Sun SITES to reach the vast collection of archives and files the Sun project makes it its business to make available. However, it's a good idea to tread lightly on the Net whenever possible, and one way of doing that is using the nearest available site to pick up a file.

There's no difference between the copy of NCSA Mosaic on the Tokyo server and the copy on the North Carolina server, for instance—but getting it from the closer site means that the file being transferred spends less time bouncing around the phone lines between computers, and less time using the resources of the computers in its path. Using the Internet as efficiently as possible is one way of taking good care of it.

Besides, there's more to `sunsite.unc.edu` than just a collection of files and archives. (This is a good place to pause and thank the administrators of `sunsite.unc.edu`, particularly Paul Jones, for allowing us to make this tour on paper.) Let's look at the top page at the site. This page is longer than most of the others we've come across thus far, as you'll see in Figures 10.10 and 10.11, but you'll soon see why.

Just below the Sun Microsystems and UNC insignia at the top of the page you'll notice nine button-type icons surrounded by a largish box. If you look more closely, you'll notice that the box is a link border. And if you roll the mouse around on the area within the border, you'll see a URL in the anchor bar at the bottom of the screen:

```
http://sunsite.unc.edu/cgi-bin/imagemap/sunbuttons
```

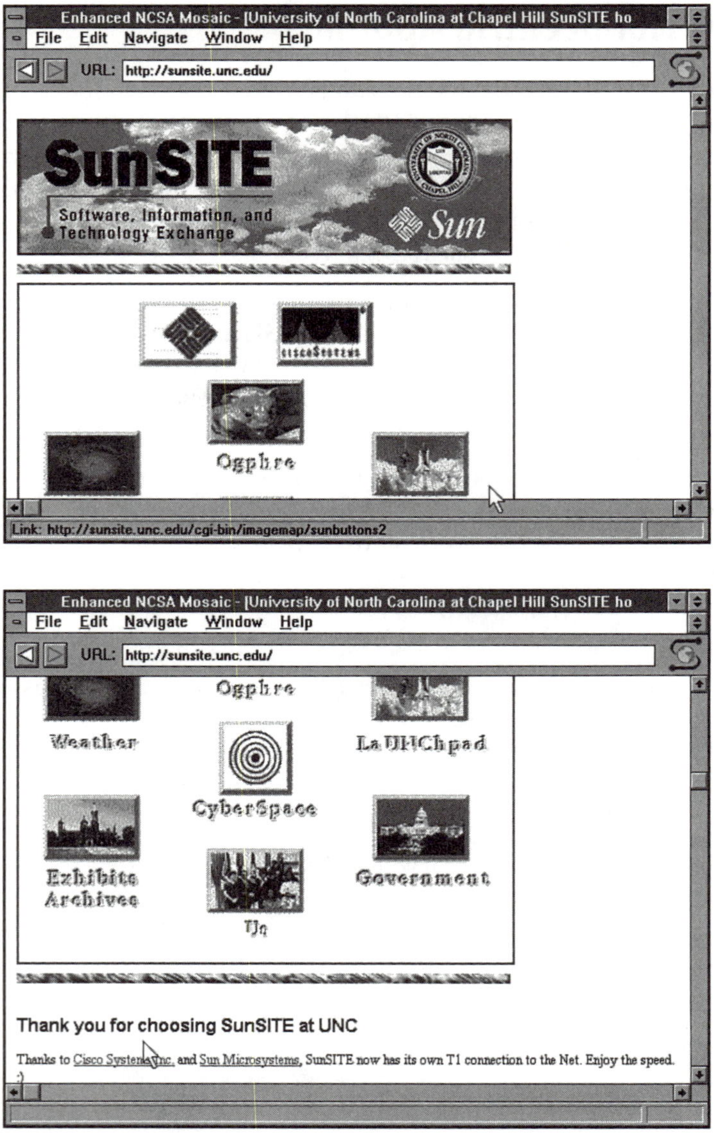

Figures 10.10 and **10.11.** The "map" of the UNC site, seen at the top of the top page.

This is a hypermedia image map, a sure sign that Mosaic is taking over the world of the Web. Every square millimeter within the link border has a link to the sunbuttons URL, which in turn connects to several (in this case, nine) links. The map lets you click on an area of one large graphic such as this one to get to any one of several links. The software reads the coordinates of the mouse-click and translates them into a request for the appropriate link. There's no way one of the old-style text-based Web browsers could handle this map—which is why just below it you'll find all the links on the image map duplicated and explained one by one, thus substantially increasing the length of the page.

We'll play with the map in a minute; we'll also see other versions of this emerging Web tool. For now, though, let's read the rest of the page, the top of which you'll see in Figure 10.12. Sun and Cisco (one of the companies that manufacturers the special computer equipment that moves Net traffic around) have links to their sites here. These links correspond to the top two areas of the image map above.

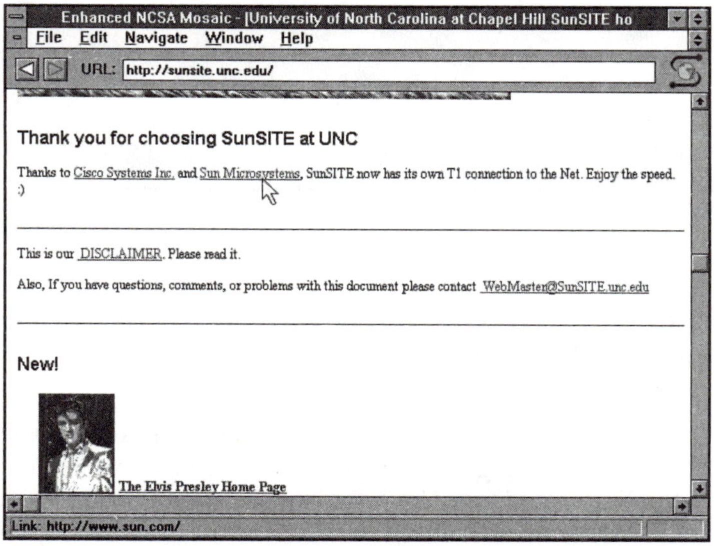

Figure 10.12. SunSITE Page with Elvis.

The Exhibits, Archives and Exhibitions link is just below; the button on the image map is in the lower left hand corner. Four sub-links are listed under the Exhibits section—Expo, a collection of links from the Vatican, Paris' Cordon Bleu cooking school, and other marvels; OTIS (Operative Term Is Stimulate), an ongoing multimedia art project; Dr. Fun, a comic strip distributed only on the Internet; and IUMA, the Internet Underground Music Archive. We saw a link to the same archive on NandO.

Let's take a detour here before we move through the rest of the top page. Click on Exhibits, either on the image map or on the text link. (It's the same link; it goes to the same place, though it looks a bit different onscreen.) This page takes a little while to load, mainly because it's huge. You see the very top of it in Figure 10.13—it goes on for *eight more screens* after that. Scroll down it (or just keep hitting Page Down). You find the Expo listing at the top; beneath that, sites are arranged roughly by topic.

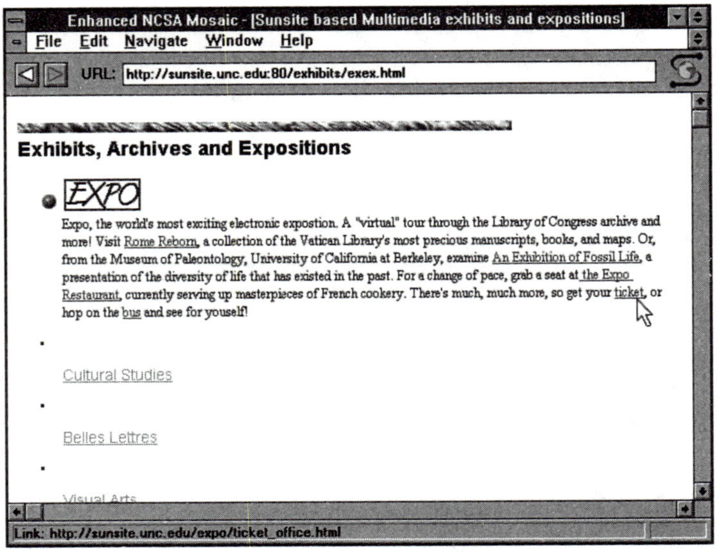

Figure 10.13. The top of the very long Exhibitions page. You've been warned—but it really is worth it.

Note the URL in the window; I clicked on the image map to reach this page. The address was translated into my mouse cursor's screen position, hence the numbers.

At the top of the page we have Expo, worth several hours all by itself. I love this site as much for its charming metaphor as for the wealth of well-chosen exhibits; the proprietor, Frans van Hoesel, uses a tour-guide metaphor to guide you from spot to spot. And like any good tour, there are day passes (links) to other sites as well as a restaurant for reviving one's energies after a grueling day of examining the treasures of the various exhibits. (The restaurant is Le Cordon Bleu, the renowned Parisian cooking school; it has recipes, photos, and suggested menus. Beware of this page if you're feeling hungry—switch off the graphics!)

Expo is kept at

```
http://sunsite.unc.edu/expo/expo/busstation.html
```

Tech Tip: To learn more about the making of the Expo exhibit, which also includes material from the Vatican, the Soviet pavilion, 1492 (an exhibit created on the anniversary's of Columbus' first voyage to North America), the Dead Sea Scrolls, a paleontology exhibit, and a multimedia tour of the ruins of the Roman palace at Spatalo, check out

```
http://rugmd4.chem.rug.nl/hoesel/expo/expo.story.html
```

The site has a wonderful selection of American culture materials; the list starts just below the Expo. The Women's Resources project is excellent, and the Soviet archives are extremely interesting (though the Dazdhbog's Grandsons link is mainly in Russian; the site gives you instructions for displaying the Cyrillic characters if you feel so disposed). By the time you read this, the Gaelic Web page should be accompanied by a Yiddish Web page. Both are significant and important resources for learning these threatened languages (and finding things to read once you do). Here's another great use for the Net; you might not know anyone living nearby who shares your interest in some of these topics, but if you're on the Net you can find a community of people that does. With any luck, Internet projects like these will preserve languages that are otherwise doomed to die.

The next section has a number of art and literary resources. Some of these are simple lists of links to other sites; some are actual creations (the award-winning "What The Welsh And Chinese Have In Common," by the way, is written by the same Paul Jones that administers this site); some are magazines or e-zines (as they call magazines that exist solely in electronic form).

While we're still in Exhibits let's look at OTIS, one of the most popular spots at `sunsite.unc.edu`. We see the OTIS's top page in Figure 10.14.

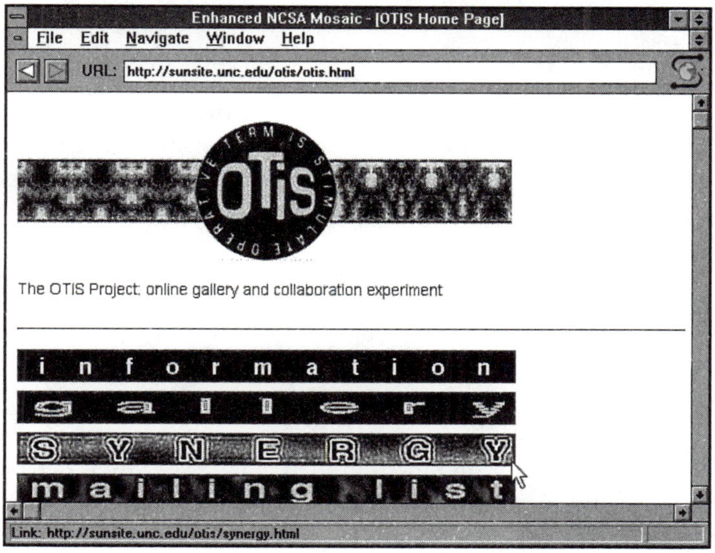

Figure 10.14. The OTIS (Operative Term Is Stimulate) Web page, found at `http://sunsite.unc.edu/otis/otis.html`.

As you see from the list, OTIS is itself a many-splendored thing, even though it's just a tiny part of the `sunsite.unc.edu` site. Clicking on any of the four links shown in the figure will bring you information on the project, let you look at the artworks, or help you to participate. Yes, you too can be part of OTIS. A glance in the

Gallery section, as seen in Figure 10.15, will hint at the variety of media (or mediums if you're the writer of this page) that can be part of the OTIS collaboration.

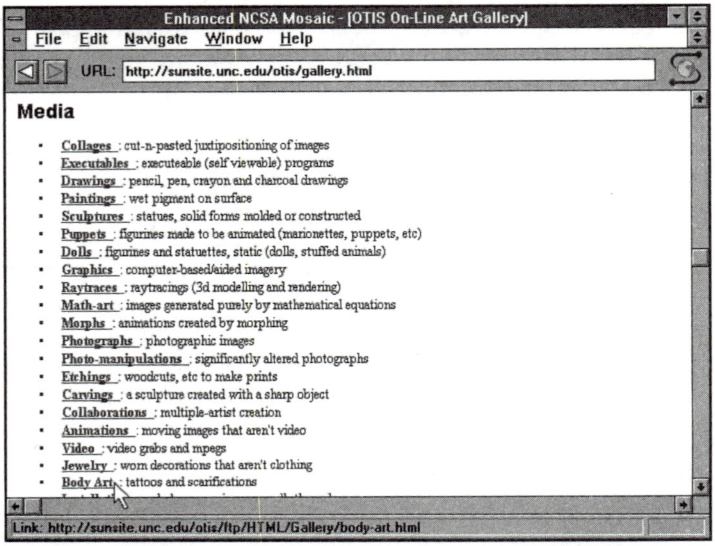

Figure 10.15. The OTIS project encourages interested artists to get involved.

This list goes on beyond the screen I'm showing you; it's followed by subject lists and other information on the kinds of art that can be contributed. (To make it brief, almost any creative medium is fair game; the categories are an organizational tool rather than a means of excluding artists.)

The OTIS project isn't the only collaborative creative project on the Web, as artists discover the possibilities of online multimedia. Many of the other links listed here, notably Cyberkind and Verbiage, are also open to contributions from the Net community.

Moving down the page, we see the Internet Underground Music Archive, Dr. Fun, and other intriguing sites (rollercoasters!). Once you add a JPG viewer to Mosaic (as I mentioned, Mosaic doesn't include such viewers but they're freely available on the Net), drop by and check out Dr. Fun—it's very funny and slightly twisted, in the tradition of The Far Side or The Neighborhood. It's also updated daily, which gives you a good reason to check in regularly.

The student projects page has a lot of charm. For instance, check out the Nancy Drew project, designed specifically for Mosaic and full of interesting links. We see the top of the Nancy Drew page in Figure 10.16.

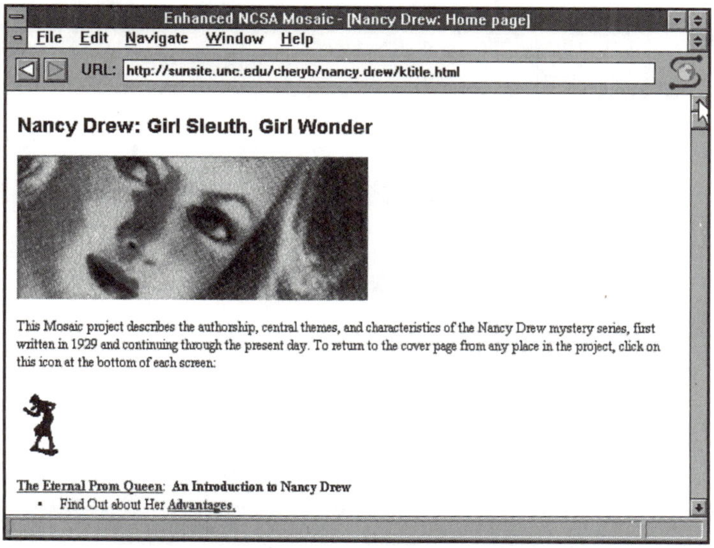

Figure 10.16. Nancy Drew, titian-haired girl sleuth, on her own Web page.

Obviously you could spend days wandering through even the top level of links in the Exhibits section. For now, though, let's return to the top page. Since we've hopped around a lot here, this is a good time to use the History option under the Navigate menu.

Back on the top page, we're ready to meet Ogphre, the Sun Site Gopher. As you'll remember from Chapter 4, Gopher was the best Net-navigation tool to come along before the advent of Mosaic; it handles all kinds of files, and it's very quick. The keepers of `sunsite.unc.edu` have chosen to group most of their Gopher-available resources under the Ogphre banner (leaving the rest of the site for true Web pages).

We've already seen one Gopher site in this chapter; NandO uses Gopher to make the daily news available. In Figure 10.17 we see the Ogphre Gopher menu. Note that some of the areas we saw on the top page (the Sun information, for instance) are duplicated once again in this menu. Since not everyone uses Mosaic yet, the proprietors are making sure that as much of the information on Sun SITES as possible is available in Gopherspace, as it's called.

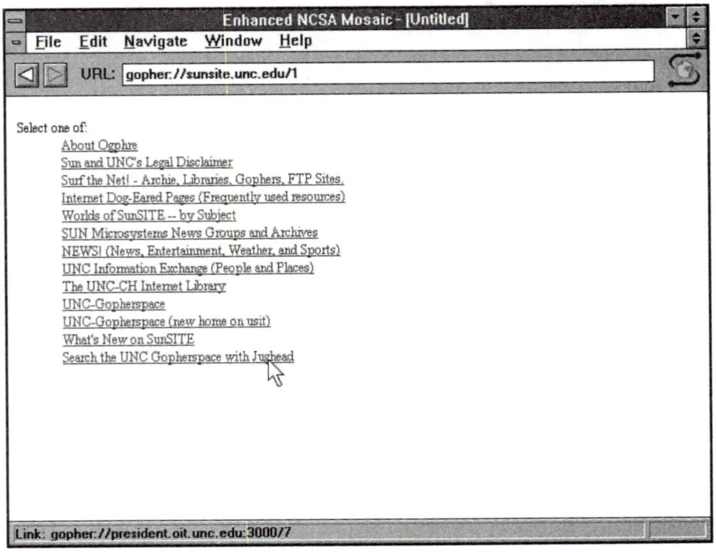

Figure 10.17. A menu from the Ogphre Gopher at UNC.

Note the icons to the left of each link; they tell you what sort of resource the link points to. You probably recognize the file folders as directories and the sheet of paper as a text file; the icon next to the final item ("Search the UNC Gopherspace with Jughead") denotes a search tool. The icon makes sense if you think of it as index cards from a library card catalog; Gopher (or Ogphre) finds resources on the site, just as a librarian uses a card catalog to find books and other materials.

The Heliocentric Information Map points you toward the other Sun Sites. As you see on the image map in Figure 10.18, this list of sites is arranged with the Sun Sites in the middle of the universe, with the university itself beyond that, with other resources in North Carolina (including NandO) beyond that, other American sites beyond that, and the world in the outermost orbit.

This is another image map, and in many ways a better one than the map on the top site page. (The organization of the universe into concentric circles lends itself well to this graphic, don't you think?) Clicking on the Sun circle (the middle of the map) shows you another good use of image maps.

The screen in Figure 10.19 shows another representation of the ring-map on the previous screen (with the Sun "icon" selected).

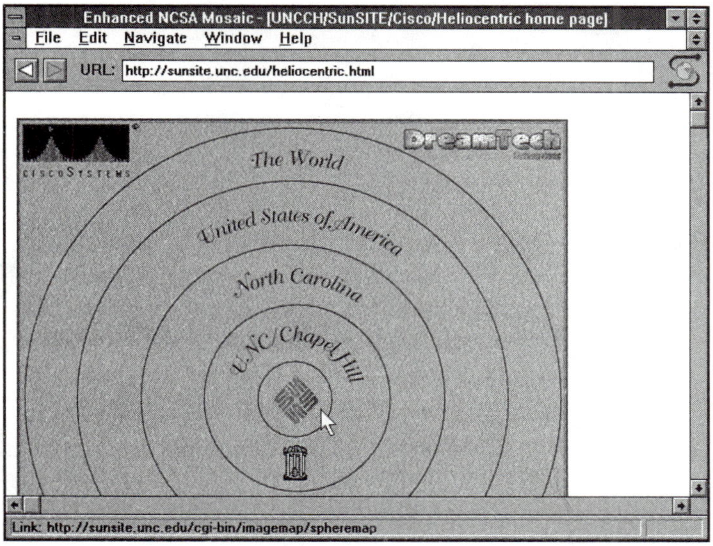

Figure 10.18. The Heliocentric Information Map, which can be reached at `http://sunsite.unc.edu/heliocentric.html`.

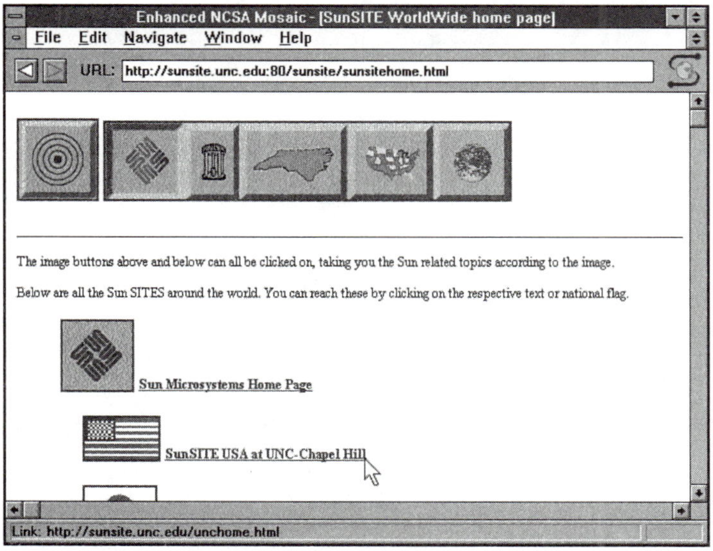

Figure 10.19. The SunSITE WorldWide Home Page.

Rolling along back on the top page, we see a section of government documents. City, state, and federal governments are rushing online (as I noted at the end of Chapter 3). One of the good aspects of that rush is easy availability of government documents. However, some government bodies take better advantage of the Net than others. The documents at this site are fairly well chosen and presented, as you see in Figure 10.20. Some of the files, such as Gore's address at UCLA, even have a few links in them.

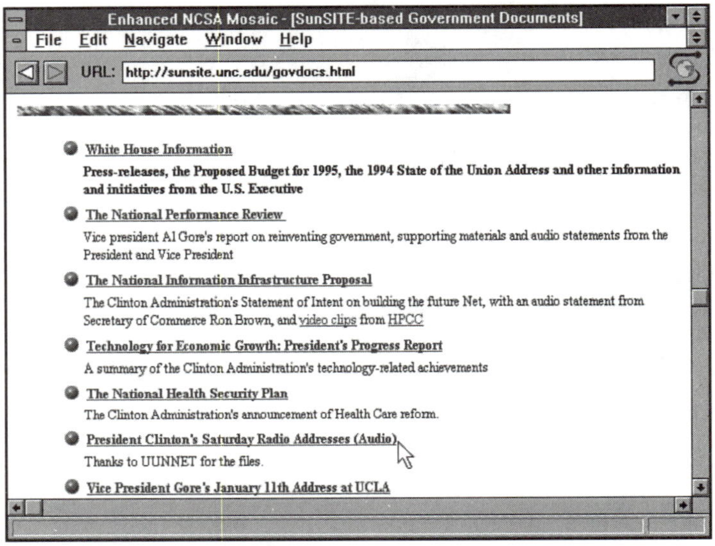

Figure 10.20. A well-presented government document, online at UNC.

> **Note:** What's the most exciting government site on the Web? I'd say it's the brand-new White House page. It's got everything from information on starting a small business to an audio file of Socks the cat. And there are plans in the works to make this a one-stop spot for filling out certain types of government forms, such as disaster-relief applications. Check it out at `http://www.whitehouse.gov` (Figure 10.21).

Finally—I told you this site was a monster—we have a link to the development group in Figure 10.22.

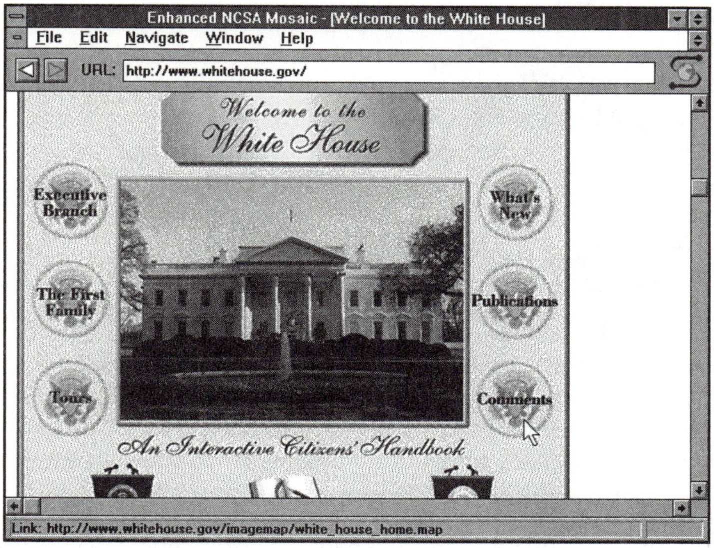

Figure 10.21. The White House welcome page.

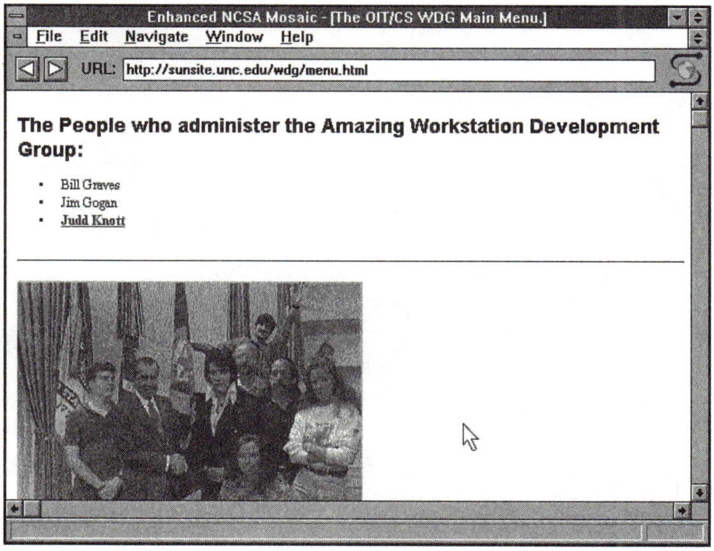

Figure 10.22. The excellent group that brings you the UNC Web site.

As you see, there are some famous folk in the crew...hey, no one said these pages had to be entirely serious. In fact, the next spot we visit is entirely geared toward fun. Take a few minutes now to explore the rich resources of `sunsite.unc.edu`. Afterwards, we'll leave North Carolina and make our way to the weird wilds of Chicago, and the famous (notorious?) bianca's SMUT-shack.

bianca—Trolling the Net

There's no purpose behind the creation of the bianca site currently at `www.bianca.com`. It didn't start as a commercial concern, it wasn't connected to an academic institution (though it did start life at Northwestern University), and it's most certainly not part of the government or military. bianca's place is just there because it amuses someone to make it so, and it amuses lots of other people that it is so.

biancaTroll, our gracious hostess, lives in the SMUT-shack. As bianca's guest, you're invited to, uh, troll through her house, looking at her stuff. The shack metaphor, like the tour-bus metaphor used by Expo, helps you to navigate the site.

Let's drop in. bianca lives at

```
http://bianca.com/shack/index.html
```

> **Note:** During the summer, bianca moved from her old digs at Northwestern University in search of a larger plot of Web territory. We're fortunate to see the site when the big move is almost complete, but you may notice a bit of sawdust and a few unpacked boxes as we wander the halls. Many thanks to bianca and to her helper Dave Thau for loaning us the keys to the house so we can wander around.

bianca's top Web page is shown in Figures 10.23 and 10.24. We're looking at the bottom of the main page here.

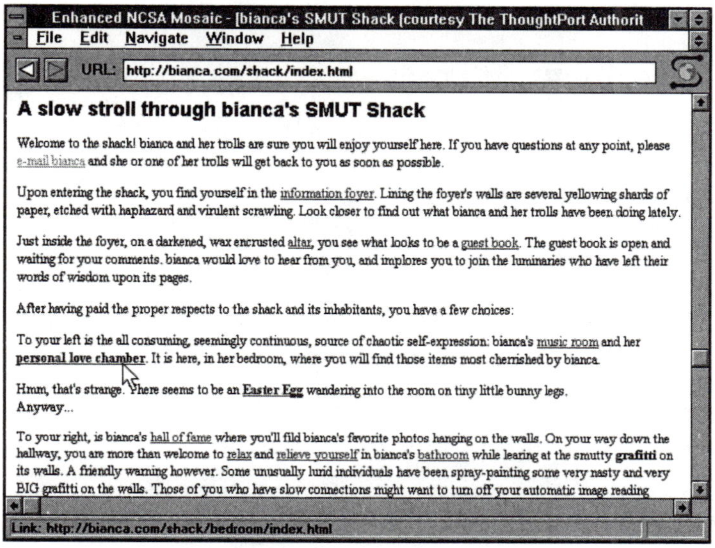

Figure 10.23. In biancaTroll's house there are many rooms…

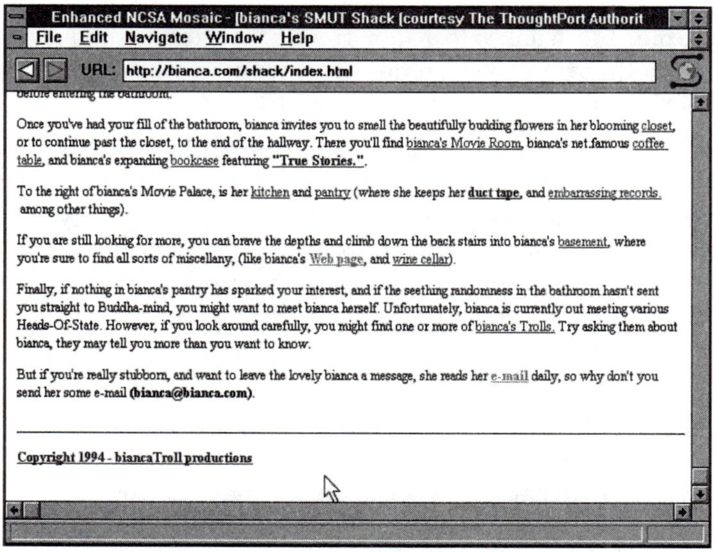

Figure 10.24. …not all of which are as they seem.

Figures 10.23 and 10.24 describe the shack in all its glory. As you see, there are a lot of links corresponding to different rooms of the shack and the things you might find there. bianca also has an image map of the shack blueprint for visual navigation. We see the map itself in Figure 10.25.

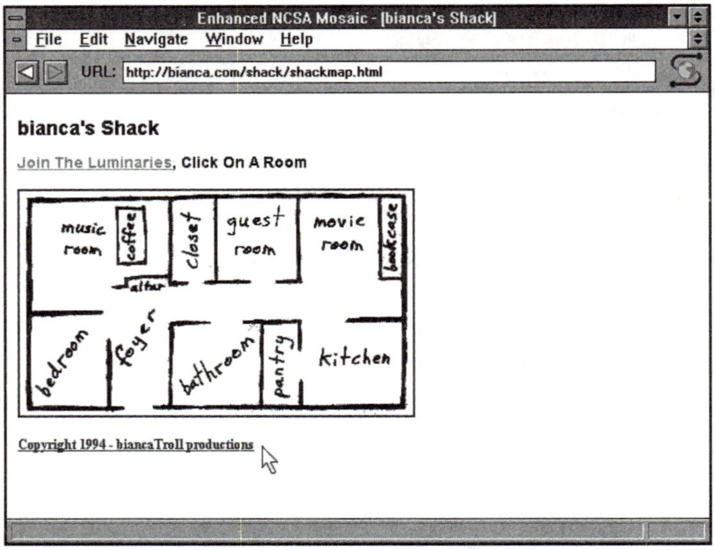

Figure 10.25. A "blueprint" of bianca's shack. It may exist only in your mind, but you'll find it's rather useful in there.

Back in Chapter 2, Josh linked to bianca's music room to browse the links she keeps there. Let's do the same. Click on the music room in the upper-left-hand corner of the map, or on the link shown in Figure 10.23.

We see the page shown in Figure 10.26. At the top of the page is a link to the graffiti-covered bathroom; beneath it you see a collection of reviews and other music information. She also includes a few semi-random thoughts on what's worth listening to, and supplies a list of pointers to other Web pages around the Net. There's the ubiquitous Internet Underground Music Archive; the popular `metaverse.com` server is listed as MTV (you'll remember the fracas over the use of the `mtv.com` domain name from Chapter 5). For obvious copyright reasons, bianca doesn't have sound clips available.

Many of the links in the music room lead to simple text files with thoughts on whatever bianca's been listening to lately. It's a quirky, opinionated collection of pages, and it shows what you, too, can do if you decide you want a page or two of your own on the Web. (Make no mistake, though—this is an ambitious site. Most personal Web pages have four or perhaps five pages to them.)

Let's head back to the top page. It's always nice to leave a note for the proprietors of a particularly good Web page, and bianca has a guest book for just that purpose. Click on the link; we see the book in Figure 10.27.

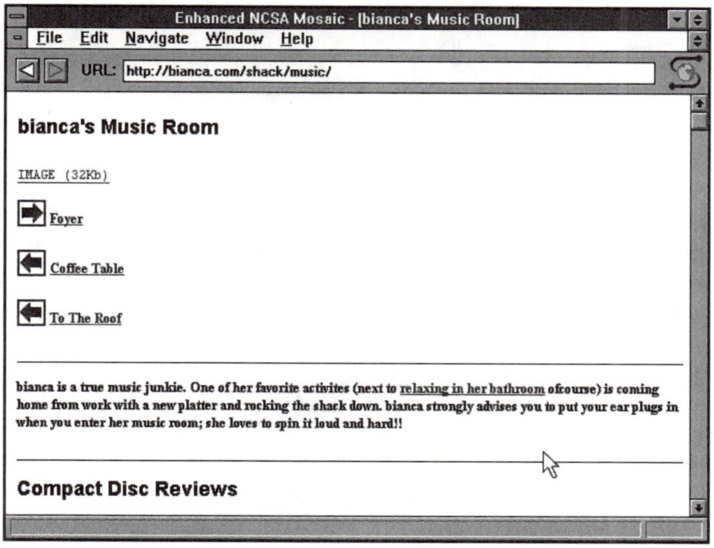

Figure 10.26. The top of the page showing you bianca's music room. There's another screen of material below this. bianca, by the way, is exceedingly polite to modem users by using fairly short pages in most cases.

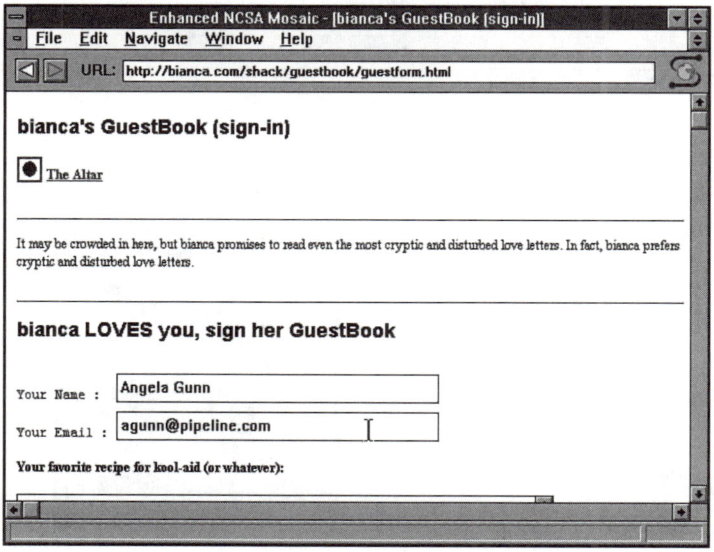

Figure 10.27. bianca's guest book helps her and her troll helpers keep track of who's dropped by.

This is a form—one of the ways Mosaic allows you to interact with what you see onscreen. By filling in the blanks, you can send a brief message to bianca and her trusty trolls. As I've mentioned, the people (and trolls) who go through the hard work of setting up and maintaining a good site love to hear your comments. Let's pause to write a note in the guest book.

Tech Tip: Once you've written the message, you should see a button that says "Submit." Clicking on that button will send your message. If, by chance, you don't see the Submit button, look for a tiny, unnamed button at the bottom-left of the page.

Once that's done, we can check out the rest of the rooms using either the map or the text links on the top page. You've seen the music room; the hall of fame in the hallway nearby is a nice example of thoughtful page design, as shown in Figure 10.28. To see the photos in the hall of fame, click on the underlined names. bianca could have automatically loaded all the photos as inline images, but as we've seen that can take a long time over a slow modem link. This page is designed to allow you to control what you see and how much time you spend here.

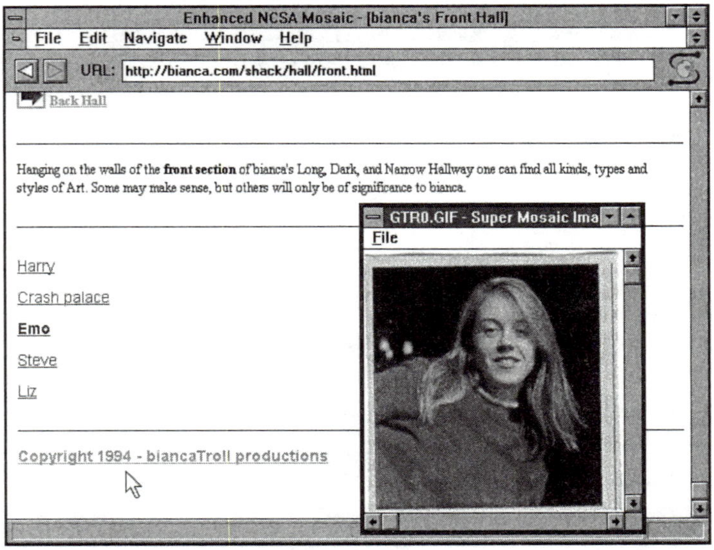

Figure 10.28. A thoughtfully designed Hall of Fame display.

If you're not scared of the bathroom I'm not either. It's actually pretty cool; the bianca site is terrific for interactivity and the bathroom is the heart of it. Click on the link. You'll enter and be given the choice to read what's on the walls or to write something of your own.

> **Warning:** If you're easily offended by coarseness or profanity, do not enter the bathroom. The Net is thankfully uncensored; however, some people get off on using that freedom to be gross. To each his own, but don't say I didn't warn you.

In Figure 10.29 we see an innocuous example of the graffiti you'll find on the walls of bianca's bathroom. Note the links! The form that allows visitors to add graffiti to the walls also allows them to enter links to other sites. A lot of these lead to other personal Web pages. I'm thinking of adding mine here too—though I don't make a habit of defacing the walls in other people's homes, bianca certainly doesn't mind.

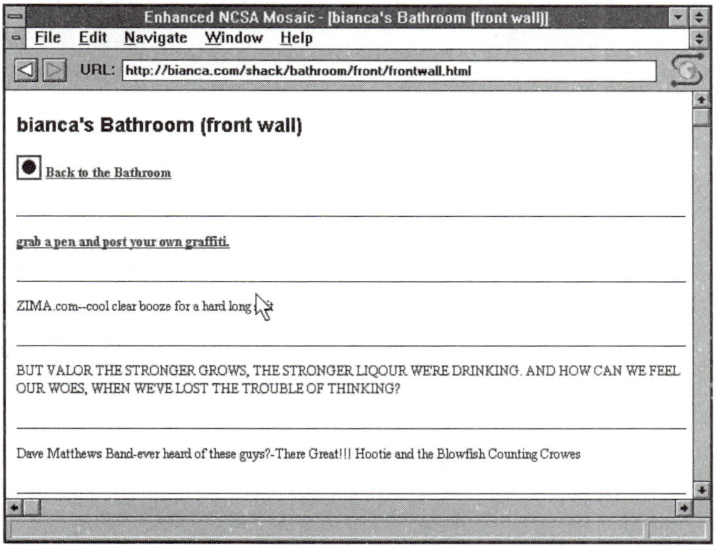

Figure 10.29. A wall in bianca's bathroom, bastion of free and cheap expression.

This is as good a place as any to mention that not every link you'll find will work properly. A number of the links submitted to the graffiti walls, for instance, don't go anywhere. Chalk it up to poorly written links, and don't take it personally. If you're feeling adventurous and really want to see a particular site, you might jot down the URL visible in the anchor line at the bottom of the screen when you position the mouse cursor directly over the link and experiment with it, using the tips on URLs at the end of Chapter 8.

Scroll through the four walls of the bathroom to see if any of these links look appealing. There's no organization, so you have to trust that serendipity thing to kick in. I found an interesting link a bit further down: It simply says "CASTLE SONNENSTEIN." The URL is

```
http://rrws6.wiwi.uni-regensberg.de/SONNENSTEIN/sonnenstein.html
```

which links to the University of Regensberg, in Germany (note the `.de` top-level domain—think Deutschland). If you check it out you'll find a game called Castle Sonnenstein, in which you're charged with rescuing a Mosaic programmer from the walls of the dread Sonnenstein academic building at the university. It's pretty nifty—it has graphics, links, and even sound clips. Worth a look.

Let's back up, though, and spend more time at bianca's place. The closet is actually a mini-greenhouse, with fairly serious gardening tips for plants of various kinds (even kinds that aren't normally grown in a closet). The movie room is, as you might expect, filled with bianca's personal recommendations as well as other good links. Her coffee table is even more idiosyncratic; periodically, she lists what can be found on the coffee table. That's it. As if you haven't guessed, bianca's shack tends toward the cluttered. The list is often a fairly funny map of what's going on in our active troll's life.

The kitchen, shown in Figure 10.30, gives you more opportunity to commune with bianca by submitting a favorite recipe and looking at some of hers.

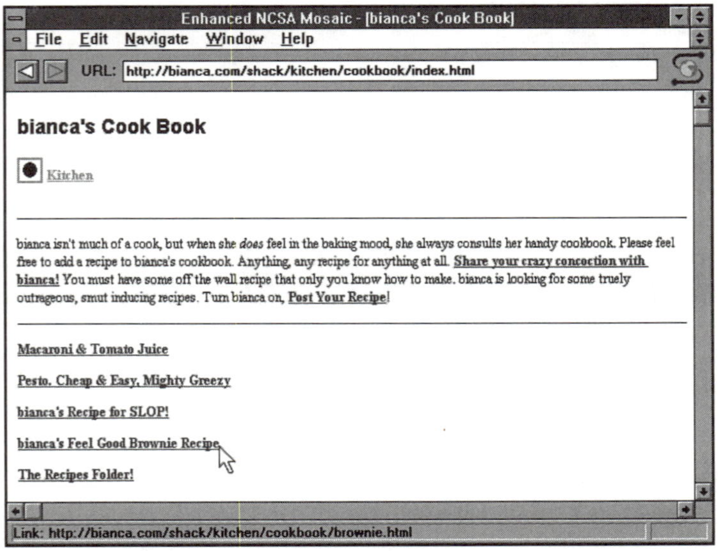

Figure 10.30. You can get anything you want at bianca's kitchen, excepting bianca.

It also has a link to a large and excellent recipes folder, located at

```
http://english-server.hss.cmu.edu/Recipes.html
```

It's geared slightly toward vegetarians, but meat-eaters will find good things here as well. This site is one of the more popular recipe repositories on the Net; if you're an adventurous cook, you might consider adding this one to your own hotlist.

The duct tape and hateful lists in the pantry are also interactive. bianca holds her shack and her world together with duct tape; your suggestions on how to make further use of this versatile product are welcome. The hateful list is similarly designed for your participation; readers not familiar with the dry wit of Sei Shonagon's Pillow Book are encouraged to read thoughts from this twelfth-century Japanese noblewoman and then add to the list. Funny, sly stuff.

Finally, you should get to know bianca's fellow trolls. There are at last count four trolls roaming the premises; each has his/her/its own section, as seen in Figure 10.31.

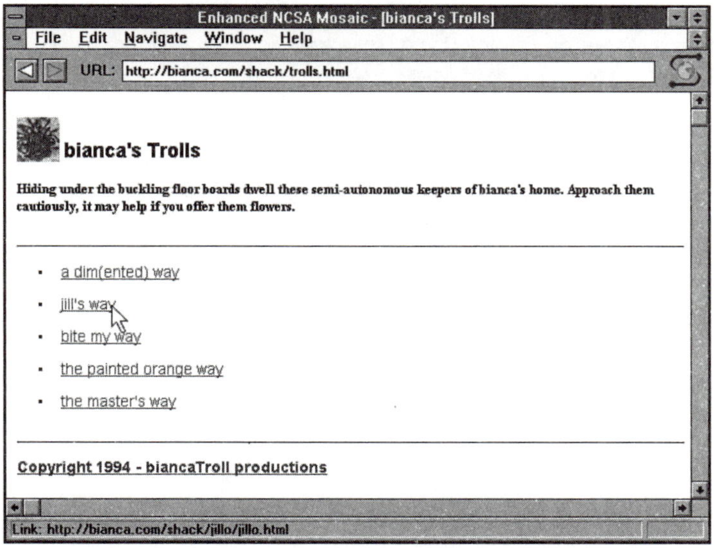

Figure 10.31. Domain of the helper trolls.

Let's look in on Jill troll, who keeps a fun collection of things to share with visitors. Jill's mom is extremely quotable, and I always check in to see if she's said anything sublime lately. However, in this craziest of shacks I wanted to show you a quiet and lovely art exhibit: Jill's postcard collection, as seen in Figure 10.32.

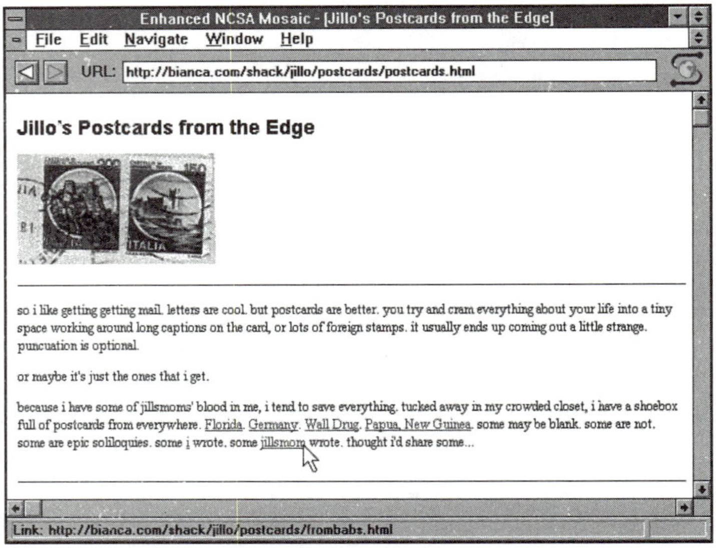

Figure 10.32. Postcards from the edge.

Jill and her mom collect postcards from everywhere. Jill has scanned in several of these, and typed in the messages on the back for your amusement. After all the frenetic touring we've done in this chapter, I find it soothing somehow to look at the pictures and hey, read someone else's mail.

On Your Own

I'll leave you here to pursue the links that amuse you. We've been to some amazing places: NandO's multimedia extravaganzas, re-shaping the face of journalism; UNC's mind-boggling Sun Site (I still can't visit without marveling that there's still so much more Net beyond it!); the interactivity and personality that characterizes bianca's Shack.

At this point, you're free to explore; you have the tools, you have the navigation skills, and you have a few places from which to start your travels. The final section of the book will simply help you to refine your skills and your software. We'll take a quick look at other tools for navigating the Web and for taking advantage of the video, sound, and graphics you'll find while Net surfing. And if these pages have inspired you, Chapter 13 will teach you the basics of Web page construction; you, too, can be a presence on the Net, by building a shack or a tour of your own.

Meanwhile, I encourage you to spend time following the many links we didn't follow at each of these three sites (believe me, we hardly scratched the surface). And for further Net surfing, check out Appendix D. I've listed hundreds of the best sites I've found, arranged roughly by topic for easy browsing. Enjoy!

PART IV

Be All You Can Be

You now have all the skills necessary to navigate the Web easily. This part will give you tips on how to make the most of everything available online, show you a few of the other Web browsers available to you, and help you design Web pages of your own.

Chapter 11 looks at a few of the other Web browsers available, both commercially and free for the downloading. Mosaic is a remarkable piece of software, but it's not the only option available for browsing the Web. Looking at some of the other programs will give you an idea of what else is available. Also, the selection of packages covered in Chapter 10 will give you a sense of how Web browsers might look and act in the future.

Chapter 12 helps you to expand your Mosaic to the worlds of graphics, video, and sound. You'll find a lot of images, audio files, and even video clips in your Net travels. The tools listed in Chapter 11 will help you see and hear everything the Net has to offer.

Chapter 13—our final chapter—will help you to build your own Web pages. Creating many of the wonderful things you'll see on the Net really isn't much different from writing in a word processor. All you need are a few special codes to tell the Web how to understand what you've written. This chapter walks you through the creation of a simple Web page and gives you tips on how they work their magic.

After Chapter 13, you'll find several appendixes with further information on where and how to continue your travels on the Net. Refer to those sections as necessary while Net surfing; they provide suggestions on how to make the most of the experience.

CHAPTER 11

Other Web Browsers

"There are countless formulas for pressing flowers."

—Kurt Cobain

Mosaic is a remarkable product, and it's attracted a lot of attention. But Mosaic is not the only means by which you can browse the Web. PC users can use shareware and freeware programs such as Cello, NetScape or Lynx; Macheads have MacWeb and other noncommercial products, and the commercial products are fast approaching market. The flood is most certainly upon us.

And the version of Mosaic we've seen in the screen shots is not the only version of Mosaic. In this chapter, we'll look at some of the other Mosaic browsers available, in part to provide for users of other versions but also to give you an idea of how these browsers are evolving, and quickly—not only can we not even begin to cram all the Mosaic browsers into this humble chapter, but major companies such as Quarterdeck will have browsers out soon after this book is published. We'll also briefly discuss some of the commercial online services that will soon provide Web-browsing abilities, particularly Delphi and America Online.

We started by examining the Enhanced Mosaic software included in this book. As I mentioned earlier, the original Mosaic was created by the National Center for Supercomputing Applications (NCSA). The Enhanced version of Mosaic is based directly on that software, as are many other popular Web browsers. There are a few differences, though. Knowing what they are will help you to follow the examples in Chapters 7, 8, and 9. We'll spend some quality time with Spyglass's Enhanced NCSA Mosaic to see how one company has chosen to make Mosaic evolve, comparing it to its freeware NCSA Mosaic ancestor.

Moving along, we'll see AIR Mosaic from Spry, a Windows browser sold as part of their AIR series TCP/IP packages. This is another browser based on NCSA Mosaic code, but it's evolved slightly differently. We'll also see two Windows browsers from Pipeline and Netcom that, though graphical like Mosaic, are based on different code entirely; we'll also see the powerful Cello freeware and discuss rising stars like NetScape, both of which work differently from Mosaic.

I haven't included any text (command-line) browsers in this chapter, though they certainly exist. Why haven't I? Mainly because throughout the book I've emphasized how very simple the Web is to navigate (and even to write for, as I'll show you in Chapter 12). Showing a text browser such as Lynx would make you think I was lying about all this simplicity.

Why use a text browser? There are a couple of reasons. First of all, the speed is incredible. Even a modem user with a slow modem can move quickly from spot to spot with a text browser. Also, we've seen that Mosaic still doesn't deal with certain aspects of the Net, or even of the Web. If wringing every last bit of performance and function out of the Internet is important to you, you might want to familiarize yourself with some of the available text browsers.

On the other hand, Mosaic is evolving very, very quickly. As you'll see in this chapter, there are a number of bright minds thinking about how best to make the Web easy to use and attractive. Mosaic and its kin become more powerful and flexible with each new version. Take a look at some of these packages and I think you'll agree.

Enhanced NCSA Mosaic from Spyglass

The first package we'll check out is a direct relation to the Mosaic you've seen in these chapters. Spyglass is located just a few miles from NCSA, and they've recently taken on responsibility for smoothing a few of Mosaic's rough edges and making it more easily available to the public (in books such as this one, for instance). Spyglass is also contributing features to the freeware version of Mosaic, so both the commercial ("payware") package and the freeware package will continue to evolve.

The screen for Spyglass's Enhanced NCSA Mosaic looks much like that of NCSA Mosaic, which you see in Figure 11.1—even the globe and those S-shaped lights have survived. However, you'll notice that somewhere between NCSA's software and its Spyglass descendant, almost all the buttons disappeared—only the forward and backward buttons remain. Also, if you look at the bottom of the screen, you'll notice a new addition in the lower-right-hand corner: A status bar shows you Mosaic's progress when loading long pages or images. Before the bar, NCSA simply told you how many bytes of the image had loaded. Luckman has this status bar, too—other packages do it differently, but all include some kind of indicator to let you know how things are progressing.

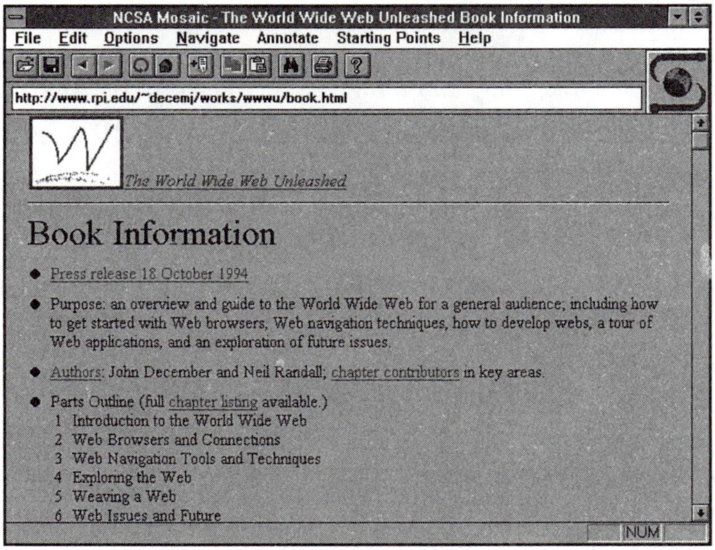

Figure 11.1. The old school: An NCSA Mosaic screen.

It looks, well, *different,* as you see from the Spyglass screen below in Figure 11.2. Like Spyglass, most of the commercial entities have streamlined the Mosaic interface even further, stripping away more tiny buttons and giving you more space for the Web pages themselves.

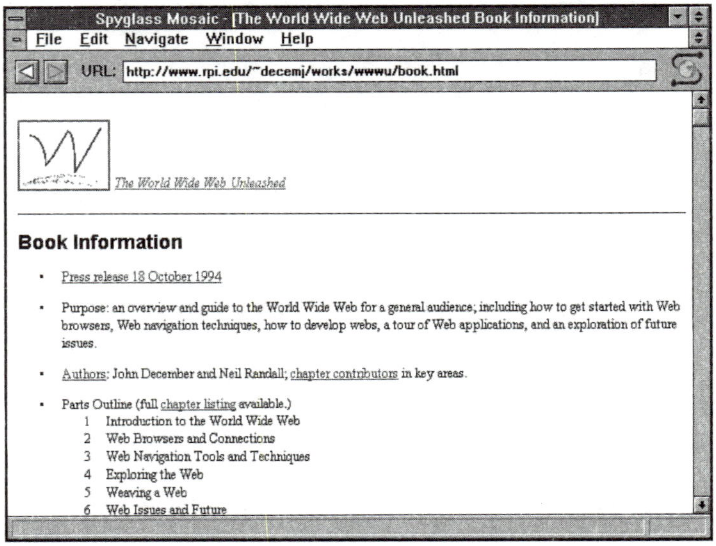

Figure 11.2. The new school: Spyglass Mosaic.

The buttons aren't the only thing that has changed. There are a number of changes in the menus; most of these streamline functions you're already familiar with. Let's walk through each menu in order, comparing them with the original NCSA selections. It won't take long, and it'll give you a sense of the kinds of things you might see in Mosaic and other Web browsers as they evolve.

FILE Menu

New Window—enables you to set up, essentially, several Mosaic sessions on one connection

Open URL—same

Open Local—same

Save As—allows pages to be saved either as HTML files or as ASCII text files; replaces the Document Source trick we saw in Chapter 7 (in other words, it works!)

Close—closes one window

Close All—closes all windows

Print—same

Page Setup—same

Printer Setup—same

Exit—same

(Missing: Save Preferences; Document Source)

EDIT Menu

Cut—the usual

Copy—the usual

Paste—the usual

Clear—the usual

Find—same

Find Again—resumes the previous search

View Source—same as File/Document source (it pops up a window rather than taking over the entire screen; nicely done)

Preferences—allows you to skip loading inline images, controls appearance of links, lets you choose a proxy server for various applications, gives display-font choices

OPTIONS menu—missing; Display Inline Images, Choose Font in the Edit/Preferences menu

NAVIGATE Menu

Back—same

Forward—same

History—same

Home—same

Hotlist—same; acts as menu editor

Add Current To Hotlist—same

Load Missing Images—reloads images when Load Inline Images switch is set to Off

Reload—same

ANNOTATE menu—missing.

STARTING POINTS menu—nearest match is Navigate/Hotlist

WINDOWS Menu

Tile—tiles your open windows

Cascade—cascades your open windows

Arrange Icons—assembles any sessions you've iconized in neat rows at the bottom of the screen

(list of windows)—the URLs currently active in the various windows you have open. Multiple windows are useful if you're pursuing several different threads and would prefer not to rely on history lists or the forward and back commands.

HELP Menu

Mosaic Help Page—a collection of local files (like regular Windows Help)

About Mosaic—version information; the Support button supplies system information that may be useful in case you need tech support

A few other things are different. For instance, once you start loading a page, you can't stop by clicking on the globe. Try hitting the Escape key instead.

Veteran Mosaic users may remember the Annotate feature, which let you keep notes about Web pages on your own hard drive. This was extremely useful for researchers. For instance, if you wanted to keep track of when you last checked a particular spot on the Web, you could make a note to yourself that Mosaic would find on your hard drive whenever you moved across the Web to that spot. Mosaic would get the page, notice that you made an annotation, and send you a message to remind you that it's available. Alas, Annotate is no more—a useful feature, but not a popular one.

On the brighter side, Spyglass Enhanced NCSA Mosaic keeps excellent track of which links you've followed. Any link you've checked within the last 24 hours, *even if you used it in an earlier session*, is shown in a different link color. (This is a feature that I never would have thought was useful…until I tried it. Now I want it in every Web browser!)

When you attempt to retrieve images, audio clips or videos, Enhanced Mosaic tells you how large the file will be and asks if you'd like to save it to the hard drive. Again, the Annotate options have been eliminated, and the hotlist isn't as immediately available as it is with NCSA Mosaic. But Enhanced Mosaic is an excellent and durable program, and looking at it as we just did is a simple and easy-to-understand way of getting acquainted with other Web browsers.

AIR Mosaic

The AIR Mosaic Windows browser from Spry, Inc. is also based on the original NSCA Mosaic. It's included with Spry's TCP/IP package along with a number of useful Internet applications. As you can see in Figure 11.3, AIR Mosaic is rather similar to packages we've already seen. Cosmetically speaking, the buttons are larger (an improvement!). The page title is shown in the Document Title window rather than at the top of the screen. And the globe has a radar-type sweep animation rather than the moving S-lights of NCSA Mosaic. (You cannot use this globe to stop Mosaic from loading a page, though. Instead, you'll click the Stop button.)

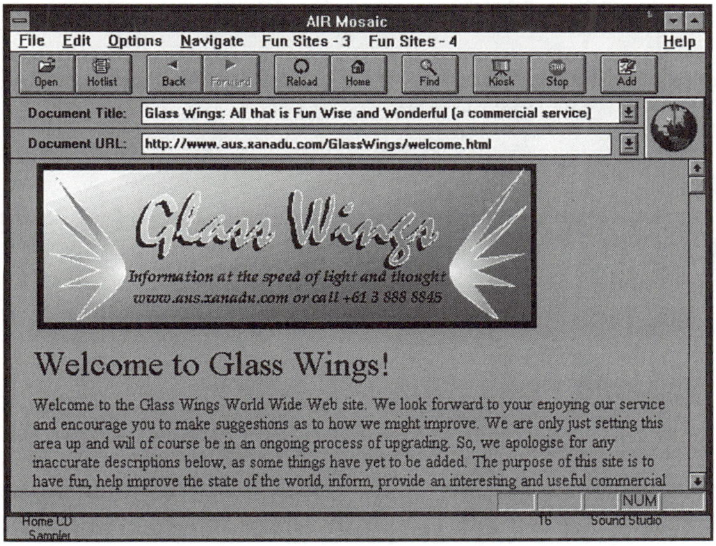

Figure 11.3. AIR Mosaic screen.

Menu arrangement is roughly similar. They're set up as follows; I've noted any differences from NCSA Mosaic—again, it's an evolutionary thing.

FILE Menu

Open URL—same

Open Local File—same

Hotlists—in NCSA Mosaic, equivalent to Navigate/Menu Editor

Save—same

Save As—same

Print—same

Print Preview—same

Print Setup—same

Document Source—same

Exit—same

(missing: Preferences, moved to Options/Configuration)

EDIT Menu

Copy—same

Find—same

OPTIONS Menu

Load To Disk Mode—same

Autoload Inline Images—in NCSA Mosaic, Display Inline Images

Kiosk Mode—allows you to load Mosaic without providing access to the rest of the system

Extended FTP Directory Parsing—same

Configuration—in NCSA Mosaic, equivalent to File/Preferences. Also contains settings for choosing a home page, selecting fonts and link color, and various other commands, as shown in Figure 11.4

Toolbar Style—allows you to see text, pictures, or both on the button bar

(missing: Show Toolbar, in Configuration; Show Status Bar, in Configuration; Show Current URL, in Configuration; Show Anchor URL, in Configuration as Show Hyperlinks; Change Cursor over Anchors, not available; Show Group Annotations, not available; Use 8-Bit Sound, in Configuration; Choose Font, in Configuration)

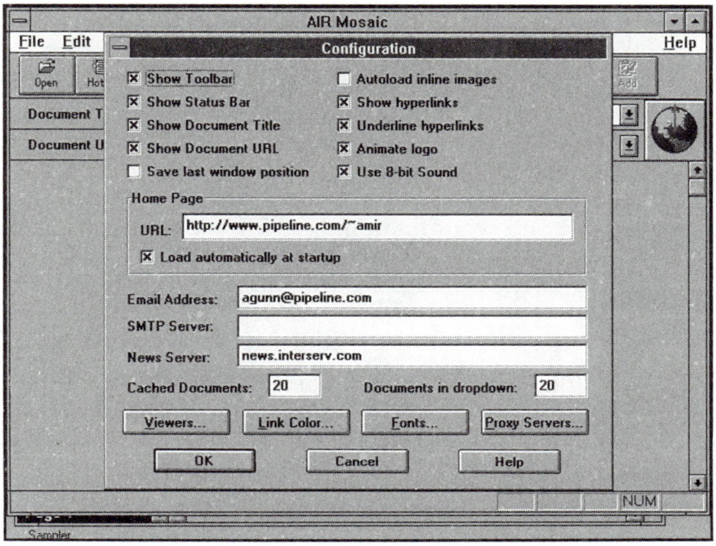

Figure 11.4. The Configuration box.

ANNOTATE menu—not available

NAVIGATE Menu

Back—same

Forward—same

Home—same

Reload—same

History—same

Cancel—in NCSA Mosaic, equivalent to click on globe

Add To Hotlist—in NCSA Mosaic, Add Current To Hotlist

(missing: Menu Editor, shown on Toolbar as Hotlist)

HELP Menu

Contents—Windows Help contents list

Using Help—Windows-style help

About AIR Mosaic—information about the software

Mail To Spry—a specialized e-mail utility for sending mail to the software developers

The Fun Sites-3 and Fun Sites-4 menu items shown in the AIR screens are my own hotlists, and will not appear on your screen. AIR allows you to make several hotlists and choose among them, displaying menu items for some and keeping others in the menu editor. This is an excellent way of keeping these things organized.

AIR Mosaic has a Kiosk mode in case you need to let other people use Mosaic on your computer (but don't want them interfering with other applications). AIR Mosaic does not offer Annotate mode, which allows you to keep a local file with comments on a particular page.

In combination with the other Internet utilities in the package, Spry AIR provides all the tools for full Internet access. (There's even a version of the LView viewer, called ImageView.) Some of the Internet front ends offered by the public-access providers also have plenty of these features. We'll look at two, both of which are currently PC-only but should have Mac versions in the near future: Pipeline for Windows and NetCruiser.

Both packages are interesting not only because of what they are (comprehensive Internet front ends) but because of what they are not, which is Mosaic-based. Each provides basic Web access. We'll also take a look at Cello, an early non-Mosaic (but graphical) Web browser for Windows.

Pipeline

The Pipeline is a New York-based public access provider, accessible around the country via SprintNet. Like many public access providers, it hasn't been around much longer than a year, but like many other providers it's growing at lightning speed. In a hotly competitive field, every successful access provider has some special feature that draws enthusiastic customers. In Pipeline's case, it's a wonderful Internet front end, also known as Pipeline.

This software is designed to work with access providers that have special Pipeline software on their servers. If your access provider doesn't have the necessary software, you won't be able to use Pipeline. This makes it different from Enhanced Mosaic and other packages that live entirely on your own computer and are independent of your access provider.

The Pipeline service provides e-mail, newsgroups, and other features in addition to the things you'll find via the Web; the Web browser is only part of Pipeline. In Figure 11.5 you see the Pipeline Web browser. The buttons are a bit obscure, but the functions they represent are normal. The usual back and forward arrows sit next to a "double-back" arrow that's equivalent to the Home button we've seen before. The Open URL (an open file), which acts as a kind of hotlist; History (two pages); and Save To Disk (multiple files) buttons are nearby. After that there's a Print button, and the universal "No" sign acts as the Stop or Cancel button.

Each of the two menu items has one option: File contains Exit, and Options contains an Expand Inline images toggle. Since Pipeline users rely on modem connections, the software is set to skip loading of inline images. Clicking on this option allows the images to load. As you see on the screen, Pipeline loads small icons in place of inline images.

Figure 11.5. The Pipeline Web browser.

Like AIR Mosaic and Enhanced Mosaic, Pipeline allows you to keep multiple windows in action. This is not, however, a Mosaic Web browser. The main difference (other than the details of the interface) is that the Pipeline Web browser doesn't require that you go through the process of configuring TCP/IP, as you did in Chapters 6 and 7. (Note: My Internet account is through Pipeline's computer, but I have my own PPP account and therefore have my own IP address, as I mentioned in Chapter 4—there's no relation between the Pipeline software we're discussing here and the software I use for my special connection. Having a PPP connection rather than relying on the one set up through the Pipeline software enables me to choose my own Web browser.

Though Pipeline's Web browser is only a part of the Pipeline software, you can set Pipeline to start up as a Web browser when you load the program. I realize I'm somewhat biased (since I use the non-Web parts of Pipeline's software on a regular basis), but I'm quite fond of this front end and the Web browser is worth checking out.

NetCruiser

Netcom, another nationwide public-access provider, also has a WWW browser in its NetCruiser software. Like Pipeline, Netcom is a full-service Internet provider; the NetCruiser front end gives you access to e-mail, news, and other delights not easily available through the Web.

As you see in Figure 11.6, NetCruiser relies mainly on icons rather than on menus. The major functions are contained on a toolbar that appears just below the main NetCruiser toolbar (on which you see the Web browser itself as a spiderweb). NetCruiser's icons correspond to the Open Local File, Save As, Hotlist, Find, Home, Back, Forward, and Stop functions in other browsers we've seen. The title appears at the top of the window, as it does with NCSA Mosaic; the current URL shows up in a small window, and both the anchor URL and a transfer percentage appear at the bottom when appropriate.

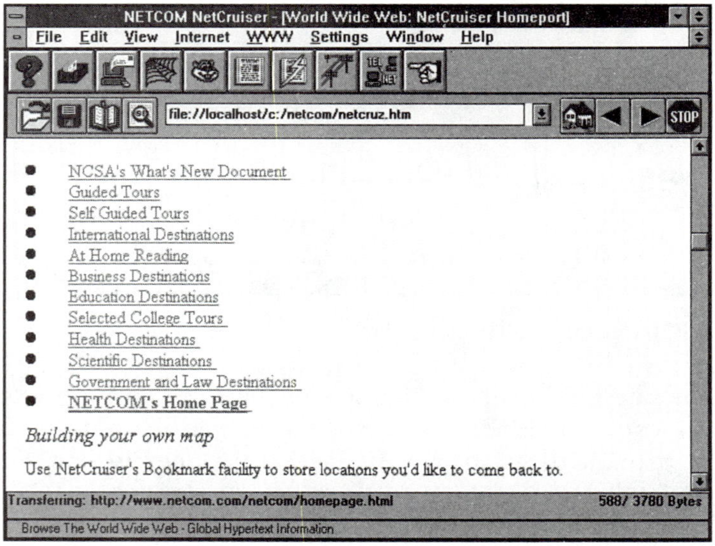

Figure 11.6. Netcom's NetCruiser.

The WWW menu item at the top of the NetCruiser window has seven of the most-used functions: Load To Disk, Back, Forward, Home, History, Reload, and Book Mark. All are exactly what you'd expect by now; Book Mark is equivalent to the Menu Editor (however, it doesn't allow you to edit the page names, which is annoying).

Like Pipeline, NetCruiser uses its own TCP/IP software, and it does not permanently assign your IP address. (In other words, when you log off, someone else will get it for a while, and you'll get a different one when you next log in.) Which is fine, but unlike users with regular TCP/IP connections you won't get to experiment with other browsers. NetCruiser is a reasonable choice if you're just starting out on the Net and don't feel too sure about what you want to do.

Macintosh versions of both Pipeline and NetCruiser are, as they say, in the works.

As you see, several companies offer non-Mosaic Web browsers that offer good basic features, especially the ability to switch easily between the browser and other tools such as e-mail. If you're new to the Internet and don't have much experience with mail readers and other utilities of that type, either software is a possible starting point.

Cello

Cello is also a non-Mosaic browser; in fact, it looks rather like NetCruiser in some respects. But Cello predates NetCruiser, and it was developed by Thomas R. Bruce for the Legal Information Institute at Cornell University. And it's freeware. It's also not reliant on a particular TCP/IP connection.

You see the Cello screen in Figure 11.7. It's quite different; the page title appears in large letters in the middle of the button bar, while the page URL appears at the bottom. The buttons are, from left to right: Up (which corresponds to Back), Stop, and Home (over to the right). You'll see links outlined with dotted boxes; unlike Mosaic, Cello does not change the color of links. Also, the cursor is a bit different; you'll see a set of crosshairs (a large thin T) when moving around the page, and a vertical arrow when the cursor is over a link. When you click on a link, a special cursor appears. You can't see the anchor URL before you click on the link, unfortunately. (Also, there's no status indicator to let you know how much or little of the page has loaded—annoying on pages with lots of graphics.)

The Cello interface is easy to configure; you can choose colors for every type of headline and for the background (any color, not just Mosaic's grey and white—actually, Cello uses a lovely creamy white background). You can also select your fonts and various other aspects of the interface.

One of Cello's big advantages over Mosaic is its support for sending e-mail. The software asks for your e-mail address, and will keep it in memory; as long as your Internet provider uses a mail protocol called SMTP, you can pop up and use the mail utility at any point.

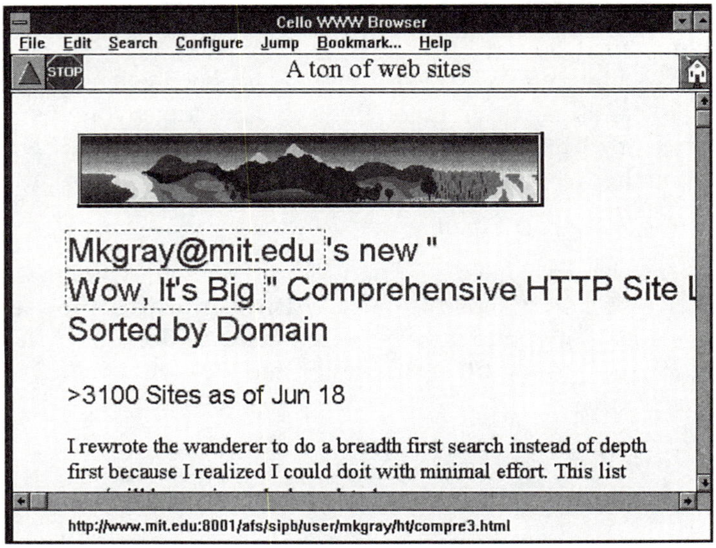

Figure 11.7. The Cello screen in all its glory.

Tech Tip: When you start Cello, a large box with software information appears. To clear the box from the screen, click on it anywhere.

Cello is arranged differently from Mosaic, as you'll see in the menus. However, most of the functions are fairly similar.

FILE Menu

Save—save a page as HTML or ASCII text

Mail file to...—mail the document you're viewing to someone

Print—as usual

Reload document—as usual

Exit—as usual

EDIT Menu

View source—in NCSA Mosaic, equivalent to Document Source

View as clean text—shows page as text file (no HTML codes!)

SEARCH Menu

Current File—in NCSA Mosaic, equivalent to Find

Search again—restarts Current File search

Index document—displays a dialog box for WAIS and other searches

CONFIGURE Menu

Files and directories—allows you to select your home page, bookmark file, style file, download directory, and cache low-water mark (amount of hard-drive space used to keep Web pages you've seen quickly available)

Links underlined only—changes appearance of links from box to underline

Background color—select background color

Automatic search dialogs—automatic search dialog popup for WAIS and other searches

Fonts—select fonts for text and headlines

Graphics—fetch automatically (in NCSA Mosaic, equivalent to Load Inline Images), Dither (a fast but homely way of uploading graphics if you use a true-color video card)

Printer—in NCSA Mosaic, equivalent to Printer Setup

Your e-mail address—add your e-mail address for future reference

Mail relay—an address to help Cello route your e-mail

News server—IP address for the Internet computer your access provider uses for handling newsgroups

WAIS gateway—IP address for an Internet computer for WAIS searches

Use your own—lets you choose your own telnet program (though it has its own), TN3270 telnet program, and text editor (Cello defaults to Notepad)

JUMP Menu

Up—in NCSA Mosaic, equivalent to Back

History—same

Bookmark—in NCSA Mosaic, equivalent to Hotlist

Launch Gopher sessions—lets you start a Gopher session by typing the domain name only

Launch telnet session—lets you begin a telnet session by typing the domain name

Launch TN3270 session—lets you begin a telnet session to a computer running the TN3270 emulation by typing the domain name only

Launch FTP session—lets you starts an FTP session by typing a domain name

Launch via URL—in NCSA Mosaic, equivalent to the URL window on the main screen

Send mail message—send e-mail

BOOKMARK menu—in NCSA Mosaic, equivalent to Hotlist

HELP Menu

Help—Windows-style help file

About Cello—software information

About the LII—information about the Legal Information Institute

Cello isn't as centered around URLs as Mosaic is. As you see from the menus, you can even reach non-Web pages such as FTP sites by typing in just the domain name rather than the full URL. They do, however, display on the screen in much the way Mosaic displays them, as you see in Figure 11.8.

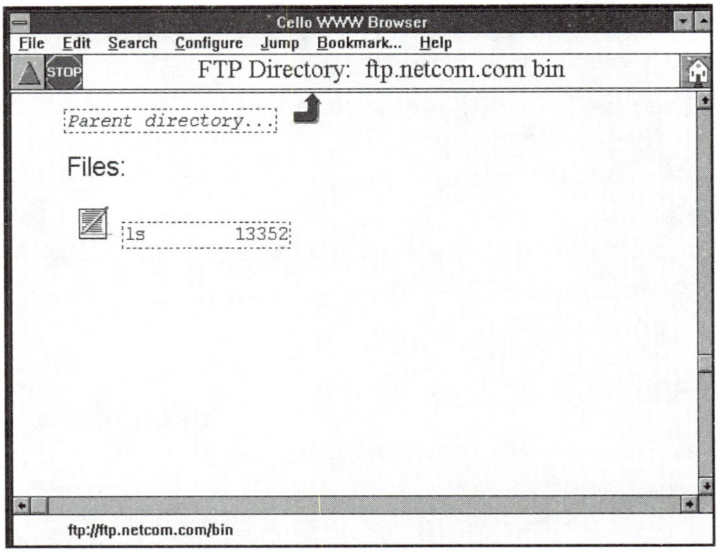

Figure 11.8. A Cello FTP session.

Overall, it's quite different from everything you've already seen, but it's an interesting program and worth trying out. And speaking of "different from everything you've already seen...."

The Next Step: NetScape

Cello evolved separately from Mosaic, but it has some similarities (after all, it's operating on the same Web!). NetScape was developed after Mosaic, and its makers at NetScape Communications (formerly Mosaic Communications) were very conscious of the good and bad things about Mosaic.

NetScape improves on Mosaic in several respects—most importantly, speed. For instance, veteran users have been dazzled by NetScape's speedy handling of graphics. Rather than making you sit there and wait while Mosaic laboriously transfers and translates every single file, NetScape brings you the graphics in such a fashion that you see them right away, first a bit muddily and then more clearly (see Figure 11.9).

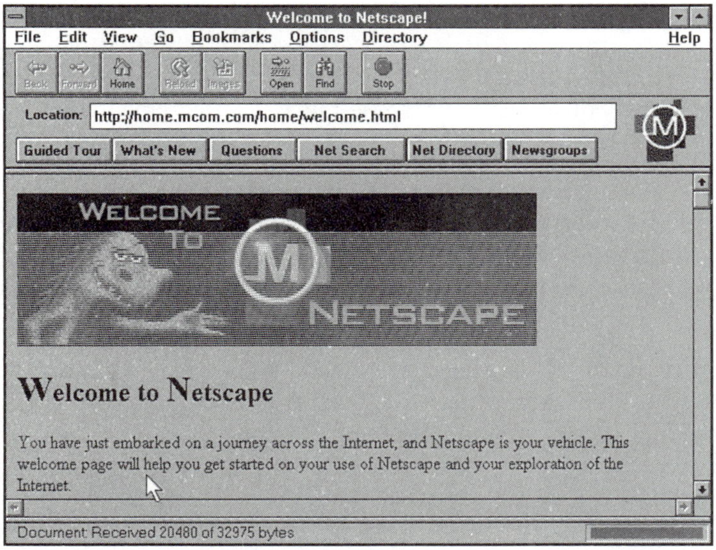

Figure 11.9. Netscape loading a graphic of "Mozilla" welcoming you to the Netscape home page.

It sounds like a trivial point (unless you frequent pages with LOTS of graphics or rely on a particularly slow modem). However, it's a tiny point that illustrates what a difference Mosaic has made to the Web. Before Mosaic, there wasn't a great demand for really efficient graphics handling, since no one was thinking of the Internet as a graphics-intensive, eye-candy kind of place. Now that Mosaic has come in to change the rules, it's clear that software developers will need to rethink their approach to the Web—deemphasizing scholarly features such as Annotate, and adding screamingly fast graphics support like NetScape's.

And Beyond: Online Services

Of course, thinking about software—how you want to look at the Net—causes you almost immediately to think about how you want to make the connection in the first place. Throughout this book I've touted the virtures of getting a full-fledged Internet connection, one that lets you choose how things will look to you. Both Netcom and Pipeline, mentioned above, use special interfaces to reach the Net. However, the point of both services is to provide Net access; almost everything contained on Netcom and Pipeline themselves is available to anyone with an Internet account.

The online services—America Online, CompuServe, Delphi, Prodigy and so forth—have distinctive services and identities in addition to unique software. If you have an account on one of these services, you're liable to call it a CompuServe account (or Prodigy account, or AOL account, or Delphi account) rather than simply an Internet account. Many of the people who subscribe to online services, in fact, never roam beyond them to see the Internet itself.

However, the online services are all moving toward granting their users greater access to the Internet, whether they use it or not. All of the online services currently offer e-mail, and some provide newsgroup, FTP, and even telnet access. Several of the services have stated that they're looking at the Web with great interest.

In the next year, you can expect to see several of the services taking tentative footsteps onto the Web. America Online has announced that they'll have a Web browser soon, perhaps by the time you read this; Delphi (which already offers excellent access to almost every facet of the Internet) has also announced a concerted move toward supplying a Web browser and other services.

Is an online service right for you? I'd suggest that unless you're primarily interested in the service and only secondarily in getting onto the Net, you will save money and have better access by choosing an access provider. The online services are fine—I'm on several of them myself—but they aren't the Internet. And they're certainly not the Web.

Now that we've discussed how you can look at the Web (via Mosaic and other programs), it's time to accessorize your Web browser. The next chapter gives information on how to look at and hear some of the things that make the Web cool: image files, video clips, and sound.

CHAPTER 12

ACCESSORIZING YOUR MOSAIC

"Still they want to dress you up..."

—Valentine Smith

In your travels, you've already seen a number of interesting items—movies, images, sound—and I've batted your mouse cursor away from most of them. It's not that these things aren't great fun (especially if you have a comparatively fast, network-based connection). We just need to add some finishing touches to your Mosaic first. To play movies, hear audio files, and get a really good look at some of those graphics, you'll need several small pieces of software known collectively as viewers. Your version of Enhanced Mosaic comes with several viewers. In this chapter, I'll describe what they are and what they can do, and give you a few tips on getting new viewers if you don't have the ones you need.

Viewers are utilities that can make sense of certain types of binary files. For instance, many of the graphics you'll find on the Net are in a format known as GIF. (This is a very common format; you'll often hear all image files referred to collectively and inaccurately as GIF files.) To look at GIFs, you'll need an image viewer that can open up the binary GIF file and translate the binary code into an image.

The most common viewer types are image viewers, sound players, video viewers, and PostScript viewers. Some of these are included with Enhanced Mosaic, but you can use Mosaic to seek them out on the Net (at the sites listed below) if you're using other software.

Which Should I Choose?

All users will find most of the viewers they need on the Net, available for download via FTP. Mac users will find that their Mosaic expects them to use certain viewers for certain file types. You'll see the list in Options/Preferences/Helper Applications. If you go onto the Internet, use FTP to get copies of these utilities, and place them in the system folder, Mosaic will automatically know how to use them on your behalf. X Window users will also find that there's a "preferred list" of viewers for their Mosaic and that their software is pre-configured to expect it.

PC users, your software also has a preferred list of viewers of its own, but you'll find that you need to check the `MOSAIC.INI` file, usually located in your `\WINDOWS` directory, to see where the Mosaic expects to find the various utilities. If you're using the version of Enhanced Mosaic that comes with this book, you'll need to look for the `LMOSAIC.INI` file in the `\LMOSAIC` directory. Also, you should examine your `MOSAIC.INI` (or `LMOSAIC.INI`) file for any surprises; it's not unusual for pointers to have the right filename for a utility but the wrong directory, in which case Mosaic can't use it.

At present, you'll need just a few tools to take advantage of the things you'll find. However, as time goes by there will doubtless be new file types available. When you happen across a file in an unfamiliar format, the first thing you should do is check the page on which you found it to see if there's information on the reader you'll need.

What About Hardware?

Beyond the system requirements in Chapters 6 and 7, Mosaic doesn't require much in the way of hardware. (If you're using Mosaic now, chances are you met those requirements. Still, the better the hardware, the happier you'll be. (So what else is new?)

Next to a faster connection and more RAM, the nicest gift you can give Mosaic is decent video. Mosaic will work on even a monochrome display, but if you're serious about looking at video and images you'll want to use at least 256-color video. And 24-bit (16.7 million-color or "true color") video makes Mosaic look great; because a certain amount of the material you'll find online (artwork and some graphics, for instance) was created with true-color display in mind, the better your video the more full-fledged your viewing experience. (And unlike sound, for instance, you'll always use video in one way or another in Mosaic.)

Sound is another matter. If your machine already supports high-quality sound output, that's fine. However, I don't recommend getting special sound hardware just for Mosaic. There's simply not enough material available yet to justify the expenditure. And modem users will find that the time and bother of downloading audio files tends to outweigh the benefits of hearing them—for now at least. Better to put that money toward more RAM, better video, or your burgeoning Internet bill.

Image Files: Get the Picture?

The most common format for image files, as I mentioned, is GIF. You'll also find a number of JPEG files available, and it's good to have viewers for both formats—fortunately, almost every good viewer can handle both types of image files, as well as the occasional BMP ("bitmap") files you'll find. Additionally, Macintosh users are familiar with the PICT format. However, there are currently no PICT viewers for the PC, so PICT files are comparatively rare online. If you're a Mac user planning to add graphics to a Web page of your own, please show your neighbors some love and stick with GIF or JPEG formats.

Enhanced Mosaic users (and Spry users), your image viewer is Imageview. It's nearly identical to Lview, the freeware viewer I list below. It handles JPEG, BMP, and GIF files.

GIF

Macintosh—JPEGView, from ftp://sumex-aim.stanford.edu or ftp://mac.archive.umich.edu

PC—LView (lview31.zip), from ftp://ftp.ncsa.uiuc.edu/Mosaic/Windows/viewers

(also available: WinGIF, WinJPEG)

JPEG

Macintosh—jpeg-view, from http://guru.med.cornell.edu/jpegview.html

PC—LView (lview.zip), from ftp://ftp.ncsa.uiuc.edu/Mosaic/Windows/viewers

(also available: WinJPEG)

TIFF

Macintosh—GIFConverter, from http://sumex-aim.stanford.edu or mac.archive.umich.edu

Audio Files: The Sound of Music (or Whatever)

Audio files are usually kept in the AU format. You may also find AIFF and WAV files online; however, it's likely that you can get away with just a AU player. Windows users usually have a WAV player, Mplayer, on their system already (it doubles as a video player). Enhanced Mosaic users, you'll find your software preconfigured for Mplayer; a AU conversion utility, Audconv, is also included.

You should understand that audio files are quite large; even a few minutes of sound can require a file of several megabytes. Modem users will find that by and large the payoff is not worth the amount of time it takes to drag an audio file across the phone line.

AIFF

PC—Wham (wham131.zip), from ftp://ftp.ncsa.uiuc.edu/Mosaic/Windows/viewers

(also WPlay for Waveout devices (`wplny09b.zip`), from `ftp://ftp.ncsa.uiuc.edu/Mosaic/Windows/viewers`)

AU

Macintosh—SoundMachine, from `http://sumex-aim.stanford.edu` or `mac.archive.umich.edu`

PC—Wham (`wham131.zip`), from `ftp://ftp.ncsa.uiuc.edu/Mosaic/Windows/viewers`

(also WPlay for Waveout devices (`wplny09b.zip`), from `ftp://ftp.ncsa.uiuc.edu/Mosaic/Windows/viewers`)

WAV

PC—Mplayer, included with Windows

> If you're looking for noisy sites, here are a few worth tuning in to:
>
> **Vincent Voice Library**—`http://web.msu.edu/vincent/`
>
> A large library of voice clips. You'll find everyone from Bogey to Betty Ford represented here.
>
> **The Metaverse**—`http://metaverse.com/knet/index.html`
>
> The ubiquitous Adam Curry has clips of both rave and blues sets available for your listening pleasure.
>
> **Internet Talk Radio**—`http://juggler.lanl.gov/itr.html` or `http://www.ncsa.uiuc.edu/radio/radio.html`
>
> A radio show? On the Internet? Sure enough. You'll find interviews with Internet movers and shakers here.

Video Clips: Let's Roll the Tape

The most common format for Net video is MPEG. There are a number of viewers available. `.AVI` files are also quite common, particularly when PC users are providing the video files. You'll also find QuickTime movies on the Net. QuickTime movies have the extension `.mov`. QuickTime is a format originally developed for the Macintosh but available to PC users with the proper viewers.

Be aware that video files are HUGE, even larger than audio files. A clip just a few minutes long will take up several megabytes of space on your hard drive. Modem users won't be seeing many video clips on the Net; it simply takes too long!

MPEG

Macintosh—Sparkle, from `sumex-aim.stanford.edu` or `mac.archive.umich.edu`

PC—Mpegplay (`mpegw32e.zip`), from `ftp://ftp.ncsa.uiuc.edu/Mosaic/Windows/viewers`

QuickTime

Macintosh—Simple Player, from `ftp://ftp.ncsa.uiuc.edu`

PC—QuickTime for Windows (`qtw11.zip`), from `ftp://ftp.cuhk.hk/pub/mov`

> To find video sites, start by looking at movie-related sites and the various literary magazines. Here are a couple of sites to see:
>
> **Kaleidoscope**—`http://kspace.com`
>
> A kind of online audition area, you'll find clips of up-and-coming actors and comedians here.
>
> **Juggling Information Service**—`http://www.hal.com/services/juggle/`
>
> I can't get enough of this place. Check out Francis Brunn's Impossible Trick. Eesh.
>
> **MPEG Movie Archive**—`http://w3.eeb.ele.tue.nl/mpeg/`
>
> Animations, supermodels, music, space, and other things—this site is comprehensive. You should check it to see if files are available on a site closer to home, though—this link goes to the Netherlands.

PostScript Viewers: Now and Then

PostScript is probably familiar to you from working with your word processor (or anything else that requires attractive typefaces). You won't find a great deal of material that requires a PostScript viewer, so you shouldn't rush onto the Net just to get one. However, if you need one, here's where to go.

Postscript

PC—GhostScript, from `ftp://ftp.cs.wisc.edu/pub/ghost`

If you never use a viewer, you'll still be able to see many of the wonders of the Internet. Any inline graphics (that is, graphics included as part of the page) will appear without special effort, for instance. But viewers and players round out the Mosaic experience, and because they're easy to get and (generally) free there's no reason you shouldn't have it all. And you might even consider augmenting your computer with a top-notch video or sound card if you find that you just can't do without all the "extras" that make the Web impressive.

We've gotten your Internet connection up and running, taken Mosaic out for a spin, considered your Web-browsing options, and outfitted your chosen software with the goods to deliver the goodies. You now have the skills and knowledge to be a good Web user. If you'd like to take the next step and become a good Web creator—if you'd like to make a few Web pages of your own—the next chapter will get you started. If you'd rather just hang out, Appendix D awaits you with hundreds of suggestions for happy Net-surfing.

CHAPTER 13

Better Living Through HTML

Home… home is where you wear your hat."

—Dr. Emilio Lizardo

You just can't stand it, can you? All these people doing amazing things on the Net, and you aren't one of them. Yet. Do you want to be? Here's the chapter that shows you how.

Constructing your own Web page is really a book in itself. This chapter (and the accompanying appendix) will give you the skills to construct a basic yet functional Web page and tell you how to go about making it available to your fellow Net surfers. I've recommended a few sources of further information in Appendix C.

But Will You Remember To Change the Litterbox?

This is not a minor responsibility, your own Web page. By placing it on the Net, you're committing to a few things.

- You must keep your page in good working order—no sloppy page-writing! This chapter should start you on the right path.
- You must keep your page up-to-date.
- You must keep your page available, as best you can, at one site; if you move, you must make sure people know how to find you.
- You must keep other people informed about your home page.

This is a simple form of netiquette. Up to now most of your actions didn't really have a major impact on the Net; the worst thing you could do was to crash your own session or possibly hog some bandwidth unnecessarily. Now that you're taking part in actually creating the Web, you owe it a bit more than a take-it-or-leave-it approach.

Once you've accepted that responsibility, you're ready to consider this task in earnest. The first thing to do is find an hospitable Web server, willing to give you a bit of space to stake your claim. The best place to start is with the company currently providing your Internet access. Many providers are willing to carry a couple of pages either for free or for a small fee. If yours isn't willing, ask your provider to recommend another site. A nearby college or university may be able to help you. And a number of companies have sprung up to accommodate corporate pages. Fees vary widely; check Appendix D under "Business" for a few starting points.

Once you know where you're going and have an idea of any restrictions the system administrator might place on your page, you can begin the planning process. And then you'll be ready to set the Web on fire. Walk with me through the creation of one of the Web pages for this book; once again, it's all much easier than it looks.

All Your Tools at Hand

You don't need anything fancy to make a simple Web page. Any ASCII text editor will do, even something as simple as Windows' Notepad. However, there are several excellent specialized text editors available for downloading on the Net. A specialized text editor has the HTML codes built-in. To make a page, you'll type in the text and format it with the menu items, just as you do with WordPerfect or Microsoft Word. The editor adds the codes—much faster and easier than doing it by hand!

Macintosh owners will like BBEditor Lite, which has HTML extensions. Get a copy by FTP at `ftp://sumex-aim.stanford.edu/info-mac/text/`. The file name is `bbedit-lite-231.hqx`.

Windows citizens can use several products, including Word for Windows itself; there's a nice set of macros called `GT_HTML.DOT` available via FTP at `ftp://ftp.gatech.edu/pub/www/`. The file name is `gt_html.zip`. I use HTML Writer, written by Kris Nosack and available via anonymous FTP at `lal.cs.byu.edu/pub/www/tools/htmlwrit.zip`.

The screen shots I show you later in the chapter were taken within HTML Writer. However, the onscreen code will be the same for Mac users—HTML is the same for all of us. The coding applies to all platforms, and other Web browsers besides Mosaic use and see essentially the same code. More thoughts on non-Mosaic users in a bit.

Planning Your Page

Before you fire up the text editor of your choice, sit down with a sketchpad and figure out what you want to create. Plan your Web page as carefully as you would an important letter or your resume.

Most Web pages are actually a collection of several pages; together they are called a Web document. Your document should have some sort of logical structure, so people understand easily how to move among them. One popular structure is the outline or tree structure. The "main" page is the trunk of the tree; other pages branch off from the truck. Here's an example:

- **Jane Doe's Home Page**—a brief biography and links to her other pages
    - **Jane's Favorite Photos**—one good photo and links to her Favorite People and Favorite Critters pages
        - **Jane's Favorite People**—photos of Jane, her beau, and her family
        - **Jane's Favorite Critters**—photos of Jane's cats and her dog
    - **Jane's Favorite Links**—Jane's list of cool sites
    - **Jane's Political Opinions**—an essay by Jane and links to other politically-oriented sites

In this example, Jane's Doe's Home Page would include links to Jane's Favorite Photos, Jane's Favorite Links, and Jane's Political Opinions. Jane's Favorite Photos would, in turn, have links to Jane's Favorite People and Jane's Favorite Critters; neither of those two pages needs links. Jane's Favorite Links and Jane's Political Opinions have links to other sites. Jane Doe's Web document is complete at six pages.

I recommend the tree metaphor for novice Web-page writers, and I've used it myself for the pages that make up the Web document for this book. It's easy to use and easy to keep organized. And it works even for really large Web sites; bianca's SMUT-Shack, for instance, uses a house metaphor to help guide you through her castle, but the site itself actually follows a very tidy tree-type outline.

When I planned the Web pages for this book, I came up with this outline:

Welcome page—greeting, description of other pages in document, links to other pages of document and to my personal Web document, maybe an inline image of the book cover

- **Sites page**—links to sites mentioned in book; book cover again
- **Sams page**—book information and link to publisher's information; book cover again
- **Table Of Contents**—one-page summary (from the front cover), summary T of C; book cover again

The information I want to include in my Web document for the book divides nicely into three sections: sites I want to offer links for, information on how to get the book, and the table of contents (and a sample of the writing). A good top welcoming page ties it all together. It also gives me a special place to offer the link for my personal Web page, which may interest some people but doesn't belong with the book's more business-like Web pages.

It's possible to put all of this on one Web page. However, you should try to avoid making your Web pages too long. Keep them no longer than the equivalent of four or five typewritten 8 1/2- by 11-inch pages. Why? Among other reasons, because even though Mosaic doesn't actually save the pages you read on your hard drive, it does use your computer's resources to hold the page information while you're reading it. A page that's too long will take a long time to load, and computers that don't have the storage space won't be able to retrieve it at all.

On that note, you should avoid adding too many in-line images to any single page. There are two reasons for this. First, graphics take a long time to travel across the Net to your computer. If you have a bunch of images on one page (or several very large images), it'll take a very long time, especially for those using modems. It's good netiquette to split them up onto several pages, as Jane did above. Secondly, not every Web user can see graphics—some non-Mosaic users only see text. Be kind to the disadvantaged and keep the graphics to the minimum necessary.

I don't need any graphics at all, but I can't resist adding a small picture of the cover. Using it on all four Web pages will tie them together visually, so I decide to brave the wrath of text-browser users and add it. (But I will make sure it's small.)

Afterwards, I wrote a draft of the text for each page and assembled the graphics. (In this case, I asked my editor to make a scan of the cover art; on my personal Web pages, I made the art in a drawing program.) With these things in hand, I'm ready to build the pages themselves.

Writing Your Page: HTML in Action

HTML (HyperText Markup Language) is remarkably simple. It bears a strong resemblance to typesetting, and if you've ever created a file in a word processor this won't be a stretch at all. Let's walk through the creation of the top (welcome) page for this book.

Almost all HTML formatting commands are contained in <pointy brackets like these>. Most commands are 2-, 3- or 4-letter codes. If you're using a specialized HTML editor, it will have menu choices that automatically add these codes. All you'll have to do is select the text to which you want to add the formatting codes. On the other hand, after a little while you'll probably find yourself typing the commands in yourself; they're that simple and easy to remember.

I start HTML Writer and choose to start a new page. The program asks for a title for the page—the line that appears at the top of the window. I want to call it "Plug-n-Play Mosaic for Windows (welcome page)," but any line of text under 64 characters will be fine.

> **Note:** Try to choose a title that makes sense to anyone who might stumble across your page. A title that says "My Home Page" or "Welcome!" doesn't help your fellow Net surfers get their bearings.

The HTML Writer program is set up to use the title as the main headline for the page. You'll see the text and formatting commands in Figure 13.1.

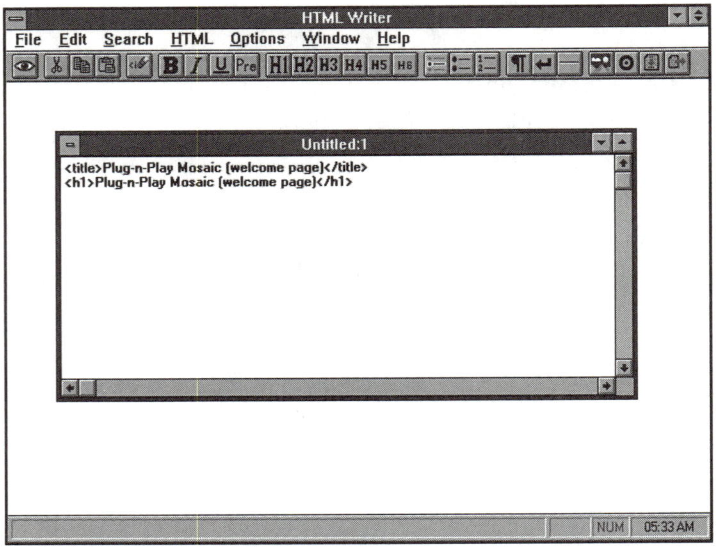

Figure 13.1. The title and main headline for my home page, as seen in HTML Writer.

As you see, the page title is surrounded by two pieces of HTML formatting code, called tags. The `<title>` tag tells Mosaic to expect whatever follows to be the title; the `</title>` tag tells Mosaic it's through with the title. (Every page on the Web has a title.) The next line starts with `<h1>`, telling Mosaic that this is a number-one-sized headline (the largest size); the `</h1>` shuts off the headline font. In most browsers, the number-one headline type is the biggest and boldest typestyle of all. There are six headline sizes, numbered `<h1>` through `<h6>`. Use the larger sizes —`<h1>`, `<h2>`, and `<h3>`—sparingly.

> **Tech Tip:** Most Mosaic formatting is "switched off" by adding the forward slash (`/`) in front of the command, just after the opening point bracket. Also, some people prefer to code in ALL CAPS. It makes no difference.

Let's look at it in Mosaic now. If you're using a specialized editor you probably have a button or menu item that lets you test your page; save the file and use the testing option to look at it. If you don't have a Test option, you can save your work as `*filename*.HTM` (any filename will do) and test it by starting Mosaic and typing the file name like this:

```
file:///c:/directory/filename.htm
```

where *directory* is the name of the directory in which you stored the file. You don't need to be connected to the Net to do this.

You'll see—oops—the screen in Figure 13.2. I'm not sure I like the second line the same size as the first, so I'll go back to the editor and change it. This is why you should preview your work often.

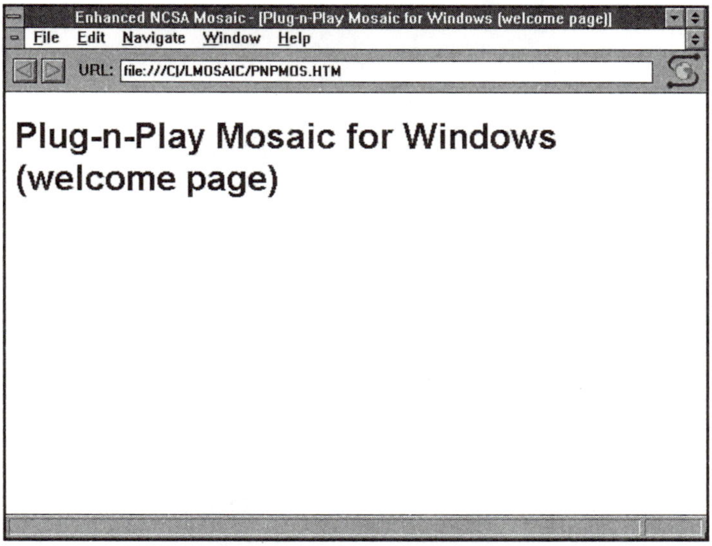

Figure 13.2. The "welcome page" headline looks awfully large here.

I go back to the editor and decide to make the `(welcome page)` line a `<h2>` headline. Now the editor screen reads

```
<title>Mosaic: Plug-n-Play Internet (welcome page)</title>
<h1>Mosaic: Plug-n-Play Internet</h1> <h2>(welcome page)</h2>
```

and looks like the screen in Figure 13.3.

Notice that the `<h1>` formatting code added the line space by itself—I didn't have to hit Return. HTML-formatted pages don't pay attention to your tabs or carriage returns. All these things are controlled by the HTML tag. For more information, please see the HTML "glossary" in Appendix C.

Warning: Avoid using extra spaces, carriage returns, or tabs in your text. Not every browser will see them as you do, and the results can be disastrous.

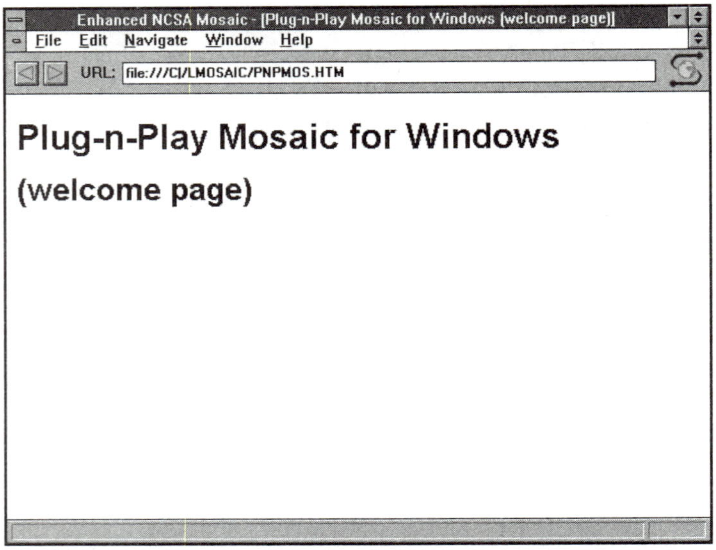

Figure 13.3. The same headline, split up into `<h1>` and `<h2>`, and looking better for it.

As you see, the headlines are real, working parts of a Web page in progress. However, I want to add a few formatting tags before we continue. These codes ensure that our page is perfectly in line with the latest standards for HTML formatting. We'll add three sets of tags: `<html>` and `</html>`, `<head>` and `</head>`, and `<body>` and `</body>`.

The `<html>` codes tell Mosaic immediately that this page is in HTML format. The `<html>` tag is the second thing on the page (what's first? We'll get there in a minute!), and the `</html>` tag is the last thing. The `<head>` tag is the third thing on the page, just after the `<html>` tag; the closing `</head>` tag comes right after the closing `</title>` tag.

Immediately after that is the `<body>` tag; you can start your headlines now and add everything else after them. The closing `</body>` tag is the second to last item on the page, just before the `</html>`. It won't make a difference in what you see onscreen, but adding these tags ensures that your pages can be read by any Web browser. (After all, you want the whole world to read this, right?) If this paragraph has you turned around, don't worry; the next time I show you the HTML Writer screen I'll be sure to put everything in its proper place.

> **Note:** So why aren't the headlines in the `<head>...</head>` area? Because the tag stands for "heading," not "headline." You can have

> plenty of headline sections on a page, but there's only one heading, and therefore one <head>...</head> area.

I'm going to add one more line here to make my page perfect. All the best Web pages have a line at the very top explaining to the rest of the Web that they conform to the latest HTML standard, Version 2.0. This line

```
<!doctype html public "-//W3O//DTD W3 HTML 2.0//EN">
```

doesn't show up onscreen, but anyone can see it by viewing the document source code. This should be the first line on the page. In Mosaic, the page still looks just as it did in Figure 13.3. In the editor, the page now looks like this:

```
<doctype html public "-//W3O//DTD W3 HTML 2.0//EN">
<html><head><title>Plug-n-Play Mosaic for Windows (welcome page)</title>
</head>
<body><h1>Plug-n-Play Mosaic for Windows</h1> <h2>(welcome page)</h2>


</body>
</html>
```

From here on, everything we add to the page will fall between the <body> and </body> tags. We can add more headlines or anything else we want, of course. From here on, we'll just assume that the first three lines of code are still there, and I won't repeat them.

Now I'll type in the main text, again between the <body> and </body> tags (and after the headlines). It doesn't need any special formatting, since when in doubt Mosaic assumes that the text is regular text. Mine reads:

```
Hello, and welcome to the Plug-n-Play Mosaic page! This page gives information on
the book by the same name from Sams Publishing. It includes a table of contents and
a list of most of the great Web pages mentioned in the book. There's also a one-
page explanation of Mosaic and the Net--astound your friends in 350 words or less.
You can also find out more about the author, Angela Gunn, by hopping to her
personal Web page. Thanks for dropping by. Enjoy!</body>
```

Let's see how that looks in Mosaic, as seen in Figure 13.4.

It's a good start, but it needs some pizzazz. First, let's break it into a few paragraphs by adding the <p> and </p> tags. I'll make three paragraphs, adding the tags in the spots shown:

```
<body><p>Hello,...page!</p><p>This page...personal Web page.</p><p>Thanks...
Enjoy!</p></body>
```

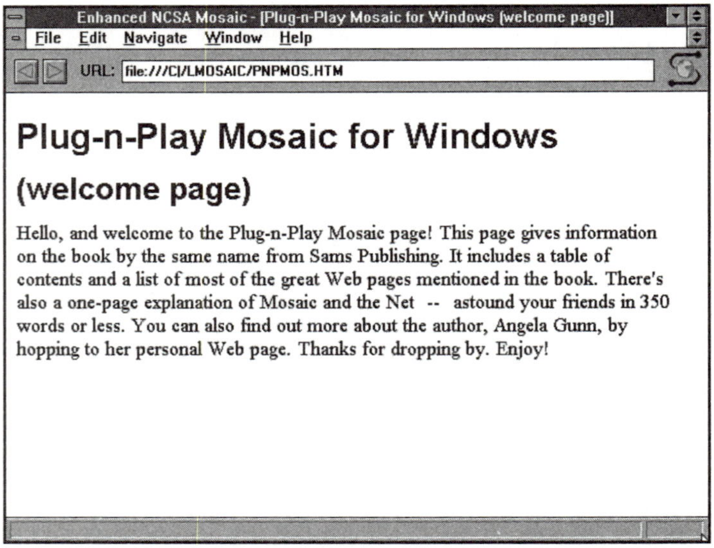

Figure 13.4. The page in progress, with a big lump of text.

We get the Mosaic screen seen in Figure 13.5.

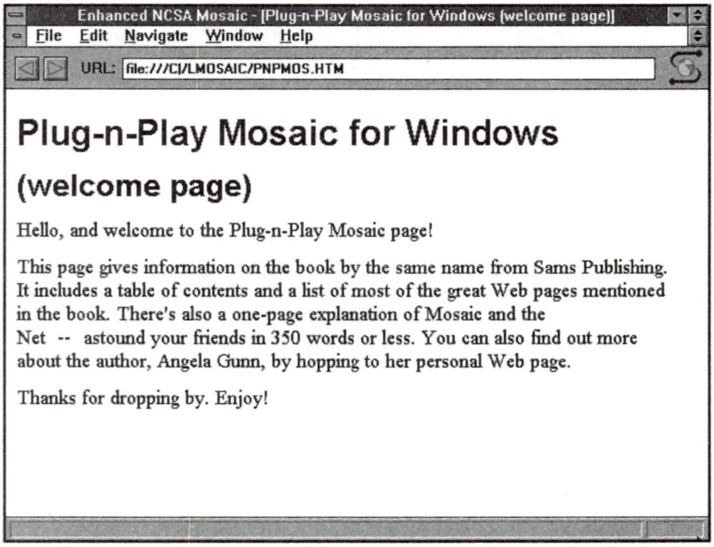

Figure 13.5. The same text is now broken into three paragraphs. Notice that Mosaic makes sure that everything fits in the margins.

Tech Tip: You don't have to use the </p> tag; when you're ready to start a new paragraph, just use another <p> tag. However, I'm sure you don't want to have to remember what you do and don't need closing tags for, so until you're feeling confident about HTML let's use closing tags for everything.

Let's add a couple more design elements. It's customary to add your e-mail address to the bottom of your Web pages, and often you'll see a straight line above the address. Let's add those now.

In the editor, I move the prompt between the final </p> and the </body> tag. First I'll have Mosaic draw a horizontal ruled (straight) line, by typing <hr> (but not </hr>—there's no such tag). After that I'll add my address in the special address font, like so: `<address>agunn@pipeline.com</address>`. The new tags make the last part of the file in the HTML editor read

```
...Enjoy!</p><hr><address>agunn@pipeline.com</address></body></html>
```

Ugly, but it looks pretty impressive in Figure 13.6. We're ready to add the good stuff—links and graphics.

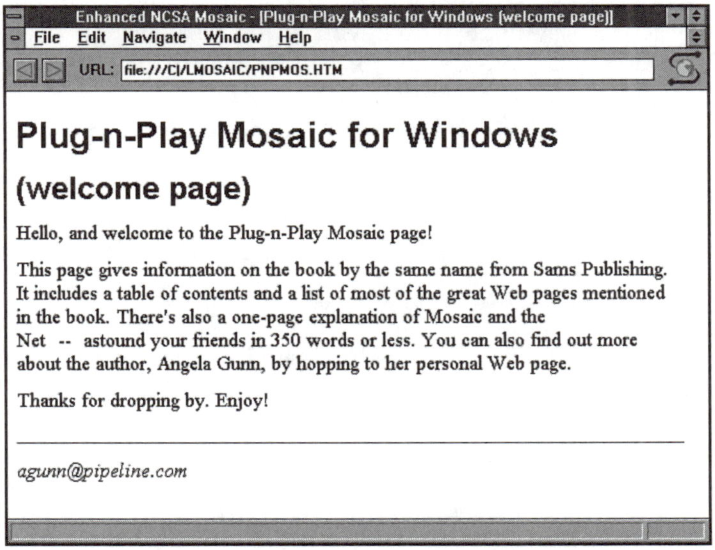

Figure 13.6. The book's home page, looking good with my address and a ruled line.

Links: A Is for Anchor

When I drew up the outline for this page I decided it would have four links (one to each branch of the tree, and one to my own home page), and I've written the text in such a way that it's easy to pick out words that make sensible links. As I wrote the text I also decided I'd like to make a link to a one-page explanation of Mosaic.

Let's make the link to the great-Web-pages page first. I plan to make the words "great Web pages" into the link to the other page. The great-Web-page page has already been written; it's a file called `greatweb.htm`. Like this welcome page, it's going to be kept at `www.mcp.com` in the directory `/sams/books/mos`. Since they will be in the same directory, I only need to remember the file's name to make my link. This is called a relative URL, since it doesn't give the full URL (absolute URL). Relative URLs are fine if you know that both the page you're on and the page to which you're linking will always remain exactly where they are.

> **Note:** On the machine I used to write these pages, my Web pages have three-letter extensions (due to DOS constraints). The pages can be converted into UNIX format before they appear on Sams server; it doesn't change anything we're discussing in this chapter. The access provider that gives you Web server space will probably take care of any conversions for you. Of course, you can leave them in DOS or Mac form too.

I position the prompt just before the word `great` and type the command to create a link to the greatweb page: `<a href="greatweb.html">`. Just after the word `pages` I type the command to end the link: `</a>`. The entire phrase looks like this:

```
...most of the <a href="greatweb.html">great Web pages</a> mentioned in the...
```

And if you check it out in Mosaic (or in Figure 13.7), you'll see that it worked; we have linkage.

> **Note:** If you're testing your files on your own computer, you'll need a special URL to help Mosaic find the files on your hard drive. The format is:
>
> ```
> file:///c:/directory/filename
> ```

where you add the name of the file (HTML page) to which you're linking and the name of the directory it's in. Note the triple forward-slashes after `file:`. Also note the forward slashes in the URL. Even if you're using a DOS machine, Mosaic can't understand the usual backwards slashes.

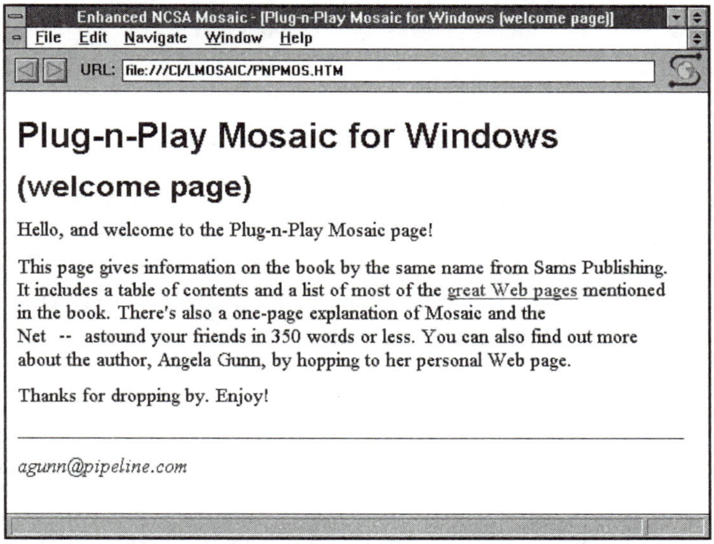

Figure 13.7. Our first link, underlined and in color (onscreen at least!).

I'll link the table of contents in the same way, with a relative URL to a file in the same directory. The file name is `pointtoc.html`, and I want to link it to the words `table of contents`, like so:

```
...includes a <a href="playtoc.html">table of contents</a> and a list...
```

The link to the Sams Publishing information is on the same server as the other pages, but it's in the `/sams/` directory with the filename `sams-publishing.html`. This requires another kind of relative URL, one that includes the directory path. We'll link it to the words `Sams Publishing`:

```
...name from <a href="/sams/sams-publishing.html">Sams Publishing.</a> It
includes...
```

I also want a link to the one-page explanation. It's at the bottom of the table of contents page, so I could just make another link there. However, it's possible to make a target link to a specific point on a page. This will let people find the explanation without wading through the table of contents. I'll just have to add a line to the table of contents page at the spot to which I want the link to connect, in addition to the usual relative URL pointing to it from the main page.

Let's do the relative URL link first, since we're already on the main page. I'm going to call the target link `explain`, and it's in the file `playtoc.html`. We'll link it to the phrase `one-page explanation`. It looks like this:

```
...also a <a href="playtoc.html#explain">one-page explanation</a> of Mosaic...
```

As you see, the file name and target name (the name of the spot we're aiming at) are separated by a `#` (pound sign). Now I need to add the target link to the file `pointtoc.html` at the spot to which I want to jump. I open the file and scroll down it to the section that begins `The Internet and Mosaic In One Page`. At the moment I've got it separated from the table of contents by a `<hr>` line, but otherwise it's not very easy to find. This target link will be just the ticket. I position the prompt right after the `<hr>` and add the link:

```
<a name="explain">
```

I try it out. By now I have almost all the links on the main page ready to roll; it looks like Figure 13.8.

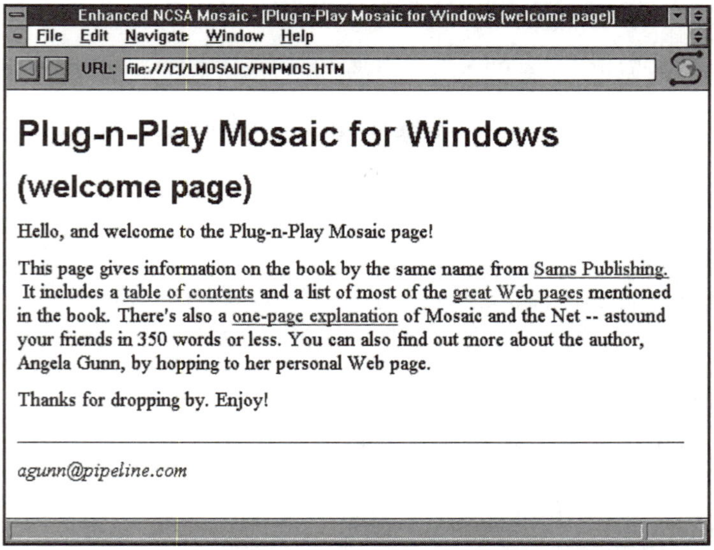

Figure 13.8. The page as it looks now, with the links we've created shown underlined (and in color).

If I test the target link, it jumps to the table of contents page and then down about halfway to the explanation section.

Just one link left—the link to my own Web pages. For this link, I need the full (absolute) URL, because the page is kept at another site altogether. The URL of the main page of my Web document is currently

```
http://www.pipeline.com/agunn/A9-main.html
```

I'll make my name the link. Now it looks like this:

```
...author, <a href="http://www.pipeline.com/agunn/ag-mail.html">Angela Gunn,</a> by
hopping...
```

It's long, but it's not very different from the other links we've created. This is the type of link you'll type most often, especially when you create your list of favorite places. (If your list of places is as long as the "greatweb" list to which this page links, by the time you're done creating the links you'll be able to type the tag in your sleep.)

Note: Test your links, both relative and absolute, often. Web pages disappear or move unexpectedly. And if your page moves or is taken off the Web, notify anyone that you know has a link to it on their own Web page.

The last link we'll need to create is to the graphic of the cover. Mosaic automatically translates .GIF files that are used as graphics, so the graphic of my cover has been stored in .GIF format. It's kept on the `www.mcp.com` site in the `/sams/books/mos` directory, so all I need is a relative URL. The name of the file is `cover.gif`. I decide to position the graphic at the top of the page, just before the text. I click to place the prompt in front of the first `<p>` tag, and type

```
<img src="cover.gif"><br>
```

The first tag explains that an image is called for and gives the relative URL.

Tech Tip: The `<img src=`*`filename`*`>` tag is also used for movies and sound clips.

The second tag, `<br>`, is a line break. Like a return in a word-processing file, it causes Mosaic to end the line and start whatever text comes next at the beginning of the next line. The <img> tag doesn't need the <br> to work, but I like the way it looks, so I'm including it.

> **Tech Tip:** The <img src=*filename*> tag assumes that you want to center your image along the bottom of the space. If you have a number of images, you might prefer to center them along the middle or at the top. To center images in the middle of the space, use the command <img align=middle src=*filename*>. To center along the top, use <img align=top src=*filename*>. In either case, *filename* should be replaced by the URL of the image file.

Let's test it once more. I've been thinking for a while that I really dislike the look of <h2> for the second headline, so I switch to <h3>—Mosaic doesn't care if you use them in order or not. Also, I'd like to italicize the name of the book in the first paragraph. That's easy with the short and simple <i>...</i> tag. It looks like this when I'm done:

```
...to the <i>Plug-n-Play Mosaic</i> page...
```

The changes are made, and the page appears in Mosaic as in Figure 13.9, complete:

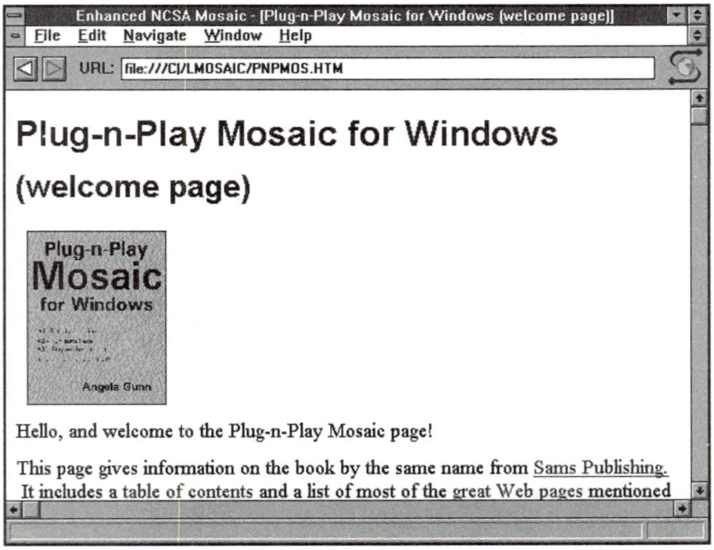

Figure 13.9. The completed page, with graphics, links, and fancy-looking text.

And on the editor screen? About half a screen's worth of text and tags, and ten minutes' worth of work (a great deal of which was spent debating the aesthetics).

One Web page later, let's recap: We've planned a page according to a simple tree structure, and assembled text and graphics we'd like to include on it. We made a simple ASCII file for the text of our page. We chose a short title and a headline, and added some tags to make them stand out. We did the same for the text, formatting it into paragraphs and adding a ruled line and my address. We created five links of various types to other pages, and inserted an inline image with a line break. Finally, we added some special formatting to the text to create italics.

These are the basic steps for creating most Web pages. We've covered both relative and absolute URLs, which account for almost all of the links you'll find. Links are perhaps the most difficult HTML tags to construct, because they're not terribly intuitive. However, there are just three major formats—URL links, target links, and links to image (and multimedia) files. You've tackled all three in this walkthrough. And emerged victorious.

How Do I...?

Trying to cram every possible HTML tag on one page, of course, would have made for a really odd page. Let's run through a few more basic tags for formatting text and sections of text. All these things, as well as some of the more arcane things like forms, are also arranged for handy reference in Appendix C.

Text Formatting

I showed you how to make italics: `<i>...</i>`. You can also make bold: `<b>...</b>`. Sometimes you'll want to show something in a monospaced (typewriter-style) font; that's `<tt>...</tt>`.

There are other type styles for specific functions. For instance, if you want to emphasize a certain piece of text, use `<em>...</em>`. This often appears as italics, though some Mosaic users prefer that it show up in color or in some other standout fashion. It's a better tag that `<i>...</i>` if you just want to make a piece of text stand out. (On our page, I used `<i>...</i>` because book titles should be in italics.)

Other tags you might use include `<cite>...</cite>`, for a citation (say, from a textbook). `<blockquote>...</blockquote>` lets you set off quoted material from the rest of your text; it may be slightly indented or it may appear as italics depending on the software used to look at the page. <strong>...</strong> makes a bit of text stand out (this often appears as bold; unless the text absolutely has to be bold, you should avoid using <b>...</b> and use this instead).

Occasionally you'll need something a little more unusual. Since HTML is used internationally, the organizations that work out these things are trying hard to be sure that characters in all languages can be used in HTML. For now there are two solutions: ASCII codes and the ISO Latin-I entities.

You may be familiar with ASCII codes from (again) word processing. Sometimes you'll need a special symbol that isn't found on your keyboard but is provided for in the computer's system. Then you'll use its ASCII number to trick your word processor into displaying the character. You can do the same thing in HTML. The tag is

```
&#asciicode;
```

where *asciicode* is the proper ASCII code. Note the other elements of the tag: ampersand, pound sign, and a semi-colon at the end.

If you're doing a certain amount of writing in a non-English language, you're probably familiar with the ISO Latin-I character entities. These enable you to use a number of characters not normally found on Anglophone keyboards—accents acutes, accents graves, cedillas, umlauts, tildes and the like, not to mention Icelandic's thorn or German's sz ligature. To produce these characters in HTML, the tag is

```
&;mnemonic
```

where *mnemonic* is one of a number of mnemonics. I've listed the mnemonics in Appendix C. They're easy; for example, Á gets you a capital A with the accent acute. Again, note the starting ampersand and the closing semicolon.

You may find on occasion that you'd like to use an ampersand in something besides a tag. In that case, you'll have to type in...a tag. Yes, a tag to avoid a tag—if you don't, Mosaic sees the ampersand and thinks you're about to give an HTML instruction. To make an ampersand without Mosaic getting confused, use

```
&amp;
```

again noting the opening ampersand and the closing semi-colon. You should also use a similar code to trick Mosaic into ignoring quotation marks (remember, HTML uses quotations in certain tags). The tag for quotation marks is

```
&quot;
```

which creates one set of marks. Don't forget to add in the other set at the end of whatever you're quoting. And a similar trick is used for pointy brackets:

```
&lt;
```

and

```
&gt;
```

are respectively the Mosaic-ignored characters for opening and closing pointy brackets.

> **Note:** ASCII and Latin-I can work together because the Latin-I is a superset of ASCII—ASCII is included in it.

Section Formatting

There are a few commands for displaying sections of text. Most of these involve various kinds of lists. The others are used to display blocks of text that Mosaic would normally try to read as HTML tags. It's also important to see how commands "nest" in HTML—nesting is what enables you to, for instance, use a .GIF file as a link.

There are five kinds of lists in proper. The first kind is the ordered (numbered) list; the second is an unordered (bulleted) list, for items that need to be listed but don't have to be in a particular sequence; the third is a definition list (or discursive list), which has an indented block of text for each listed item. The fourth is a menu list, which has neither bullets nor numbers; it's like an unordered list, but it's spaced to take up a bit less room. Finally there's the directory list, which is good for listing short items (under 20 characters—for instance, you could use a directory list for the months of the year).

Ordered, unordered, menu, and directory lists share a particular format. It looks like this:

```
<listtag>
<li>Item one</li>
<li>Item two</li>
<li>Item three</li>
</listtag>
```

The <li>...</li> tags in front of each item indicate to the browser that this is a new item and needs a fresh line. The *<listtag>*, of course, changes according to what sort of list it is. Ordered lists have the <ol>...</ol> tag. Unordered lists have the <ul>...</ul> tag. Menu lists have—had—the <menu>...</menu> tag. Directory lists have the <dir>...</dir> tag.

Don't get confused and type *listtag*. That's only a placeholder for one of the four types of tags listed. The point is to show you that they all work the same.

> **Tech Tip:** Like <p> with its optional </p> above, <li> doesn't really require the closing </li> tag. I show it here so you don't have to remember which tags do and don't need to be "closed;" when you're feeling more fluent in HTML, you can skip using the </li> tag.

Definition lists are a bit different. Items in definition lists travel in pairs: every defined term has a definition. A good HTML editor will alert you if you try to make a definition list and don't have everything paired off properly.

A definition list looks like this:

```
<dl>
<dt>First thing to define</dt>
<dd>Its definition</dd>
<dt>Next thing to define</dt>
<dd>Its definition</dd>
</dl>
```

You might also see it looking like this, which is slightly more correct but a little congested:

```
<dl>
<dt>First thing<dd>Its definition
<dt>Second thing<dd>Its definition
</dl>
```

Now and then you might want to include a large block of text that includes characters that could give Mosaic trouble (for instance, you might want to show how to write out a link). In that case, use the preformatted-text tag, which looks like

```
<pre>...</pre>
```

and often appears in a typewriter-style (monospaced) font. Mosaic will not attempt to interpret anything between the tags. This makes it useful for displaying, for instance, large chunks of HTML-formatted text.

You may need to add a hidden comment in your page—something you can't see with the browser but can see if you're looking at the document source code. In those cases, use the tag

```
<!-- your message here -->
```

and Mosaic won't attempt to read it or display it. This is useful if, for instance, you want to remind yourself when you last checked a link. Note that there's no space between the exclamation point and the double hyphen. You can put one between the last two hyphens and the closing bracket; it won't make a difference.

> **Warning:** Even though comments can't be seen with Mosaic or other browsers, anyone can see them by viewing the source code. Don't say anything damning or rude in your comments.

Finally, let's look at a nested tag. Of course, everything on a proper HTML page is nested between the `<html>...</html>` tags, so you see that in theory you could combine these formats any which way as long as you did it in an orderly fashion, like so:

```
Start of first thing
Start of second thing
Start of third thing
End of third thing
End of second thing
End of first thing
```

One of the most popular nested tags is a GIF file that acts as a link. To do that, you construct the link with the image-file tag inside the link tags, like so:

```
<a href="somewhere"><img src="graphicfile"></a>
```

where `"somewhere"` is replaced by the URL of the page to which you're linking and `"graphicfile"` is the the URL of the GIF file.

However, remember that not everyone's browser can support graphics. For their sake, we'll add a little something extra to this tag:

```
a href="somewhere"><img src "graphicfile" alt="Picture this!"></a>
```

The text-browsing types will now see the words `"Picture this!"` in place of your image. You can substitute anything you like for the `"Picture this!"`, as long as you enclose it in quotation marks.

When All Else Fails

Sometimes you can't get the look you want no matter what you do. Or you may find the whole process frustrating. If all else fails, there's one thing left to do to get good code:

Steal it.

I highly recommend this, actually, even if you're not entirely lost. By finding a well-made page and viewing the document source code, you can learn a lot about how other people have created their works. It's not right to claim someone else's work as your own, of course, but there's no problem with loading a copy of a good page to disk to dissect it later. And if you open that page in your own text editor, you can always change the text and URLs between the tags, plugging in the things you want to say. If you're meticulous about catching every phrase, URL, and reference to specific e-mail addresses, who'll know?

> **Warning:** Do NOT appropriate others' GIF files, movies, or sound clips without asking permission; use the e-mail addresses on the pages. And don't appropriate their text, either. The only thing I'm suggesting you "borrow" is the coding scheme.

Call it an homage.

What Lies Ahead

The book stops here, to coin a weak pun. Of course, that can only mean that here's where the real adventure starts.

The rest of the book is given over to tips and tricks to make the most of your Netsurfing sessions. For starters, I've included a list of Internet providers in Appendix A. The Luckman Mosaic software includes access to Portal, one of the largest Internet providers, but if you'd like to check out others you'll find good information here.

Appendix B answers a number of questions. Overall, the material we've covered applies equally to all platforms—HTML and Mosaic are about as universal as such things get—but I have addressed a few special concerns there. Also, I've added a bit more information about the NCSA (freeware) Mosaic, which you may have found on line and want to try out. Appendix C digs deeper into HTML. A full list of tags is there (and notes on some of the finer points of page construction), along with sources on the Net that can provide you with more guidance.

In Appendix D I've listed some of the best and most interesting Web sites I've found recently. There's a little something there for everyone, I think. When you start browsing the Web on your own, be sure to drop by the home page for this book at `http://www.mcp.com/sams/books/mos.html`; I'm keeping a version of the site list there for easy exploration.

After that is the glossary.

After that is the index.

After that—see you online!

Internet Access Providers

Although the software that's included on our disks provides you with a very quick and easy way to get an Internet account with Portal Communications, this may not necessarily be the most cost-effective way for you to get on the Internet with Mosaic. You may be better off with a provider in your area with a local phone number.

This appendix lists companies and organizations that provide dialup SLIP or PPP Internet accounts for individuals. For more information on different types of Internet access and what to look for in an access provider—especially in relation to accessing the World Wide Web with Mosaic—see Chapter 6, "Dialup Connections SLIP and PPP."

Geographical and Area Code Summary—U.S. and Canadian Providers

Following is a listing of North American Internet provider names arranged by the state or province that the provider services, and then by area code. Details and contact information for each provider follow in the next section.

Alabama

205

Nuance Network Service

Alberta

403

Alberta SuperNet Inc.

CCI Networks

Arizona

602

CRL

Evergreen Internet

British Columbia

604

Cyberstore Systems Inc.

DataFlux Systems Limited

Wimsey Information Services

California

213

CRL

310

CERFnet
CRL
Netcom

408

Netcom
Portal

415

CERFnet
CRL
Institute for Global Communications (IGC)
Netcom

510

CCnet Communications
CERFnet
CRL
HoloNet
Netcom

619

CERFnet
CTS Network Services
Netcom

707

CRL

714

CERFnet
Digital Express Group (Digex)
Netcom

818

CERFnet
Netcom

909

Digital Express Group (Digex)

916

Netcom

Colorado

303

CNS
Colorado SuperNet
Netcom

719

CNS
Colorado SuperNet

District of Columbia

202

Clarknet

Florida

305

CyberGate
IDS World Network

407

IDS World Network

Georgia

404

CRL
Netcom

Illinois

312

CICNet
InterAccess Co.
Netcom

708

CICNet
InterAccess Co.
XNet Information Systems

815

InterAccess Co.

Louisiana

504

Neosoft

Manitoba

204

MBnet

Maryland

301

ClarkNet
Digital Express Group (Digex)

410

ClarkNet
Digital Express Group (Digex)

Massachusetts

617

Netcom
North Shore Access

Michigan

313

Msen

810

Msen

Missouri

314

Neosoft

Nevada

702

Evergreen Internet

New Hampshire

603

MV Communications, Inc.

New Jersey

609

Digital Express Group (Digex)

908

Digital Express Group (Digex)

New York

212

Echo
Netcom
Panix

516

Panix

718

Echo
Mindvox

North Carolina

704

Interpath
Northcoast Internet
Internet Access, Inc.

910

Interpath

919

Interpath

Ohio

614

OARNet

Ontario

416

UUNorth Incorporated

519

Hookup Communication Corporation

Oregon

503

Agora

Netcom

Teleport

Pennsylvania

412

Telerama

Rhode Island

401

IDS World Network

Quebec

514

Communications Accessibles Montreal, Inc.

Texas

214

Netcom

Texas Metronet

512

Netcom

713

Neosoft

817

Texas Metronet

Utah

801

Evergreen Internet

Virginia

703

ClarkNet
Digital Express Group (Digex)
Netcom

Washington

206

Netcom
Teleport

Packet Network/Toll-Free Access

CompuServe Packet Network

IDS World Network

PSINet

HoloNet

SprintNet

Neosoft
Portal

Tollfree/800 Access

CERFnet
CICNet
CNS
CRL
Msen
Neosoft

Tymnet

Holonet

Providers in United States and Canada

Agora

Area code(s)	503
E-mail address	`info@agora.rain.com`
Dialup number	503-293-1772
Services provided	Shell, Usenet, FTP, telnet, Gopher, Lynx, IRC, mail, SLIP/PPP coming

Alberta SuperNet Inc.

Area code(s)	403
Voice phone	403-441-3663
E-mail address	`info@supernet.ab.ca`
Services provided	Shell, e-mail, Usenet, FTP, telnet, Gopher, SLIP/PPP

CCI Networks

Area code(s)	403
Voice phone	403-450-6787
E-mail address	`info@ccinet.ab.ca`
Services provided	Shell, e-mail, Usenet, FTP, telnet, Gopher, WAIS, WWW, IRC, Hytelnet, SLIP/PPP

CCnet Communications

Area code(s)	510
Voice phone	510-988-0680
E-mail address	`info@ccnet.com`
Dialup number	510-988-7140, login as **guest**
Services provided	Shell, SLIP/PPP, telnet, e-mail, FTP, Usenet, IRC, WWW

CERFnet

Area code	619, 510, 415, 818, 714, 310, 800
Voice phone	800-876-2373
E-mail address	`sales@cerf.net`
Services provided	Full range of Internet services

CICNet

Area code(s)	312, 708, 800
Voice phone	800-947-4754 or 313-998-6703
E-mail address	`info@cic.net`
Services provided	SLIP, FTP, telnet, Gopher, e-mail, Usenet

ClarkNet (Clark Internet Services, Inc.)

Area code(s)	410, 301, 202, 703
Voice phone	800-735-2258, ask for extension 410-730-9764
E-mail address	`info@clark.net`
Dialup number	301-596-1626, login as **`guest`**, no password
Services provided	Shell/optional menu, FTP, Gopher, telnet, IRC, news, Mosaic, Lynx, MUD, SLIP/PPP/CSLIP, and much more

CNS

Area code(s)	303, 719, 800
Voice phone	800-748-1200
E-mail address	`service@cscns.com`
Dialup number	719-520-1700, 303-758-2656
Services provided	Shell/menu, e-mail, FTP, telnet, all newsgroups, IRC, 4m, Gopher, WAIS, SLIP, and more

Colorado SuperNet

Area code(s)	303, 719
Voice phone	303-273-3471
E-mail address	`info@csn.org` or `help@csn.org`
Services provided	Shell, e-mail, Usenet news, telnet, FTP, SLIP/PPP, and other Internet tools

Communications Accessibles Montreal, Inc.

Area code(s)	514
Voice phone	514-931-0749
E-mail address	`info@cam.org`
Dialup number	514-596-2255
Services provided	Shell, FTP, telnet, Gopher, WAIS, WWW, IRC, Hytelnet, SLIP/CSLIP/PPP, news

CRL

Area code(s)	213, 310, 404, 415, 510, 602, 707, 800
Voice phone	415-837-5300
E-mail address	`support@crl.com`
Dialup number	415-705-6060, login as **newuser**, no password
Services provided	Shell, e-mail, Usenet, UUCP, FTP, telnet, SLIP/PPP, and more

CTS Network Services (CTSNet)

Area code(s)	619
Voice phone	619-637-3737
E-mail address	`support@cts.com`
Dialup number	619-637-3660
Services provided	Shell, e-mail, Usenet, FTP, telnet, Gopher, IRC, MUD, SLIP/PPP, and more

CyberGate

Area code(s)	305
Voice phone	305-428-4283
E-mail address	`sales@gate.net`
Services provided	Shell, e-mail, Usenet, FTP, telnet, Gopher, Lynx, IRC, SLIP/PPP

Cyberstore Systems Inc.

Area code(s)	604
Voice phone	604-526-3373
E-mail address	`info@cyberstore.ca`
Dialup number	604-526-3676, login as **guest**
Services provided	E-mail, Usenet, FTP, telnet, Gopher, WAIS, WWW, IRC, SLIP/PPP

DataFlux Systems Limited

Area code(s)	604
Voice phone	604-744-4553
E-mail address	`info@dataflux.bc.ca`
Services provided	Shell, e-mail, Usenet, FTP, telnet, Gopher, WAIS, WWW, IRC, SLIP/PPP

Digital Express Group (Digex)

Area code(s)	301, 410, 609, 703, 714, 908, 909
Voice phone	800-969-9090
E-mail address	`info@digex.net`
Dialup number	301-220-0258, 410-605-2700, 609-348-6203, 703-281-7997, 714-261-5201, 908-937-9481, 909-222-2204, login as **new**
Services provided	Shell, SLIP/PPP, e-mail, newsgroups, telnet, FTP, IRC, Gopher, WAIS, and more

Echo

Area code(s)	212, 718
Voice phone	212-255-3839
E-mail address	`info@echonyc.com`
Dialup number	212-989-3382
Services provided	Conferencing, e-mail, shell, complete Internet access including telnet, FTP, SLIP/PPP

Evergreen Internet

Area code(s)	602, 702, 801
Voice phone	602-230-9339
E-mail address	`evergreen@libre.com`
Services provided	Shell, FTP, telnet, SLIP, PPP, others

HoloNet

Area code(s)	510, PSINet, Tymnet
Voice phone	510-704-0160
E-mail address	`support@holonet.net`
Dialup number	510-704-1058
Services provided	Complete Internet access

Hookup Communication Corporation

Area code(s)	519, Canada-wide
Voice phone	800-363-0400
E-mail address	`info@hookup.net`
Services provided	Shell, e-mail, Usenet, FTP, telnet, Gopher, WAIS, WWW, IRC, Hytelnet, Archie, SLIP/PPP

IDS World Network

Area code(s)	401, 305, 407, CompuServe Network
Voice phone	401-885-6855
E-mail address	info@ids.net
Dialup number	401-884-9002
Services provided	Shell, FTP, Gopher, telnet, Talk, Usenet news, SLIP

Institute for Global Communications (IGC)

Area code(s)	415
Voice phone	415-442-0220
E-mail address	support@igc.apc.org
Dialup number	415-322-0284
Services provided	E-mail, telnet, FTP, Gopher, Archie, Veronica, WAIS, SLIP/PPP

InterAccess Co.

Area code(s)	312, 708, 815
Voice phone	800-967-1580
E-mail address	info@interaccess.com
Dialup number	708-671-0237
Services provided	Shell, FTP, telnet, SLIP, PPP, etc.

Interpath

Area code(s)	919, 910, 704
Voice phone	800-849-6305
E-mail address	info@infopath.net
Services provided	Full shell for UNIX, SLIP, and PPP

MBnet

Area code(s)	204
Voice phone	204-474-9590
E-mail address	`info@mbnet.mb.ca`
Dialup number	204-275-6132, login as **mbnet** with password **guest**
Services provided	Shell, e-mail, Usenet, FTP, telnet, Gopher, WAIS, WWW, IRC, Archie, Hytelnet, SLIP/PPP

Msen

Area code(s)	313, 810, 800
Voice phone	313-998-4562
E-mail address	`info-request@msen.com`
Services provided	Shell, e-mail, telnet, FTP, Usenet, Gopher, IRC, WAIS, SLIP/PPP

MV Communications, Inc.

Area code(s)	603
Voice phone	603-429-2223
E-mail address	`info@mv.mv.com`
Dialup number	603-424-7428
Services provided	Shell, Usenet, FTP, telnet, Gopher, WAIS, SLIP/PPP

Neosoft

Area code(s)	713, 504, 314, 800, SprintNet
Voice phone	713-684-5969
E-mail address	`info@neosoft.com`
Services provided	Shell, Usenet, FTP, telnet, Gopher, SLIP/PPP, etc.

Netcom On-Line Communications Services

Area code(s)	206, 212, 214, 303, 310, 312, 404, 408, 415, 503, 510, 512, 617, 619, 703, 714, 818, 916
Voice phone	800-501-8649
E-mail address	`info@netcom.com`
Dialup number	206-547-5992, 212-354-3870, 214-753-0045, 303-758-0101, 310-842-8835, 312-380-0340, 404-303-9765, 408-261-4700, 408-459-9851, 415-328-9940, 415-985-5650, 503-626-6833, 510-274-2900, 510-426-6610, 510-865-9004, 512-206-4950, 617-237-8600, 619-234-0524, 703-255-5951, 714-708-3800, 818-585-3400, 916-965-1371; login as **guest**
Services provided	Shell, e-mail, Usenet, FTP, telnet, Gopher, IRC, WAIS, SLIP/PPP

North Shore Access

Area code(s)	617
Voice phone	617-593-3110
E-mail address	`info@shore.net`
Dialup number	617-593-4557, login as **new**
Services provided	Shell, FTP, telnet, Gopher, Archie, SLIP/PPP

Northcoast Internet

Area code(s)	707
Voice phone	707-444-1913
Services provided	Shell, FTP, telnet, Gopher, SLIP/PPP

Nuance Network Services

Area code(s)	205
Voice phone	205-533-4296
E-mail address	`info@nuance.com`
Services provided	Shell, Usenet, FTP, telnet, Gopher, SLIP/PPP

OARNet

Area code(s)	614
Voice phone	800-627-8101
E-mail address	`info@oar.net`
Services provided	Shell, SLIP/PPP

Panix Public Access UNIX and Internet

Area code(s)	212, 516
Voice phone	212-787-6160
E-mail address	`info@panix.com`
Dialup number	212-787-3100, 516-626-7863, login as **`newuser`**
Services provided	Shell, Usenet, FTP, telnet, Gopher, Archie, WWW, WAIS, SLIP/PPP

Portal Communications Company

Area code(s)	408, SprintNet
Voice phone	408-973-9111
E-mail address	`info@portal.com`
Services provided	Shell, e-mail, Usenet, FTP, telnet, Gopher, IRC, SLIP/PPP

PSI

Area code(s)	North America, Europe, and Pacific Basin; send e-mail to `numbers-info@psi.com` for list
Voice phone	703-709-0300
E-mail address	`all-info@psi.com`
Services provided	Complete Internet services

Teleport

Area code(s)	503, 206
Voice phone	503-223-4245
E-mail address	`info@teleport.com`
Dialup number	503-220-1016
Services provided	Shell, e-mail, Usenet, FTP, telnet, Gopher, SLIP/PPP

Telerama

Area code(s)	412
Voice phone	412-481-3505
E-mail address	`sysop@telerama.lm.com`
Dialup number	412-481-4644
Services provided	Shell, e-mail, telnet, Usenet, FTP, Gopher, IRC, SLIP/PPP

Texas Metronet

Area code(s)	214, 817
Voice phone	214-705-2900
E-mail address	`info@metronet.com`
Dialup number	214-705-2901, 817-261-1127; login as **`info`** with password **`info`**
Services provided	Shell, e-mail, Usenet, FTP, telnet, Gopher, IRC, SLIP/PPP

UUNorth Incorporated

Area code(s)	416
Voice phone	416-225-8649
E-mail address	`uunorth@north.net`
Dialup number	416-221-0200, login as **`new`**
Services provided	E-mail, Usenet, FTP, telnet, Gopher, WAIS, WWW, IRC, Archie, SLIP/PPP

VNet Internet Access, Inc.

Area code(s)	704, public data network
Voice phone	800-377-3282
E-mail address	`info@vnet.net`
Dialup number	704-347-8839, login as **new**
Services provided	Shell, e-mail, Usenet, FTP, telnet, Gopher, IRC, SLIP/PPP, UUCP

Wimsey Information Services

Area code(s)	604
Voice phone	604-936-8649
E-mail address	`admin@wimsey.com`
Services provided	Shell, e-mail, Usenet, FTP, telnet, Gopher, WAIS, WWW, IRC, Archie, SLIP/PPP

XNet Information Systems

Area code(s)	708
Voice phone	708-983-6064
E-mail address	`info@xnet.com`
Dialup number	708-983-6435, 708-882-1101
Services provided	Shell, e-mail, Usenet, FTP, telnet, Gopher, Archie, IRC, SLIP/PPP, UUCP

Australia

Aarnet

Voice phone	+61 6-249-3385
E-mail address	`aarnet@aarnet.edu.au`

Connect.com.au P/L

Areas serviced	Major Australian capital cities (2, 3, 6, 7, 8, 9)
Voice phone	1 800 818 262 or +61 3-528-2239
E-mail address	`connect@connect.com.au`
Services provided	Shell, SLIP/PPP, UUCP

Germany

Contributed Software

Voice phone	+49 30-694-69-07
E-mail address	`info@contrib.de`
Dialup number	+49 30-694-60-55, login as **`guest`** or **`gast`**

Individual Network e.V.

Area serviced	All of Germany
Voice phone	+49 0441 9808556
E-mail address	`in-info@individual.net`
Dialup number	02238 15071, login as **`info`**
Services provided	UUCP throughout Germany; FTP, SLIP, telnet, and other services in some major cities

Inter Networking System (INS)

Voice phone	+49 2305 356505
E-mail address	`info@ins.net`

Netherlands

Knoware

E-mail address	`info@knoware.nl`
Dialup number	030 896775

NetLand

Voice phone	020 6943664
E-mail address	`Info@netland.nl`
Dialup number	020 6940350, login as **new** or **info**

Simplex

E-mail address	`simplex@simplex.nl`
Dialup number	020 6653388, login as **new** or **info**

New Zealand

Actrix

Voice phone	(04) 389-6316
E-mail address	`john@actrix.gen.nz`

Switzerland

SWITCH - Swiss Academic and Research Network

Voice phone	+41 1 268 1515
E-mail address	`postmaster@switch.ch`

United Kingdom

Almac

Voice phone	+44 0324-665371
E-mail address	`alastair.mcintyre@almac.co.uk`

Cix

Voice phone	+44 49 2641 961
E-mail address	`cixadmin@cix.compulink.co.uk`

Demon Internet Limited

Voice phone	081-349-0063 (London) 031-552-0344 (Edinburgh)
E-mail address	`internet@demon.net`
Services provided	SLIP/PPP accounts

The Direct Connection (UK)

Voice phone	+44 (0)81 317 0100
E-mail address	`helpdesk@dircon.cu.uk`
Dialup number	+44 (0)81 317 2222

Note to Providers: If you would like to be included in future versions of this list, for use in subsequent editions of this book as well as other Sams Internet books, send an e-mail message to Mark Taber <mtaber@netcom.com>.

APPENDIX B

NCSA Mosaic: Tips for Mac (and Windows) Users

Users of Macintosh computers have gotten less ink in these pages, but rest assured that it's because the PC side needs more explanation. (You've always known that those things were a pain, right?) The ease with which Mosaic melds with the rest of your system is just another example of why you chose (or were given) a non-PC in the first place.

This appendix gives additional information on the Macintosh and Windows versions of the original NCSA Mosaic (the freeware). Since the software in the back of this book is PC-only, I'll assume that you've chosen to download a copy of MacMosaic. Good choice; the MacMosaic software is powerful, flexible, and above all, free. We'll walk through all the menu options available and make sure that you're ready to go. You should by now have skimmed Chapters 8 and 9, which describe the PC software; if you haven't, you might flip to them now to familiarize yourself with the basic concepts behind Mosaic. Also, since I spend a few paragraphs in this appendix describing NCSA Mosaic for Windows, you may feel comfortable with just that refresher course.

As I was saying, this appendix also includes information on getting the Windows version of NCSA Mosaic. You don't need it because a version of Enhanced Mosaic is included in the back of the book, but you might find it on the Net and want to give it a whirl. Also, because I used NCSA as the "gold standard" of comparison in Chapter 11, you may want to explore it more fully for yourself.

NCSA Mosaic (Windows and Macintosh)

NCSA Mosaic is the original version of the software and the progenitor of most of the other Web browsers currently available. As such I use it as the "gold standard" for comparing other browsers, especially in Chapter 11—its wide availability, existence on multiple platforms, and extremely reasonable price make it an excellent pacesetter for the many Mosaic-come-lately software packages that are becoming available.

A brief review of the interface components is in order. As shown in Figure B.1, we see the usual URL window at the top of the screen, the anchor window at the bottom of the screen, the Mosaic globe in the upper-right corner, and a large collection of buttons and menu items.

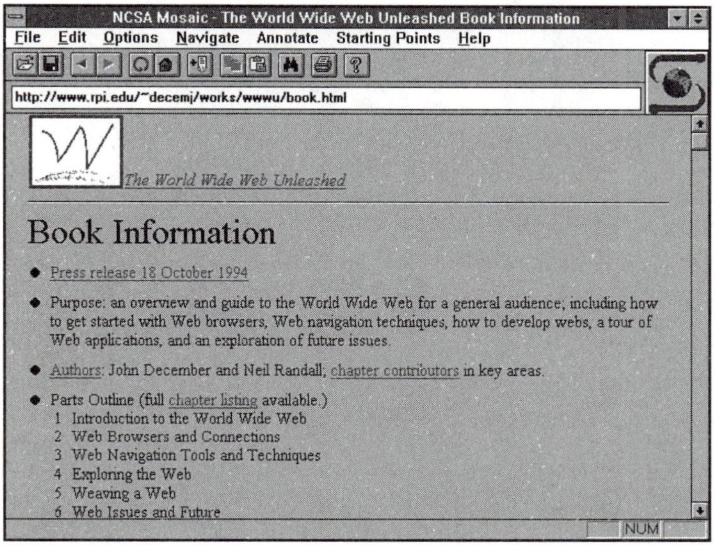

Figure B.1. The NCSA Mosaic for Windows screen.

The NCSA Mosaic software has certain drawbacks. First and foremost, it's *quite* slow. Certain features (annotate, anyone?) didn't always work as one might wish. And some features were never implemented (even though menu items and buttons exist for them!). Still, I highly recommend that anyone genuinely interested in exploring Mosaic get a copy of the original and goof around with it for awhile. (Hey, can you ever have too much Mosaic? I think not.)

The buttons perform the following functions, left to right:

File folder—open URL

Diskette—save to file

Backward arrow, forward arrow—go backward, go forward

Circular arrow—reload

House—go to home page

Two pages—copy

Clipboard and page—paste

Page with arrow—find text on current page

Printer—print

Question mark—about NCSA Mosaic for Windows

The menus in NCSA Mosaic are arranged in the following groups. Since the functions are much like those we saw in Chapters 8 and 9, I won't describe them unless they vary greatly from what you've already seen.

FILE Menu

- Open URL—also available via button
- Open Local File
- Save
- Save As
- Save Preferences
- Print—also available via button
- Print Preview
- Print Setup
- Document Source
- Exit

EDIT menu

- Copy
- Find

OPTIONS Menu

- Load to Disk
- Show Toolbar
- Show Status Bar
- Show Current URL
- Show Anchor URLs
- Change Cursor Over Arrows
- Extended FTP Directory Parsing—lets you choose how much info Mosaic gives you about files in FTP sites
- Display Inline Images
- Show Group Annotations
- Use 8-bit sound
- Choose Font

Most of these options are found in Luckman Mosaic in the Edit/Preferences menu.

NAVIGATE Menu

Back—also available via button

Forward—also available via button

Reload—also available via button

Home—also available via button

History

Add Current To Hotlist

Menu Editor

ANNOTATE Menu

Annotate

Edit this annotation

Delete this annotation

The annotate feature does not exist on most commercial Mosaic software. For a full description of the Annotate feature, please see Chapter 11.

STARTING POINTS Menu

Various pre-loaded lists of good URLs

HELP Menu

Online documentation—actually a tiny specialized hotlist for Mosaic help

FAQ page

About Windows Mosaic

Note that the Help button calls a help file that lives on your hard drive, while the help ("Online Documentation") in this menu goes online to seek out information.

Note that NCSA Mosaic is still being developed and improved. You may see "extra" menu items in beta versions of Mosaic—most of those are there so the software writers can easily tweak the Mosaic in progress. You may safely ignore these options.

Macintosh Software (NCSA Mosaic for Macintosh)

Interface

The MacMosaic interface differs from that of the PC, but most of the differences are cosmetic. I've chosen to focus on the NSCA version of MacMosaic in this appendix, because it's free and easy to find.

The Back, Forward and Home interface buttons in the main window are quite familiar to you by now (but in MacMosaic they're much, much larger). The familiar globe has moved to the left side of the window. The middle URL window acts as the History list, and the Search function is used for forms-based activities such as searches. Just below that, a status line shows the progress of loading pages and displays the appropriate anchor URL when the mouse rolls over a link.

As for the menu choices, you'll see that they're much the same as those we saw with the NCSA PC platform in Chapter 11 and this appendix.

FILE Menu

New Window—same

Clone Window—creates a new window and loads a copy of the page in the current window

Open URL—same

Open Local—same

Reload—same

Close—closes the current window

Save As—saves in either text or HTML format

Page Setup—the usual

Print—the usual

Mail Developers—send e-mail to the authors of NCSA Mosaic

Quit—the usual

EDIT Menu

Undo—the usual

Cut—the usual; not applicable to Web pages displays

Copy—the usual; not applicable for Web page displays

Paste—the usual; not applicable to Web page displays

Clear—the usual; not applicable to Web page displays

Find—same

Find Again—resume Find

Show Clipboard—the usual

OPTIONS Menu

Hide URLs—toggle switch to hide the URL window on main screen

Show Status Messages—toggle switch to hide the status (anchor) line on main screen

Load To Disk—same

Auto-Load Images—same as Load Inline Images

Use Temp Items—dictates where Mosaic stores temporary files

Remove Temp Files—deletes all temporary files; useful if your computer crashes mid-session

Use HTTP .9—a developer's feature

Flush Cache—clear both document and images caches

Preferences—set home page, news server, WAIS gateway, user name, e-mail address, anchor colors, and helper applications (viewers).

Style—fonts

NAVIGATE Menu

Back—same (same as left-arrow button)

Forward—same (same as right-arrow button)

Home—same (same as home button)

Network Starting Points—a hotlist

Internet Resources Meta-Index—a hotlist of search tools

NCSA Demo Page—a Mosaic tour

NCSA What's New Page—a link with additions to the MacMosaic software and to the Web

MacMosaic Home Page—the NCSA Macintosh for Mosaic Web page

MacMosaic Features—information on current and past versions of NCSA Mosaic for Macintosh

ANNOTATION Menu

Text—same

Audio—record an audio-file annotation (if your hardware is capable of doing so)

Edit Annotation—same

Delete annotation—same

HOTLIST Menu

Hotlist Interface—begin New hotlist, Open hotlist, Save hotlist, Save As a different hotlist, Edit hotlist

Add This Document—adds the current URL to the hotlist

(Your hotlists appear here)

BALLOON HELP Menu

About Balloon Help—the usual

Show Balloons—the usual

MacMosaic Documentation—link to NCSA Mosaic for Macintosh document

HTML Help—link to A Beginner's Guide To HTML

URL Help—link to A Beginner's Guide To URLs

FAQ—link to Frequently Asked Questions about NCSA Mosaic for Macintosh

Note that there's no option to view the document source code. To see document source for a particular page, choose Options/Load To Disk and then choose File/Reload. The page will be saved to your hard drive as an ASCII text file.

APPENDIX C

HTML and Home Page Construction: The Quick Reference

This reference section covers the following topics:

- Basic page structure
- Writing your links
- URL links, hypermedia links, absolute and relative URLs, target links, text links
- HTML and HTML 2
- Forms and image maps: One step beyond
- Alphabetical list of basic HTML commands
- HTML commands by function
- ISO Latin-1 character entities
- For further information
- A selection of editors available online

Basic Page Structure

No matter what the content of your Web page, it should follow certain guidelines. Here's the basic structure:

```
<doctype html public "-//W3O//DTD W3 HTML 2.0//EN">
<html><head><title>YOUR PAGE'S WINDOW TITLE HERE</title>
</head>
<body><h1>PAGE HEADLINE</h1>
PAGE CONTENTS
<hr><address>YOUR-USERNAME@YOUR.EMAIL.ADDRESS</address>
</body>
</html>

<html><head><title>YOUR PAGE'S WINDOW TITLE HERE</title>
<link  rev="made" href="mailto:YOUR-USERNAME@YOUR.EMAIL.ADDRESS">
<h1>PAGE HEADLINE</h1></head>
<body><p>FIRST PARAGRAPH</p>
<p>NEXT PARAGRAPH</p>
<hr>
<address>YOUR-USERNAME@YOUR.EMAIL.ADDRESS</address>
</body>
</html>
```

The line breaks shown above are not important; you could (if you wished) write your entire page as one long block of text and codes. In addition, I've shown the tags in lowercase, but you could uppercase them to make it easier to locate them on a long page. (Of course, the material shown above in all capital letters should be replaced with your specific page and address information.)

Writing Your Links

There are three major types of link tags on the average page: URL links, hypermedia links, and target links.

URL Links

A URL link connects the user to another location. URL links follow the form

```
<a href="URL">...</a>
```

where *URL* is replaced by the absolute or relative URL of the page to which you're linking.

Hypermedia Links

A hypermedia link brings up an image file, a video clip, a sound file, or some other resource. Hypermedia links follow the form

```
<img src="URL">...</a>
```

where *URL* is replaced by the absolute or relative URL of the file to which you're linking. This format will load the hypermedia file as an inline image; that is, it will not be a link. If you'd like to make the file a link, the hypermedia link (first half only—no closing </a>) must be nested within a URL link, like so:

```
<a href="URL"><img src="URL"></a>
```

where the first *URL* is the name of the link, and the second *URL* is the name of the hypermedia file.

The hypermedia link tag takes several formatting arguments. There are three arguments that define the positioning of the file:

```
<img src="URL" align="top">
<img src="URL" align="middle">
<img src="URL" align="bottom">
```

The default value is align="bottom".

There's also an argument to provide for text-only browsers. By using

```
<img src="URL" alt="X">
```

you can give text-browser users an alternate image (in this case, the letter X) in place of the hypermedia file. By using a null set in that argument (that is, alt="") you'll keep the text-only browser from seeing anything in the spot where graphical browsers see the image.

Relative Versus Absolute Links

URL links and hypermedia links include a URL, which may be either absolute (the whole URL, with domain name and full file name and directory information) or relative (a partial URL, usually with the directory information and/or the file name). Here's the same link expressed as a relative URL and as an absolute URL:

```
<a href="looks.html">...</a>
```

and

```
<a href="http://www.pipeline.com/~agunn/personal/looks.html>...</a>
```

You must use absolute links whenever the link goes to a page not on the same server as the page you're writing. In addition, absolute links are often preferable to relative links for pages on the same server. If the file including the links moves to another computer or directory, all relative links must be changed. Finally, if you're writing a page with links that other users might want to see independently of the page itself (that is, if they might want to view the document source code for the page and make note of the links for later use, as with a page of references), it's easier on the users if they can see the entire URL.

Why use relative links? It's primarily a speed and elegance issue; if you know the page to which you're linking is and will always be located in the same directory on the same server, using a relative URL eliminates a domain-name lookup. It also makes the page much easier to read.

Target Links

Target links are not links in the true sense (they can't take you to another page); rather, they allow other links to arrive at a particular spot on a page. This is useful if you have a page with a great deal of information on it; target links can be inserted at section headings, and users can hop quickly to the section they need.

Target links follow the structure

```
<a name="TARGET">...</a>
```

where *TARGET* is any word that describes the spot to which you're linking. To reach a target link on another page, construct a URL link (relative or absolute) with the structure

```
<a href="PAGENAME.html#TARGET">...</a>
```

where the name of the page file is followed immediately by a pound sign (#) and the word used as the target. To link to a target on the same page, use a URL link with the format

```
<a href="#TARGET">...</a>
```

This is known as a local link.

Text Links

Additionally, there is a format for including text files in an HTML page. It bears a close resemblance to the format for hypermedia links:

```
<inc srv  "FILENAME">
```

where *FILENAME* is replaced by the URL for the file you wish to include. The file will appear in the browser's regular text font. If you prefer that it appear in some other stylefont, the tag may be nested—for instance, if you'd like the text to appear in italics, this tag would look like this:

```
<i><inc srv "FILENAME"></i>
```

Note that unlike the hypermedia tag, the text tag does not currently include the "=" sign. The text-link HTML format is still under development.

HTML and HTML+

HTML (HyperText Markup Language) is what's known as an SGML (Standardized General Markup Language). SGMLs are created to work over many different types of computers, which is why we're able to include Mac and PC information in one book.

The latest version of HTML is called HTML 2. It's compatible with the earlier version, known simply as HTML. However, some commands used under HTML are no longer used by HTML 2, and HTML 2 uses several commands that HTML doesn't have. In our examples, I've chosen to show you the most current HTML 2 coding, and I encourage you to use it. If you find an older HTML document and decide to use it as a blueprint, do your best to include the HTML 2 codes.

To get the latest information on the emerging HTML 2 specification, check in periodically via anonymous FTP at

```
ftp://15.254.100.100/pub/
```

Forms and Image Maps: One Step Beyond

Forms

Forms such as those used for searches and on bianca's graffiti walls are beyond the scope of this book, as are images maps such as the `sunsite.unc.edu` map or bianca's shack blueprint. However,

```
http://www.ncsa.uiuc.edu/SDG/Software/Mosaic/Docs/fill-out-forms/
```

has tips on coding and a sample form if you're inclined to try your hand at building one, and

```
http://south.ncsa.uiuc.edu/forms.html
```

has a forms-creation tutorial as well. The specifications for forms creation are still under development. Also, there's a fair amount of additional work in ensuring that the information users enter in the form is properly understood by the HTTP server (and then transferred to another file or to e-mail). Check the links at this site for more information.

Image Maps

Image maps, in which the coordinates of a mouse click are interpreted by a mapping server, are somewhat less complicated to create. However, a number of the maps you'll find online are poorly designed. Also, remember that an image map will add bulk to your page—since not everyone can view such maps, you'll need to duplicate all the links as normal text-based pointers. And images, as we've seen, take much longer to move across the Net that text does. However, if you're still interested, there's a good tutorial at

```
http://wintermute.ncsa.uiuc.edu:8080/map-tutorial/image-maps.html
```

which will acquaint you with the wonders of the `<ismap>` tag.

Alphabetical List of Basic HTML Commands

<!–...–>—comments; text you want to add to the document but don't necessarily want to appear onscreen. The text must be placed between the pair of double hyphens. *Beware*—even though the material in the brackets won't show via Mosaic, it will show up if the reader views the document source code. Be careful not to put in anything damning or confidential.

<a href="#...">...</a>—local URL link—if you're making links to another spot on the same page (a local link, that is), this is how you make the link you jump from. For example, if you're making a link to jump from the top of the page to a spot near the bottom, this is the command that goes at the top. SEE <a name=...> for more info.

<a href="URL...">...</a>—URL link

<a name=...>...</a>—target link

<address>...</address>—font for address. For multi-line addresses, use <br> to create line breaks. (You need only use the address tags at the start and end of the address section.)

<b>...</b>—bold text

<body>...</body>—marks everything below the headline block at the top of the page.<body> should immediately follow </head>, and </body> is the second to last thing on the page (followed by </html>)

<blockquote>...</blockquote>—a block of quoted text

—line break; like a Return in a word processor. Only one is necessary. Appears as a line break; additional text will start on the next line.

<cite>...</cite>—citation text; a type style for indicating the name of a source of information, such as a textbook

<dd>—definition in definition list; should appear in tandem with (and just after) a line tagged with <dt>...</dt>. The next command should be either a new <dt> term or the closing argument for definition lists (</dl>). Definitions appear in pairs.

<dir>...</dir>—a list format for short (under 20 character) unordered items; individual list items take the <li> tag

<dl>...</dl>—definition list (or discursive list); starting and ending arguments are needed. The <dl> should be followed immediately by the first <dt> line, which marks off the term being defined.

<dt>...</dt>—term in definition list; should appear in tandem with a line tagged with <dd>...</dd>. The next item should either be the definition or the term (<dd>).

<emp>...</emp>—emphasized text (often appears as italics)

<h1>—header of the first degree (most browsers show this as the largest, boldest headline font)

<h2>—header of the second degree

<h3>—header of the third degree

<h4>—header of the fourth degree

<h5>—header of the fifth degree

<h6>—header of the sixth degree

<head>...</head>—marks the section at the top of the page in which you give the title. <head> should be the third thing on the page (right after <html>), and </head> should be followed immediately by <body>.

<hr>—horizontal ruled line. There is no closing tag; only one is necessary. These are useful for separating sections on long pages, and often appear just before the address at the end.

<html>...</html>—the first and last commands on a well-written page

<i>...</i>—italics

<img src="URL">—adds an inline hypermedia file—an image, video clip, or sound clip (one that can't be clicked on as a link). The name and location of the hypermedia replace URL. See the links discussion (above) for the list of arguments available.

<inc srv "URL">—adds inline text from another file; the name and location of the text file replace URL.

<li>...</li>—list item; only <li> is necessary, but it's preferable that you use both. Items in lists don't need <br> lines; the <li> argument automatically makes a line break.

<listing>...</listing>—marks off large blocks of pre-formatted text

<ol>...</ol>—ordered (numbered) list. Items appear as list with Arabic numerals; list items are enclosed by <li>...</li>.

<p>...</p>—paragraph break. only <p> is necessary, but it's preferable that you use both. Additional text will start after one blank line.

<strong>...</strong>—strong text (often appears as bold)

<title>...</title> page title; appears at the top of your screen window, but does not appear on the page itself

<tt>...</tt>—a monospaced (typewriter-style) font

<u>...</u>—underline; not widely used

<ul>...</ul>—unordered (bulleted) list; items on the list are enclosed by <li>...</li>

&#(*a number*);—an ASCII character; the ISO Latin I Character Entity Set is also available for non-English alphabets (see below).

&—ampersand ("and sign"); otherwise HTML and Mosaic think you're trying to give a command

>—*SEE* &lt

<...>—open pointy-bracket (<) and closing pointy-bracket (>); whatever you type between these codes is not read by Mosaic, just displayed. This is useful for showing URLs and other examples of HTML coding onscreen.

"—quotation marks; add one at the beginning and one at the end of whatever you're quoting

HTML Commands by Function (A Reverse Dictionary)

Address—<address>...</address>

Alternate display (argument for display of inline images)—alt="X" (where X is some text symbol or phrase)

Ampersand (for display only)—&

Body text area—<body>...</body>

Bold text—<b>...</b>

Bracket, closing (for display only)—>

Bracket, opening (for display only)—<

Characters, ASCII—&#*xxx*;, where *xxx* is the ASCII code number

Characters, non-English—&*xxx*;, where *xxx* is the mnemonic code (see list below)

Citation text—<cite>...</cite>

Comments—<! — . . . —>

Defined term (in block)—<dt>

Definition in block—<dd>

Definition block—<dl>...</dl>

Document area (entire document)—<html>...</html>

Emphasized text (often like italics)—<emp>...</emp>

Headline area—<head>...</head>

Headlines—<h*x*>...</h*x*>, where *x* is a number between 1 and 6

Inline images, movies, sound—<img src="..." (options)>

Inline text (from another file)—<inc srv "...">

Italics—<i>...</i>

Line (onscreen design element)—<hr>

Line break (starts new line but doesn't make a space)—

List, with bullets—<ul>...</ul>

List, numbered—<ol>...</ol>

List, unordered with short items—<dir>...</dir>

List item (individual item on list)—<li>...</li>

Local target link—<a href="#...">...</a>

Monospaced (typewriter-style) text—<tt>...</tt>

Paragraph break (starts a new line after making a space)—<p>...</p>

Preformatted text (long)—<listing>...</listing>

Quotation block—<blockquote>...</blockquote>

Quotation marks (for display only)—&quot

Remote (other place) link—<a href="URL...">...</a>

Ruled line (onscreen design element)—<hr>

Strong text (often like bold)—<strong>...</strong>

Target (jump-to-here) link—<a name=...>...</a>

Title (of Mosaic window)—<title>...</title>

Typewriter-style (monospaced) text—<tt>...</tt>

ISO Latin-I Character Entities

If you need non-English letters or symbols, these codes will create them. The general format is

`&character;` *(note beginning ampersand and closing semi-colon)*

The ISO Latin-I characters mainly cover Western European languages; support for other character sets, such as Kanji, is not yet standardized. (However, you will find working implementations of Kanji, the Cyrillic alphabet, and other character sets on the Internet.) Also note that monetary symbols (other than $) are not supported.

`á`—small a, acute accent

`Á`—capital A, acute accent

`â`—small a, circumflex accent

`Â`—capital A, circumflex accent

`à`—small a, grave accent

`À`—capital A, grave accent

`å`—small a, ring

`Å`—capital A, ring

`ã`—small a, tilde

`Ã`—capital A, tilde

`ä`—small a, dieresis or umlaut mark

`Ä`—capital A, dieresis or umlaut mark

`æ`—small ae diphthong (ligature)

`Æ`—capital AE diphthong (ligature)

`ç`—small c, cedilla

`Ç`—capital C, cedilla

`ð`—small eth, Icelandic

`Ð`—capital Eth, Icelandic

`é`—small e, acute accent

`É`—capital E, acute accent

`ê`—small e, circumflex accent

`Ê`—capital E, circumflex accent

`è`—small e, grave accent

`È`—capital E, grave accent

`ë`—small e, dieresis or umlaut mark

`Ë`—capital E, dieresis or umlaut mark

`í`—small i, acute accent

`Í`—capital I, acute accent

`î`—small i, circumflex accent

`Î`—capital I, circumflex accent

`ì`—small i, grave accent

`Ì`—capital I, grave accent

`ï`—small i, dieresis or umlaut mark

`Ï`—capital I, dieresis or umlaut mark

`ñ`—small n, tilde

`Ñ`—capital N, tilde

`ó`—small o, acute accent

`Ó`—capital O, acute accent

`ô`—small o, circumflex accent

`Ô`—capital O, circumflex accent

`ò`—small o, grave accent

`Ò`—capital O, grave accent

`ø`—small o, slash

`Ø`—capital O, slash

`õ`—small o, tilde

`Õ`—capital O, tilde

`ö`—small o, dieresis or umlaut mark

`Ö`—capital O, dieresis or umlaut mark

`ß`—small sharp s, German (sz ligature)

`þ`—small thorn, Icelandic

`Þ`—capital THORN, Icelandic

`ú`—small u, acute accent

`Ú`—capital U, acute accent

`û`—small u, circumflex accent

`Û`—capital U, circumflex accent

`ù`—small u, grave accent

`Ù`—capital U, grave accent

`ü`—small u, dieresis or umlaut mark

`Ü`—capital U, dieresis or umlaut mark

`ý`—small y, acute accent

`Ý`—capital Y, acute accent

`ÿ`—small y, dieresis or umlaut mark

For Further Information

These sites contain further information on HTML and on page creation.

`http://info.cern.ch/hypertext/WWW/Provider/Style/Overview.html`—Hypertext Style Guide

`http://life.anu.edu.au/education/hypermedia.html`—really comprehensive; several HTML editors are also available at this site

`http://rugmd4.chem.rug.nl/hoesel/index.html`—the story behind the Expo exhibit (see Appendix D, under Museums and Libraries)

`http://www.bu.edu/html-intro.html`—concise guide to creating HTML documents; also contains links to specialized information on proxy gateways, interactive games, WAIS, PGP/PEM encryption, and so forth

`http://www.maths.qmw.ac.uk/hyperspace/`—Hyperspace GR hypertext

`http://www.ncsa.uiuc.edu/demoweb/html-primer.html`—beginner's guide to HTML

`http://www.ncsa.uiuc.edu/General/Internet/WWW/DocProduction.html`—how-to

`http://www.ncsa.uiuc.edu/General/Internet/WWW/HTMLQuickRef.html`—HTML quick reference guide

`http://www.vuw.ac.nz/non-local/gnat/www-primer.html`—World Wide Web Primer

A Selection of Editors Available Online

`aim.stanford.edu/info-mac/text/bbedit-lite-231.hqx`—BBELite HTML editor for Macintosh (via anonymous FTP)

`ftp.gatech.edu/pub/www/gt_html.zip`—Word for Windows HTML macros (via anonymous FTP)

`lal.cs.byu.edu/pub/www/tools/htmlwrit.zip`—HTML Writer for Windows (via anonymous FTP)

APPENDIX D

Things To See, Places To Do: The World's Great Web Sites

Here for your Web surfing enjoyment we have several hundred interesting, informative, bizarre, or just generally neat Web pages. This page reflects my interests and the interests of the many kind Net.citizens who have suggested sites for exploration. Any of these can be an excellent starting point for a fresh Web surfing experience.

Remember that the Internet is an ever-changing creature. Web pages come and go, and sometimes they come and go and come and go and come and go. These pages were all active and available last time I checked, but there are bound to be one or two that have headed south between the time I type these words and the time you read them.

Also, remember that some Web sites are a bit flighty and hard to reach. Usually that's due to popularity (so many people are checking it out that it can't handle any more visitors), but sometimes a site experiences technical difficulties and its pages are inaccessible. If you aren't able to reach a page that you're reasonably sure exists, keep trying. (If possible, avoid some of that Net gridlock by logging in at off-peak hours. If you're a night owl, you're in luck.)

I've chosen to list only World Wide Web pages; there are plenty of great FTP and Gopher sites available also.

Finally, an HTML version of this page is included in this book's copy of Enhanced Mosaic; its filename is `greatweb.htm`. Once Mosaic has loaded this file, you can get to any of the sites listed here just by clicking on the underlined name. You can use Mosaic to open this file either through the *Plug-n-Play Mosaic* Home Page, or by loading the `greatweb` file directly (from the main menu of Enhanced Mosaic just select File and then Open URL…, type in the URL, press Enter, and you're on your way!).

Note: You'll find the most up-to-date electronic version of this directory online at the URL `http://www.mcp.com/sams/books/mos/greatweb.html`.

Overview

Sites of General Interest

The Asylum

Another strange and wonderful place at CalTech

http://www.galcit.caltech.edu/~ta/cgi-bin/asylhome-ta

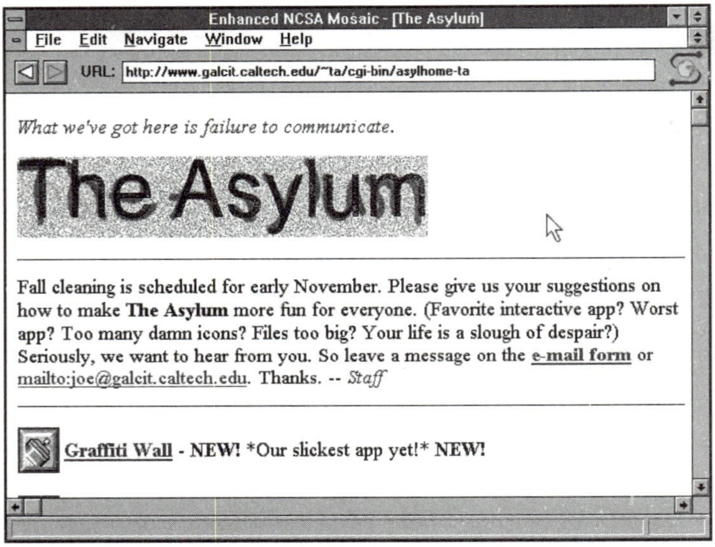

Figure D.1. The Asylum.

Best of the Web '94 Recipients

Several categories of worthy competition; expect the 1995 awards soon

http://wings.buffalo.edu/contest/awards/index.html

bianca's SMUT-Shack

Music, art, and general bad behavior, with your gracious hostess biancaTroll

http://bianca.com/btp/

Cool Site Of The Day
Always a fresh place to check out, thanks to Glenn Davis
`http://www.infi.net/cool.html`

Cyber Sight
Another unique spot with really creative ideas (and good links)
`http://cybersight.com//cgi-bin/cs/s?main.gmml`

Matt Gray's Comprehensive HTTP Site List
Over 10,000 links at last count
`http://www.mit.edu:8001/afs/sipb/user/mkgray/ht/compre3.html`

Planet Earth Home Page
Features a huge number of links, and it's well-organized too
`http://white.nosc.mil/info.html`

Really "Different" Sites
From your friends at CalTech
`http://www.galcit.caltech.edu/~aure/htmls/strangepts.html`

ToyBox
Notre Dame's eclectic document
`http://orange-room.cc.nd.edu/ToyBox/ToyBox.html`

UCLA's Useful Stuff Wisdom and Lore Page
A semi-random but decent collection of links to various fun spots
`http://cad.ucla.edu/repository/useful/useful.html`

University of North Carolina at Chapel Hill SunSITE
All roads lead to North Carolina
`http://sunsite.unc.edu`

Whole Internet Catalog Top 50 Sites
Changes regularly
`http://nearnet.gnn.com/gnn/wic/top.toc.html`

Yahoo - A Guide to WWW
Over 27,000 links!
`http://akebono.stanford.edu/yahoo`

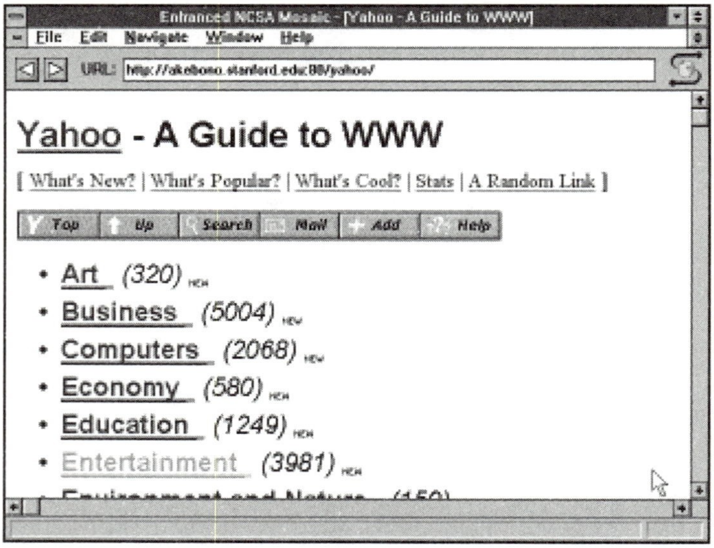

Figure D.2. The Yahoo Guide.

Art and Literature

Arts Network for Integrated Media Applications (ANIMA)
Comprehensive resource for creative Net types
`http://wimsey.com/anima/ANIMAhome.html`

Bad Subjects
A journal of high and low culture
`http://english-server.hss.cmu.edu/Bad.html`

Big Time Television
Hypertext and HP Lovecraft
`http://daneel.acns.nwu.edu:8082/`

Cybercafe
ARTEC and interSPACE, cultural stuff with plenty of museum links, a little like bianca's place
`http://cybercafe.demon.co.uk`

Edinburgh's Fringe Festival Page
`http://www.gold.net/lynx/fringe/`

Etext Archives
Good literature site
`http://etext.archive.umich.edu/`

FineArt Forum Online

`http://www.msstate.edu/Fineart_Online/home.html`

The Gutenberg Project

Index to electronic texts

`http://info.cern.ch/roeber/Misc/Gutenberg.html`

Kaleidospace

For independent artists of all types, with sound and video clips

`http://kspace.com`

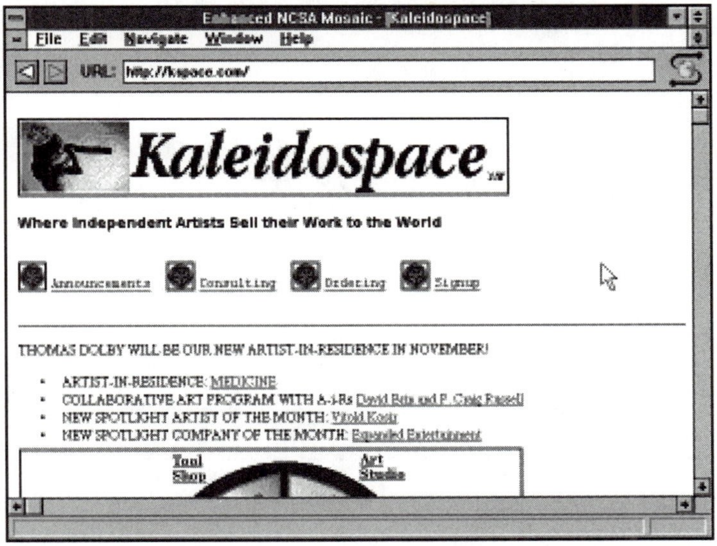

Figure D.3. Kaleidospace.

Nancy Drew Home Page

`http://sunsite.unc.edu/cheryb/nancy.drew/ktitle.html`

Tango!

`http://imtsun3.epfl.ch:8000/tango//welcome.html`

Book Stacks Unlimited

It's all here, including newsgroups

`http://www.books.com`

Underground.Net

Excellent art/music site, featuring many unsigned bands and renegade creators

`http://underground.net/underground.html`

Virtual Library: Literature

`http://sunsite.unc.edu/ibic/IBIC-homepage.html`

Zstuff on the Web

Humor and The Doomsday Brunette, a group-participation, interactive detective story

`http://zeb.nysaes.cornell.edu/`

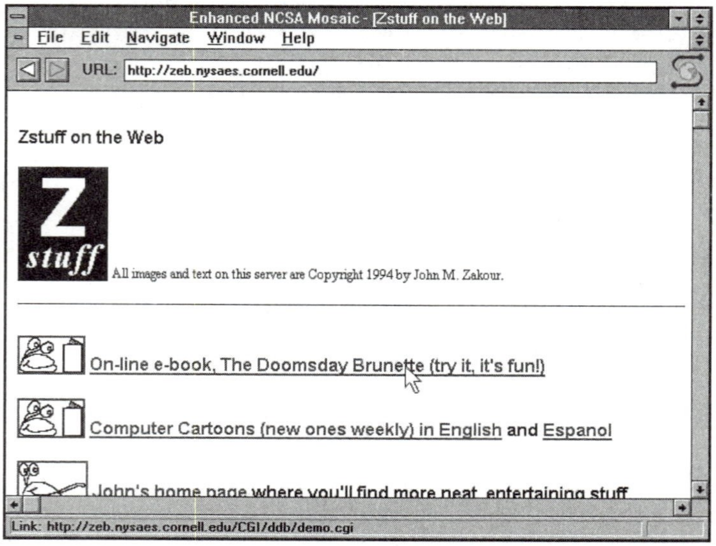

Figure D.4. Zstuff on the Web.

Business

BizNet Technologies

Advertising for a number of regional businesses; they'll also provide space for your own Web page for a small fee

`http://www.biznet.com.blacksburg.va.us/index.html`

Cable Television Labs

`http://www.cablelabs.com/`

Commercial Web Sites
List of commercial web sites (also a server for commercial page makers)
`http://www.directory.net/`

Downtown Anywhere
Another commercial site for pages and so forth
`http://www.awa.com`

FTP Software
Very new. Tech support numbers, cool touch-map for info, product info, tech stuff
`http://www.ftp.com`

Hyatt Hotels
`http://www.travelweb.com/thisco/common/tweb.html`

Internet Ad Emporium
This one's for Cafe Mam (organic coffee)
`http://mmink.cts.com/mmink/dossiers/cafemam.html`

Joel Maloff's Home Page
With business Internet stats
`http://uunorth.north.net:8000/pages/joelhome.html`

Lexis/Nexis
Information about the massive database of magazine and newspaper articles
`http://www.meaddata.com/`

The NetCenter
Ads from a variety of businesses
`http://netcenter.com`

Pizza Hut
Yes, you can get that to go
`http://www.pizzahut.com`

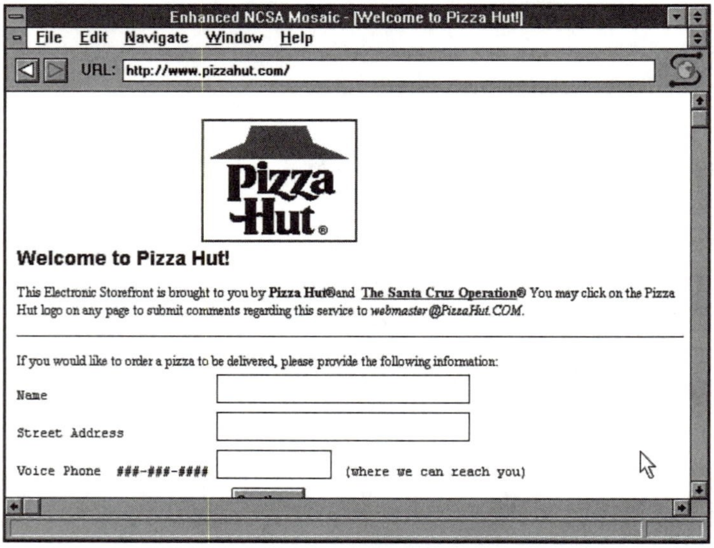

Figure D.5. Pizza Hut.

QMS Printer Products
Also information on beautiful Mobile, Alabama
`http://www.qms.com`

Spyglass, Inc.
From the creators of Spyglass Enhanced NCSA Mosaic
`http://www.spyglass.com`

The UNCAT Database
Hard-to-find books on titles from businesses, nonprofit groups, trade associations, museums and self-published authors
`http://www.sapphire.com/UNCAT/`

Unisphere
A commercial venture
`http://www.nando.net/uni/uni.html`

Comics

Bloom County List
Ack! Pfffbt!
`http://menger.eecs.stevens-tech.edu/~sahirns/bloom.html`

The Calvin And Hobbes Gallery
`http://www.seas.upenn.edu/~lzeltser/calvin.hobbes`

Cerebus: Campaign '93
The scanned image is a little muddy but it's a loving homage
`http://www.maths.tcd.ie/pub/cerebus/crazed-ferret/Cerebus.html`

Dilbert
Daily strip
`http://nearnet.gnn.com/gnn.arcade/comix/dilbert.html`

The Dr. Fun Page
Daily strip—available only on the Web
`http://sunsite.unc.edu/Dave/drfun.html`

Reviews from the Forbidden Planet
Large comics site with reviews and commentary; strong on DC/Vertigo and some of the independents
`http://www.maths.tcd.ie/mmm/ReviewsFromTheForbiddenPlanet.html`

Zippy the Pinhead
Text only (it has its charm that way)
`http://www.cis.ohio-state.edu/htbin/zippy`

Education

American Universities
List of all American schools that have Web pages
`http://www.clas.ufl.edu/CLAS/american-universities.html`

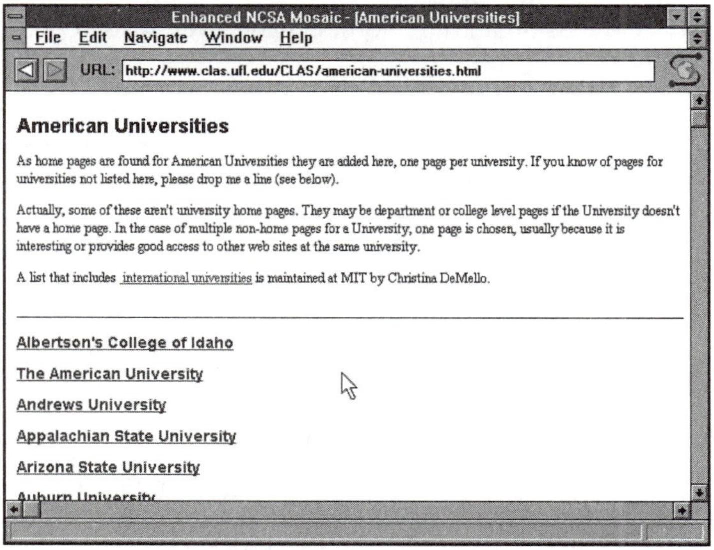

Figure D.6. American Universities.

Bradley University
http://www.bradley.edu

CalTech
http://www.caltech.edu/

Columbia University
http://www.cc.columbia.edu

Minority On-Line Information Service
Scholarship information
http://web.fie.com/web/mol/

MIT
Lots of links, especially campus stuff; also Madlibs and other silliness
http://www.mit.edu

Monta Vista High School
http://www.mvhs.edu/

Penn's School of Engineering and Applied Science
http://www.seas.upenn.edu

Plugged In
A youth center; working to build national network
http://www.pluggedin.org

Trinity College Dublin, School of Mathematics
http://www.maths.tcd.ie

UC Santa Cruz Info Slug
Useful and well-organized information on a variety of topics
http://www.ucsc.edu/

University of Pennsylvania
Extremely comprehensive and well-managed; good place to start if you're looking for college information
http://www.upenn.edu

Et Cetera

Americom Area Decoder
Area, country, city code lookups
http://www.xmission.com/~americom/aclookup.html

Ask Joe
Advice column from the MIT Freshman Fishwrap
http://fishwrap.mit.edu/News/AskJoe/AskJoe.html

Brittanica Online

`http://www.eb.com/`

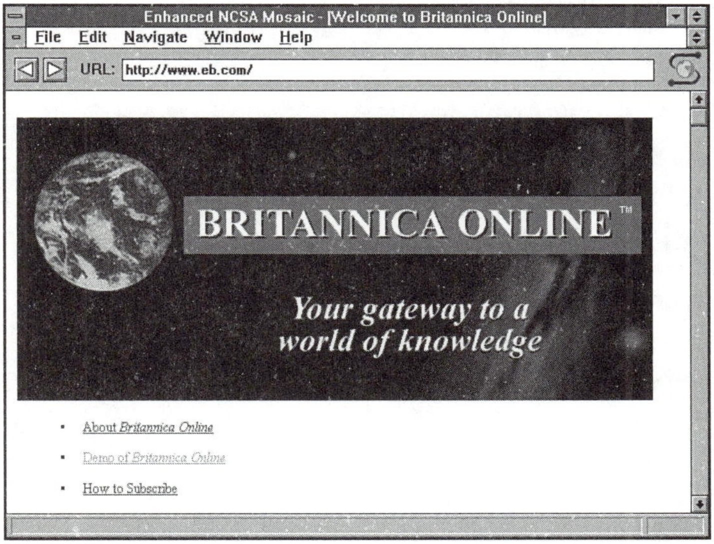

Figure D.7. Brittanica Online.

First-aid information

`http://www.seas.upenn.edu:80/~lzeltser/first.aid.html`

Internet Talk Radio

Yes, these are sound files

`http://www.ncsa.uiuc.edu/radio/radio.html`

The Legal Information Institute

Good for U.S. Supreme Court information

`http://www.law.cornell.edu/`

MPEG Movie Archive

Animations, supermodels, music, space, and other things

`http://w3.eeb.ele.tue.nl/mpeg/`

North Carolina Discoveries

From NandO

`http://www.nando.net/ncd`

The Obituary Page

Obituaries and This Day In Death (and birth)

`http://catless.ncl.ac.uk/Obituary/README.html`

U.S. Holocaust Memorial Museum

http://www.ushmm.org/index.html

Vincent Voice Library

Many sound clips

http://web.msu.edu/vincent/

Your Daily Biorhythm Chart

http://cad.ucla.edu:800/biorhythm

Food and Drink

Bartender's List

http://schiller.wustl.edu/~sam/drinks.html

Boston Restaurant Related Lists

Lists restaurants, menus, reviews from Boston, northeast, rest of United States and rest of the world!

http://www.osf.org:8001/boston-food/related-lists.html

Dining Out

Restaurant-related sites on the Web

http://cornelius.ucsf.edu/"troyer/dish/diningout.html

Hot Hot Hot

A Pasadena, California-based specialty hot-shop

http://www.hot.presence.com/hot.

Intellectics

Austrian commercial site offering wine, olive oils, liqueurs

http://www.intellectics.co.at/intellectics/

List of Food Sites

http://www.vuw.ac.nz/who/Amy.Gale/recipe-archive.html

Recipes

A wide range of recipes available on the Net

http://alpha.acast.nova.edu/fun/food.html

The Recipes Folder

Very large list of recipes

http://english-server.hss.cmu.edu/Recipes.html

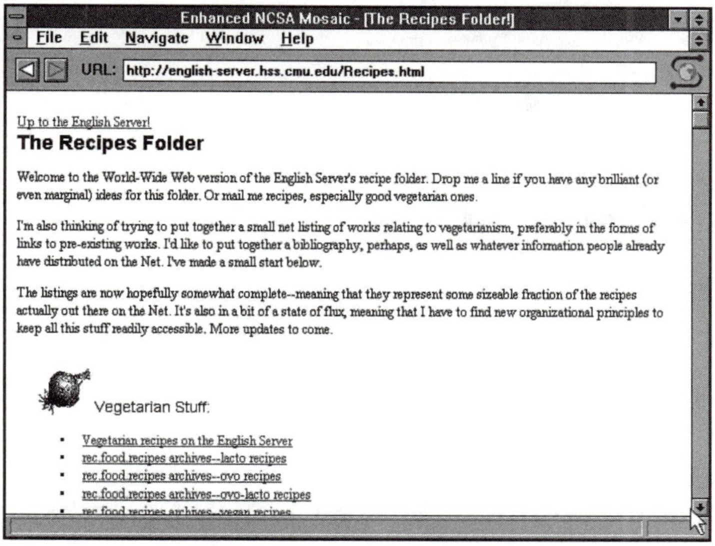

Figure D.8. The Recipes Folder.

Recipes for Traditional Food in Slovenia
For a change of pace
`http://www.ijs.si/slo-recipes.html`

Restaurant Le Cordon Bleu
The renowned cooking school
`http://sunsite.unc.edu/expo/restaurant/restaurant.html`

Some Great Recipes
Chocolate truffle recipes
`http://tns-www.lcs.mit.edu/people/hhh/recipes/recipes.html`

Spencer's Beer Page
Home brewing; includes resources, labels, and recipes
`http://guraldi.itn.med.umich.edu:80/Beer`

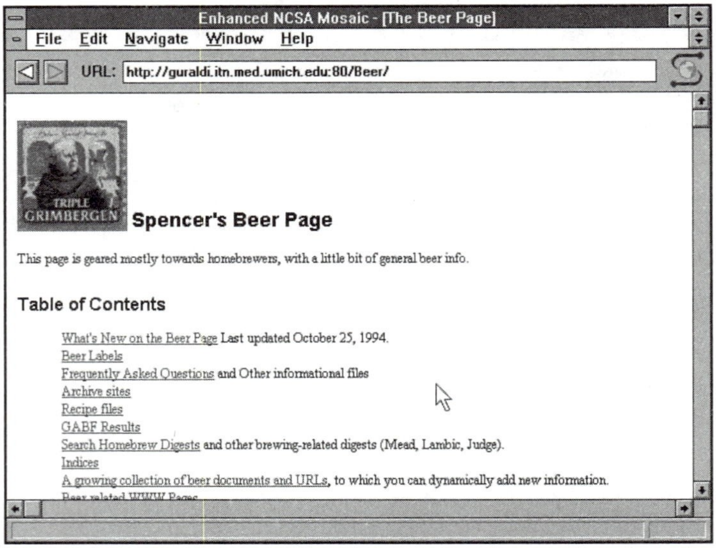

Figure D.9. Spencer's Beer Page.

Triangle Vegetarian Society

`http://www.trinet.com/tonc/tvspage.html`

Vegan-L FAQ

Vegan recipes and information

`http://www.bath.ac.uk/~mapnjd/veganl.html`

Wine Enthusiasts Web Site

Tasting notes, etc.

`http://augustus.csscr.washington.edu/personal/bigstar-mosaic/wine.html`

Fun and Games

BU's Interactive WWW Games

`http://www.bu.edu/Games/games.html`

Castle Sonnenstein Game

`http://rrws6.wiwi.uni-regensberg.de/SONNENSTEIN/sonnenstein.html`

Games Domain

Huge lists of sites

`http://wcl-rs.bham.ac.uk/~djh/index.html`

Internet Pizza Server

Cyber-pizza; truly unique—give it a whirl

`http://www2.ecst.csuchico.edu/~pizza/`

LEGO Information
Clubs, ideas, activities, theme song, pictures, product lists, factory tour notes, and previews of the latest LEGO stuff
`http://legowww.itek.norut.no/`

Lite-Brite
Remember the old Lite-Brite toy? Here it is again
`http://www.galcit.caltech.edu/~ta/lb/lb.html`

The North Pole
Hey, it's for charity; starts Thanksgiving Day and lasts 'til Xmas. Really neat.
`http://north.pole.org/santa/`

Palindromes!
Feel free to chime in
`http://www2.ecst.csuchico.edu/~beej/palindromes.html`

WWW Hunt
Another scavenger hunt; good practice!
`http://www.glacit.caltech.edu/~ta/hunt/wwwhunt.html`

Zarf's List of Interactive Games
`http://www.cs.cmu.edu:8001/afs/cs.cmu.edu/user/zarf/www.games.html`

Internet Information

About the Internet
InterNIC Stats and history info; good for background
`http://www.internic.net/infoguide/gopher/about-internet.html`

Clearinghouse for Subject-Oriented Resource Guides
`http://www.lib.umich.edu/chhome.html`

Cygnus Support Information Gallery
`http://www.cygnus.com/`

Entering the WWW: A Guide to Cyberspace
`http://www.eit.com/web/www.guide/`

GNU Project Overview
`http://info.desy.de/gnu/www`

The HCI Bibliography Project
Human-computer interaction studies
`http://www.tu-graz.ac.at/CHCIbib`

Interesting WWW Uses

http://www.cs.colorado.edu/homes/mcbryan/public_html/bb/8/summary.html

The Internet Index

Harper's Index-style Internet information

http://www.openmarket.com/info/internet-index/current.html

Internet RFC

http://www.cis.ohio-state.edu/hypertext/information/rfc.html

Internet Society

Official information

http://info.isoc.org/home.html

List of Registered WWW Servers

http://info.cern.ch/hypertext/DataSources/WWW/Geographical.html

The Mother-of- All-BBSs

http://www.cs.colorado.edu/homes/mcbryan/public_html/bb/summary.html

NCSA Mosaic Home Page

http://www.ncsa.uiuc.edu/SDG/Software/Mosaic/NCSAMosaicHome.html

Reasons Why the Information Superhighway is So Annoying

http://enterprise.osd.mil/wtishs.html

Web Servers Directory

http://info.cern.ch/hypertext/DataSources/WWW/Servers.html

World Wide Web FAQ

Frequently asked questions about the Web

http://sunsite.unc.edu/boutell/faq/www_faq.html

Magazines and Other Publications

CyberKind

A literary magazine

http://sunsite.unc.edu/ckind/title.html

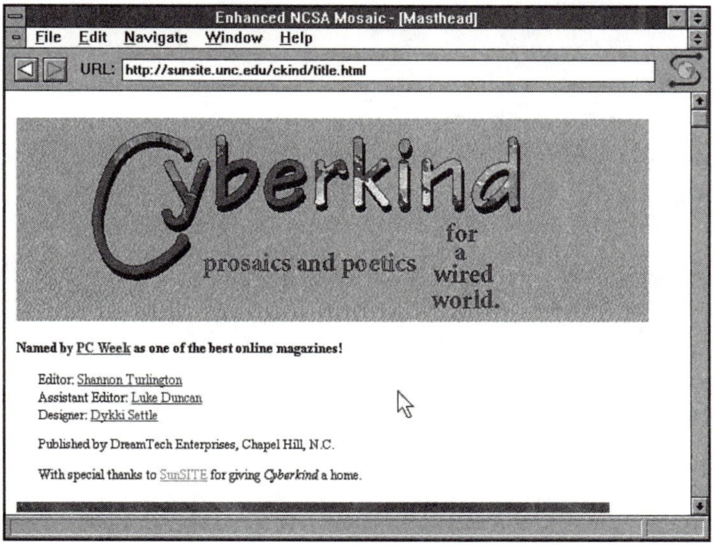

Figure D.10. CyberKind.

E-zine list
Comprehensive list of e-zines
`http://www.ora.com/:8080/johnl/e-zine-list/`

The Gate
The San Francisco Chronicle and the San Francisco Examiner
`http://sfgate.com/`

Global Network Navigator
`http://nearnet.gnn.com/gnn/gnn.html`

International Teletimes
General-interest e-zine
`http://www.wimsey.com/teletimes.root/teletimes_home_page.html`

Lake Tahoe News Network
`http://www.enet.net/eg/egnet/bonanza.html`

NandO.Net
The Raleigh (NC) News and Observer
`http://www.nando.net/`

NWHQ
A hypermedia magazine of original literature and artwork; available only on the Internet
`http://www.wimsey.com/~jmax/`

Verbiage
A magazine of short fiction
`http://sunsite.unc.edu/boutell/verbiage/index.html`

Vibe
`http://vibe.www.com/`

The Web's Edge
Factsheet Five online; the place to go if you're interested in e-zines
`http://kzsu.stanford.edu/uwi.html`

Wired
`http://www.wired.com`

Ziff Communications
Ziff Web server, with links to *PC Magazine*, *PC Week*, and other computer publications
`http://www.zis.ziff.com`

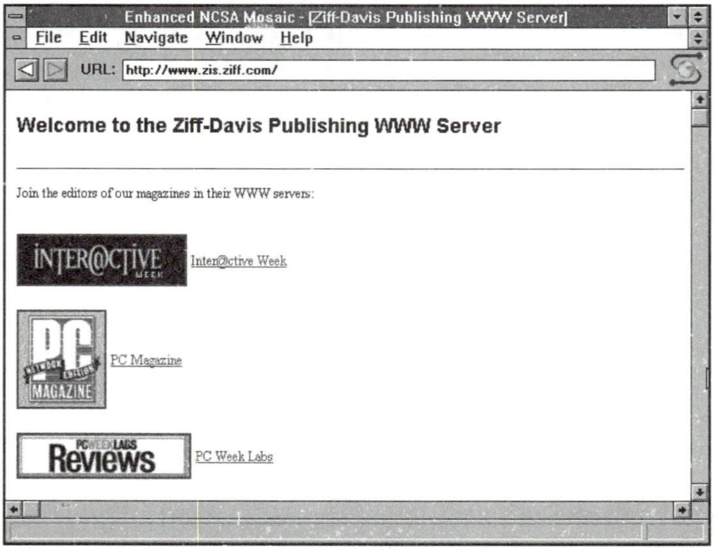

Figure D.11. Ziff Communications.

Movies

Ann Arbor Film Cooperative

`http://www.css.itd.umich.edu/groups/aafc/`

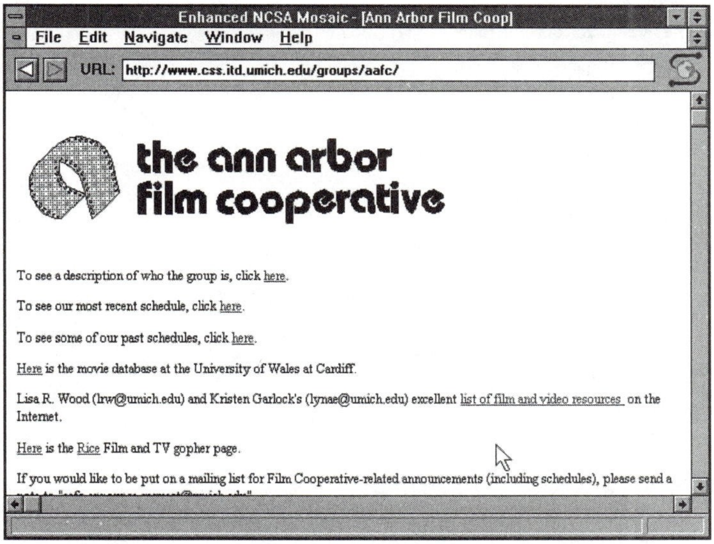

Figure D.12. Ann Arbor Film Cooperative.

Art Hole

Animations

`http://www.mcs.net/~wallach/arthole.html`

Cardiff's Movie Database Browser

Very large and searchable

`http://www.msstate.edu/Movies/`

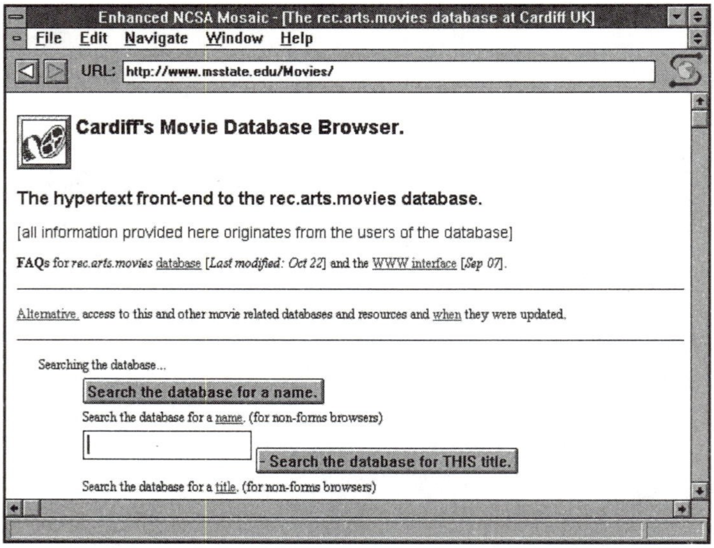

Figure D.13. Cardiff's Movie Database Browser.

Hong Kong Movies Home Page
`http://www.mdstud.chalmers.se/hkmovie`

The Horror Web Page
Horror movies and literature; many GIFs
`http://www.ee.pdx.edu/~caseyh/horror/horror.html`

Kjetil's Quentin Page
Quentin Tarantino's Reservior Dogs, with many GIFs (if you haven't seen the movie, these will give away the plot and denouement)
`http://www.nvg.unit.no/~eddie/tarantino.html`

Star Wars Home Page
`http://stwing.resnet.upenn.edu:8001/~jruspini/starwars.html`

Museums and Libraries

ANIMA: Nexus Home Page
Online projects by various artists; astonishing
`http://wimsey.com/anima/NEXUShome.html`

Australian National University Art History
`http://www.ncsa.uiuc.edu/SDG/Experimental/anu-art-history/home.html`

Expo Shuttle Bus
Le Cordon Bleu, Vatican, Soviet pavilion, 1492, Dead Sea Scrolls, paleontology, Spatalo; not to be missed
`http://sunsite.unc.edu/expo/expo/busstation.html`

Krannert Art Museum
`http://www.ncsa.uiuc.edu/General/UIUC/KrannertArtMuseum/GuideContents.html`

Le WebLouvre
`http://mistral.enst.fr/~pioch/louvre`

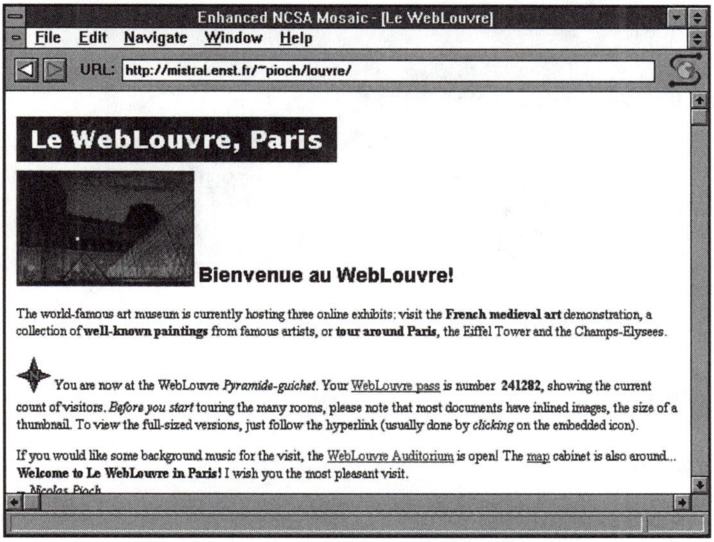

Figure D.14. Le WebLouvre.

Library of Congress
Exhibits, prints and photos; catalogs via telnet
`http://lcweb.loc.gov/homepage/lchp.html`

Music

biancaTroll's Music Room
`http://www.bianca.com/biancaTroll/music/music.html`

Concerts in the Bay Area
`http://www.usfca.edu/usf/neufeld/concerts.html`

The Elvis Aron Presley Home Page
`http://128.194.15.32/~ahb2188/elvishom.html`

Empty.tv.com

Anti-Metaverse site; excellent satire

`http://www.galcit.caltech.edu/~ta/mtv/main.html`

The Internet Underground Music Archive

`http://sunsite.unc.edu/ianc/index.html`

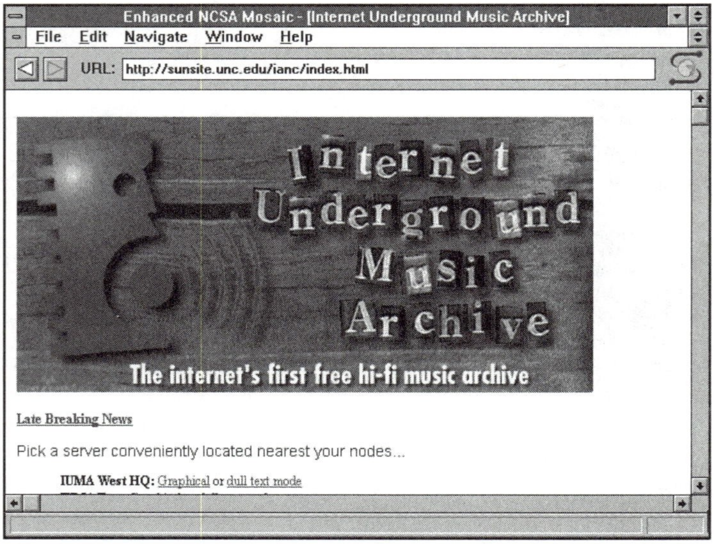

Figure D.15. Internet Underground Music Archive.

Jazz Information Server

`http://www.acns.nwu.edu/WNUR/jazzbase`

Mammoth Records Internet Center

`http://www.nando.net/mammoth/`

Metaverse

Main page to Adam Curry's Web site

`http://metaverse.com/index.html`

Music Kitchen

Includes Beastie Boys, Breeders, and other bands

`http://www.nando.net/music/gm/`

Nirvana Home Page

`http://www.ludd.luth.se/~burrito`

REM Archive

Guitar tabs for REM songs

`http://www.halcyon.com/rem/`

WNUR-FM Rock Information Base

`http://www.acns.nwu.edu/WNUR/rock/`

Personal Pages

Justin Hall

Vast and wonderful

`http://raptor.sccs.swarthmore.edu/jahall`

Amir Rosenblatt

`http://www.pipeline.com/~amir`

Tom Jennings

`http://wps.com//`

Lenny Zeltser

`http://www.seas.upenn.edu:80/~lzeltser/lenny.html`

Beej's Place

Excellent and strange

`http://www2.ecst.csuchico.edu/~beej/`

Political and Social

Amnesty International

`http://cyberzine.org/html/Amnesty/aihomepage.html`

Animal Rights Resource Site

`http://www.gate.net/~dgraft`

Bay Area Model Mugging

`http://www.ugcs.caltech.edu/~rachel/bamm.html`

Computer Professionals For Social Responsibility

`http://www.cpsr.org/home`

Cypherpunks

Important info about privacy and free speech

`http://soda.berkeley.edu/pub/cypherpunks/Home.html`

The Drum

African and African-American issues

`http://drum.ncsc.org/`

EarthWeb

Global activism

`http://www.earthweb.com:2800/`

Electronic Frontier Foundation

http://www.eff.org

Environmental Protection Agency

http://www.epa.gov/

The Noam Chomsky Archive

http://www.contrib.andrew.cmu.edu:/usr/tp0x/chomsky.html

Queer Resources Directory

Good lesbian/gay resources and information

http://vector.casti.com/QRD/.html/QRD-home-page.html

Resources for Diversity

One-stop shopping; ideal starting point

http://alpha.acast.nova.edu/diversity.html

Richard Boddie for Senate

A Libertarian home page

http://www.lp.org/lp/ca/Boddie.html

San Carlos Page

http://www.abag.ca.gov/abag/localgov/city/sancarlos/schome.html

The White House

http://www.whitehouse.gov/

Women and Computer Science

Women's issues; great list of resources

http://www.ai.mit.edu/people/ellens/gender.html

Women Home Page

Excellent list of various women's resources

http://www.mit.edu:8001/people/sorokin/women/index.html

Women's Resources

http://sunsite.unc.edu/cheryb/women/wshome.html

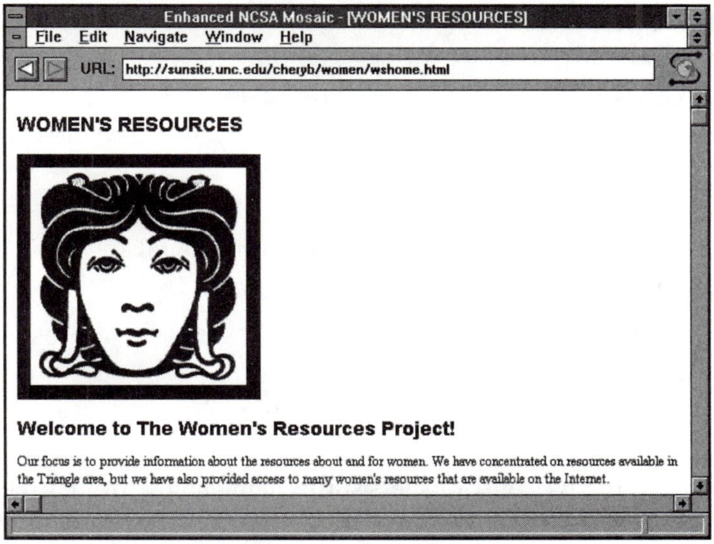

Figure D.16. Women's Resources.

Religion and Spirituality

Baha'i Information Page

http://herald.usask.ca/~maton/bahai.html

Catholic Resources on the Net

Catholic history, prayers, liturgies

http://www.cs.cmu.edu:8001/Web/People/spok/catholic.html

Christian Resource List

Comprehensive and fairly ecumenical

http://saturn.colorado.edu:8080/Christian/list.html

Discordia/Slack

http://io.com/user/blade/fnord.html

Edinburgh Christian WWW

Protestant site with good resources

http://www.dcs.ed.ac.uk/misc/local/ecwww/

Global Jewish System

http://www.huji.ac.il/www_jewishn/www/t01.html

I-Ching

Hexagram reading

http://cad.ucla.edu/repository/useful/iching.html

Islamic Resources

http://sparc.latif.com/welcome.html

The Jerusalem Mosaic

Jerusalem in photos, maps, song, and history; not to be missed

http://shum.cc.huji.ac.il/jeru/jerusalem.html

Judaism and Jewish Resources

http://sleepless.acm.uiuc.edu/signet/JHSI/judaism.html

The Orthodox Christian Page

http://www.york.ac.uk/~em101/Orthodox.html

PaganLink

http://www.tardis.ed.ac.uk/~feorag/html/plhome.html

Spirit-WWW

Much alternative consciousness stuff; channeling, astrology, healing, UFOs, light, out-of-body experiences, yoga, Vedic culture, theosophy

http://err.ethz.ch/~kiwi/Spirit.html

Tarot

Online tarot; three-card layout

http://cad.ucla.edu/repository/useful/tarot.html

Unitarian Universalist Resource List

http://vector.casti.com/QRD/.html/UUA/uu-toc.html

The WWW Bible Gateway

Christian bible search tool; references several editions

http://unicks.calvin.edu/cgi-bin/bible

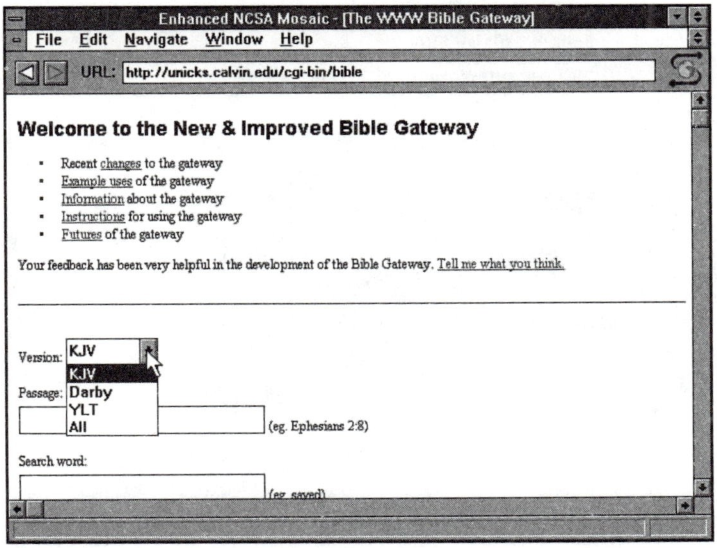

Figure D.17. The WWW Bible Gateway.

Sciences

Comet Shoemaker-Levy 9 Home Page

`http://newproducts.jpl.nasa.gov/s19/s19.html`

Gallery Of Interactive Geometry

Cool even if you don't understand the theory behind it

`http://www.geom.umn.edu/apps/gallery.html`

HCC Dinosaurs

`http://www.hcc.hawaii.edu/dinos/dinos.1.html`

NASA

`http://hypatia.gsft.nasa.gov/NASA_homepage.html`

National Oceanic and Atmospheric Administration

Great information on the environment and its various ecosystems

`http://www.noaa.gov/`

Net Frog

Interactive frog dissection

`http://curry.edschool.Virginia.EDU:80/~insttech/frog/`

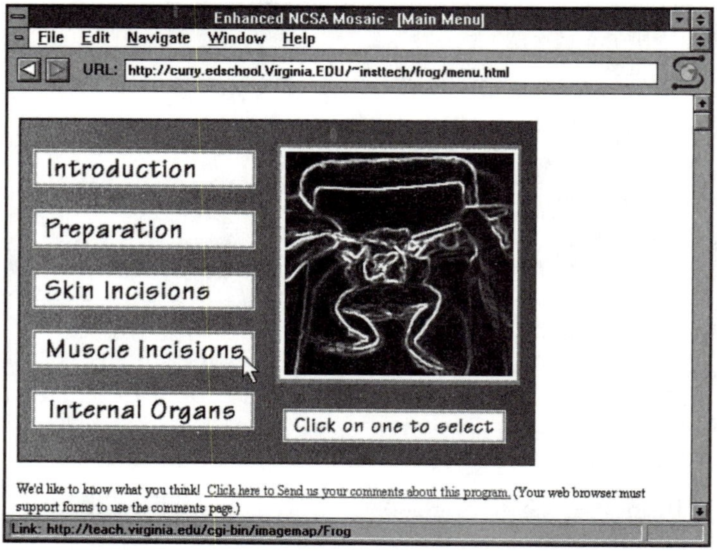

Figure D.18. Net Frog.

North Carolina Zoo

`http://www.nando.net/sproject/zoo/zoo1.html`

Science Horizons

`http://horizon.horizon.com/`

Search Tools

GLIMPSE

A tool to search entire file systems

`http://glimpse.cs.arizona.edu:1994/`

JumpStation

`http://www.stir.ac.uk/jsbin/js`

Unified Computer Science Technical Report Index

`http://cs.indiana.edu/cstr/search`

W3 Catalog

`http://cui_www.unige.ch/w3catalog`

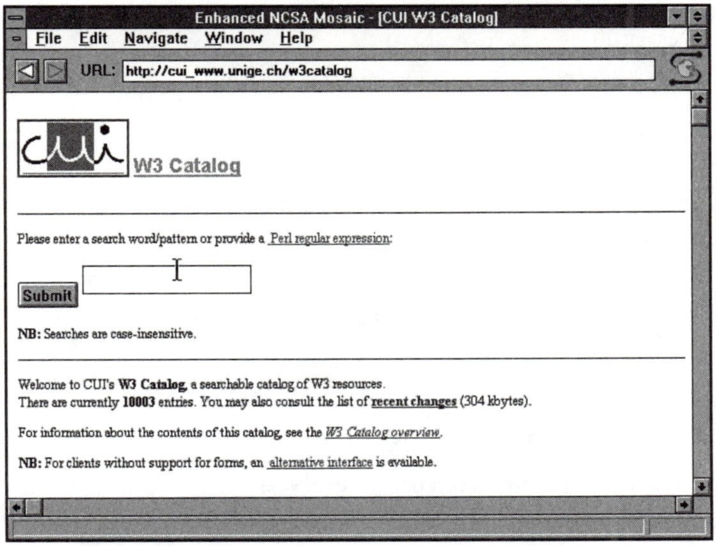

Figure D.19. W3 Catalog.

W3 Search Engines

`http://cui_www.unige.ch/meta-index.html`

WWW Searching Tools

`http://www.cs.washington.edu/info/search.html`

WWW Virtual Library: Subject Catalog

`http://info.cern.ch/hypertext/DataSources/bySubject/Overview.html`

WWW Wanderer

`http://www.mit.edu:8001/afs/sipb/user/mkgray/ht/web-groth.html`

WWWW - The World Wide Web Worm

`http://www.cs.colorado.edu/home/mcbryan/WWWW.html`

Sports and Hobbies

Aquanaut

Comprehensive; with images, weather, marketplace, database of diveable wrecks

`http://www.opal.com/aquanaut`

The Canadian Football League Home Page

`http://www.ee.umanitoba.ca/CFL/`

Cichlid Home Page
Still more aquarium information
`http://trans4.neep.wisc.edu/~gracy/fish/opener.html`

The Climbing Archive
Exercise programs, climbing oriented
`http://www.dtek.chalmers.se/Climbing/Body/orig-index.html`

Figure Skating Home Page
`http://www.cs.yale.edu/HTML/YALE/CS/HyPlans/loosemore-sandra/skate.html`

Fish Information Service (FINS)
`http://www.actwin.com/fish/`

The Gay Games
`http://vector.casti.com/QRD/events/gaygames`

The Global Cycling Network (VeloNet)
`http://cycling.org/`

GolfData On-Line
`http://www.gdol.com/`

The Internet Runner
`http://www.recreation.com/running/home.html`

Juggling Information Service
An extraordinary juggler's page; quite comprehensive
`http://www.hal.com/services/juggle`

The Krib
Aquarium and tropical fish index
`http://marge.phys.washington.edu/fish/`

The Paddling WWW Server
Canoeing, kayaking, and rafting
`http://www.recreation.com/paddling/home.html`

Speleology Information Server
`http://speleology.cs.yale.edu/`

SurfNet
`http://sailfish.peregrine.com/surf/surf.html`

The Tennis Server
`http://arganet.tenagra.com/Racquet_Workshop/Tennis.html`

Tom's Herp Page
Snakes! UK-oriented; young but growing quickly
`http://www.abdn.ac.uk/~psy152/herps/herpstuff.html`

UI Rugby Server

http://rugby.phys.uidaho.edu/rugby.html

Ultimate Frisbee

http://www.cs.rochester.edu/u/ferguson/ultimate/

University of Queensland Underwater Club

Scuba

http://www.uq.oz.au/spra/uquc/home.html

World Wide Web of Sports

http://tns-www.lcs.mit.edu/cgi-bin/sports

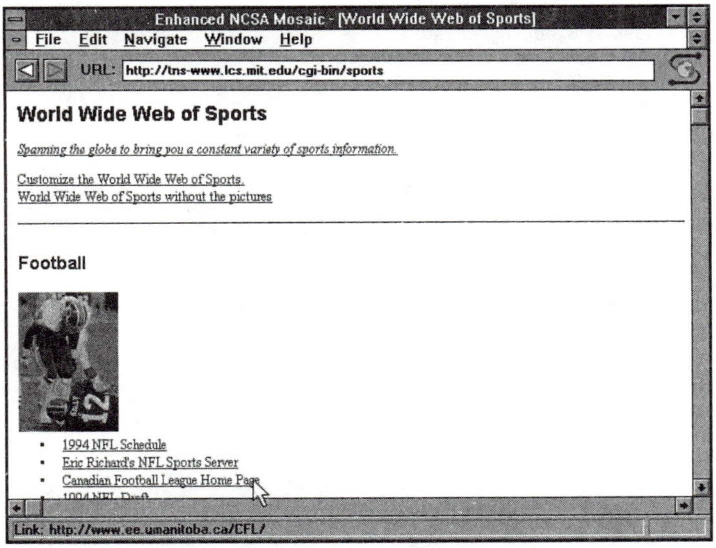

Figure D.20. World Wide Web of Sports.

Television

The Creative Internet Page

Various music and TV from CalTech's Asylum

http://www.galcit.caltech.edu/~ta/creative.html

The Gate's Fun and Games Department

Various TV shows

http://sfgate.com/fun/index.html

The Late Show with David Letterman Web Server

http://bingen.cs.csbsju.edu/letterman.html

Miranda's Muppet Fest

http://www.cs.wustl.edu/~mir/muppets/

The Monty Python Page

http://alfred.u.washington.edu:8080/~uffda/python.html

The Simpsons Archive

http://www.digimark.net/TheSimpsons/

Star Trek Picture and Sound Page

Star Trek images and sound files

http://moose.uvm.edu/~jfabian

Weather

Harvey's Cyberspace Jump Station: Weather

http://ice.ucdavis.edu/Cyberspace_Jump_Station/weather.html

Weather World

http://www.atmos.uiuc.edu/wxworld/html/top.html

Glossary: Plug-n-Play Mosaic

absolute URL—when writing a Web page, a link that uses the full three-part URL of the resource or page to which the link will lead. *Compare* relative URL.

access—the ability to get onto the Internet. To get access, you will need an account either with a public-access provider or on a smaller local area network (LAN).

access provider—*see* public access provider.

account—on computers, the username and password that allow you to connect to a particular access provider or LAN. if you have an account on an access provider, your username and password allow you to connect to the computers and use them.

anchor—the "guts" of a link; the URL of the file or Web page to which a link will take you.

annotation—a note concerning a particular Web page. Mosaic allows you to write an annotation for a Web page; when you load that page again, Mosaic reminds you that you made the annotation and offers to show it to you. Annotations are not part of the Internet; they stay on your computer. *Compare* comment.

anonymous FTP—the process by which many Internet files are available to any Internet user for downloading.

applications—a computer program, particularly that "does something" that's obvious to you, the user. Mosaic, word processors, and spreadsheet programs are all applications. *Compare* utility.

Archie—a method of searching the Internet for files that you can transfer to your own computer via FTP.

archive—a collection of older files of various kinds; often, a collection of programs.

ASCII—the American Standard Code for Information Exchange; the simplest and most common way for computers to display "normal" letters and numbers. *See* text file.

audio file—a "sound clip" that is in binary-file form and transferable over the Internet.

automagic—a process that performs certain complex Internet operations seemingly by magic; a term of admiration.

backbone—one of the massive communications lines that connect major portions of the Internet. The backbone is to your telephone line as Godzilla is to a gecko.

bandwidth—the amount of data a connection can carry, usually expressed in kilobytes (or megabytes) per second. Large files are known colloquially as "high-bandwidth" files because they take up much of the connection's capacity as they move around the Internet.

binary—the language of ones and zeroes spoken by all computers. Binary code is the closest possible representation of the actual electrical pulses that make a computer do its work.

binary file—a file composed of ones and zeroes; often a program or image file. A binary file usually requires applications or utilities to turn it into a form useful to the average user.

bookmark—in this case, a Mosaic reference to a favorite spot on the Internet.

browser—a program that allows you to use the hypertext/hypermedia capabilities of the Web.

bug—something in a program that does not work properly. Also, an unplanned feature.

bulletin-board system (BBS)—a computer system that offers files, e-mail, and sometimes discussion groups to callers. Smaller than, but similar to, an online service.

CERN—a major European physics laboratory, located in Switzerland; birthplace of the World Wide Web.

chat—typed Internet-based conversations that take place in real time. An exercise in group imagination.

client—a computer that asks for data and uses programs on another computer (called a server). When you log into the Internet, your computer is a client of your access provider's computer.

comment—notes written in a computer program on (in this case) a Web page. Notes are normally not seen by the reader, but since they're part of a public file on the Net it's possible for comments to be seen. *Compare* annotation.

communications software (comm software)—a program that allows your computer to talk to your modem, so your modem can in turn talk to the outside world. Popular comm software includes Microphone, Procomm Plus, and Telix. Windows includes a basic comm program called Terminal.

COM port—another phrase for serial port (sometimes called the SLIP port). External modems (and some mice) plug into COM ports.

configure—to give a piece of software the information it needs to work properly. Usually a one-time process.

conversion—the process of changing a file from one format to another.

CSLIP—Compressed SLIP, known as Van Jacobson compression, which sends a smaller version of the TCP packet information. Used by some public-access providers and useful with such applications as telnet.

cyberspace—the entirety of the Internet, online services, BBSs, and other online computer-based realms. A state of mind.

database—any collection of information, but usually understood as an organized collection of information on a particular topic.

demand load timeout—the amount of time the TCP/IP software waits quietly before asking again for packets.

developer—a person or group that plans, creates, and programs software.

dialer—a simple communications program used by your TCP/IP to connect your computer to the public access provider's computer.

dialup accounts—Internet accounts that do not have an IP address but depend on the access provider's computer to talk to the Internet on their behalf. A dialup account allows you to use many of the Internet's functions, but you won't be able to run Mosaic.

direct connection—an Internet account that connects your computer directly to the Internet. If you have a direct account, you rely on your access provider's account only to make the initial connection; your computer will talk to the Internet by itself. You need a direct connection to use Mosaic.

directory—a section of a computer's hard drive that holds certain files. A directory inside a directory is a subdirectory.

DNS—*see* domain name server

document—a hypertext file with all its links. Also, a collection of Web pages that share an identity (for instance, the Web pages for this book).

document source—the ASCII-and-HTML-coded text file that tells Mosaic how to create the page you see onscreen. You can view any Web page's document source code.

domain address—the IP address of the computer (belonging to your access provider) you use to connect to the Internet.

domain name—the name of the computer (belonging to your access provider) you use to connect to the Internet.

domain name server—a computer on the Internet that translates domain names into domain addresses.

dots—the periods that separate sections of Internet addresses.

download—to move a file from one computer (on the Internet, in this case) to your own computer's hard drive. Many of the programs you'll find on the Internet, such as games, must be downloaded for you to use them.

driver—a small program that lets hardware talk to other hardware.

electronic mail—*see* e-mail.

e-mail—short for electronic mail. E-mail is probably the most popular use for the Internet; it allows you to send messages and files to another person. All you need is their address, sometimes called their e-mail or Internet address.

FAQ—Frequently Asked Question; a file of information on a particular topic. You'll find many FAQs on the Internet, many put there by kind volunteers.

feature—the capability of software to do a particular thing. Also, an institutionalized bug.

file—any set of information on a computer. A file can contain anything that can be placed on a computer.

file transfer—the process of moving files from one computer to another via modem.

firewall—a security device that shields a computer or network of computers from the Internet while still allowing certain kinds of access.

formatting—codes added to a file to make it behave in certain ways, such as the HTML codes that turn ASCII text files into Web pages.

forms—sections of Web pages that allow readers to type in information.

freeware—software programs made available online free for the downloading. The author of a freeware program does, however, retain copyright on the work. *Compare* shareware, public domain.

FTP—File Transfer Protocol; also (colloquially) the process of transferring files on the Internet via FTP.

gearhead—someone who doesn't need the glossary. A techno-whiz. Someone genuinely interested in how computers work.

GIF—Graphics Interchange Format; a format for storing image files. Image files are often referred to as GIFs.

Gopher—a method of indexing Internet files for easy searching; also, the method of navigating such files. Files that are available via Gopher are said to exist in "Gopherspace," which, like the Web is just another way of organizing the Internet.

hacker—someone with a keen intellectual curiosity about other people's computers. Also, someone with a malicious streak about other people's computers.

home page—the Web page your copy of Mosaic automatically loads when you start Mosaic. *Compare* Web page.

hosts file—a older method of translating domain names into domain addresses, replaced by the domain name server.

hotlist—a list of the URLs for your favorite Web pages.

HTML—Hypertext Markup Language, the formatting system that turns ordinary files into Web hypertext (or hypermedia) documents.

hypermedia—a system of connecting files together via links. Hypermedia documents may include text, images, video clips, and sound clips. *Compare* hypertext.

hypertext—a system of connecting separate text files together. Documents that use hypertext are made up of several files, but you see them on your computer as just one document. *Compare* hypermedia.

info-harvesting—the process of finding information on the Internet. Includes almost everything one might do on the Net, including file transfer, research, searches, and just plain reading.

image—a broad category that covers any photo or artwork on the Net.

image map—an image with multiple links to various other places. Depending on where you click on an image map, you'll go to different places.

inline image—a graphic on a Web page that does not contain a link to another place; it's there for illustration only.

installation—the process of setting up and configuring software to work on your computer.

interface—how computers and their programs look to the user. PCs, X Window machines and the Mac all have a graphical interface composed of small pictures called icons.

Internet—the vast system of computers that Mosaic navigates.

internet—short for internetworking; used as part of the name of various processes and protocols, and refers to any two computers connecting together. Computers may use an internet protocol without connecting to the Internet.

Internet Registry—the organization in charge of assigning Internet addresses to access providers; run by the InterNIC Registration Service.

information superhighway—also known as the infobahn or the I-way. A mirage, at least for now. Get over it.

IP—Internet Protocol; *see* TCP/IP.

IP address—your computer's unique address on the Internet, assigned by your access provider and interpreted by a domain name server.

keyword—a word used to search for information on a particular topic. Many files on the Internet are indexed by their keywords so various search programs can find them.

LAN—Local area network; a group of computers (often in an office) that are jointly connected to a central "server" computer and share e-mail and files.

link—a possible connection to another file that's part of a hypertext or hypermedia document. On the Web, a link can lead to a file on a computer thousands of miles away.

load—to retrieve a file or Web page on the Net. Also, to start a piece of software on a computer by putting the software's files in RAM (random-access memory).

local file—a file on your own computer.

local user—to a network administrator, one of the users on her or his system.

login—to connect to your Internet access provider's computer. Also, to connect your computer to a LAN by typing in your name and password. Interchangeable in colloquial use with logon.

logoff—to break the connection between your computer and the access provider or LAN. Interchangeable in colloquial use with logout.

logon—*see* login.

logout—*see* logoff.

login name—*see* username.

mailing list—e-mail that is regularly distributed to a group of users who have asked to receive it. A mailing list is usually devoted to one subject.

Maximum Segment Size (MSS)—the maximum amount (in bytes) of information in the packets in which your Internet requests travel. *Compare* Maximum Transmission Unit.

Maximum Transmission Unit (MTU)—the maximum size (in bytes) of the packets in which your Internet requests travel. *Compare* Maximum Segment Size.

menu—a list of options available in a program.

modem—a piece of computer equipment that allows your computer to communicate with other computers over the telephone lines. It does this by changing the computer's binary language into the analog system used by telephones, and converting analog signals from the phone lines into the computer's language of ones and zeroes.

MOO—like MUD, a chat area on the Internet.

Mosaic—a graphical front end for the Internet that lets users hop from spot to spot via hypermedia links. Available for PCs, Macintosh and X Window machines.

mouse—a piece of computer equipment that lets user operate the computer by moving a pointer to items seen onscreen and clicking a button. A mouse is one of the types of equipment known as a "pointing device." Other types include trackballs and digital pens.

MSS—*see* Maximum Segment Size.

MTU—*see* Maximum Transmission Unit.

MUD—stands for multi-user dungeon; a chat area on the Internet.

multimedia—anything that combines text, video, sound, and/or images.

multi-user games—a computer game that allows two or more people to play at the same time. Players are aware of each other and usually "play together" or compete in some fashion.

navigation—the process of finding one's way around. In Mosaic, navigation consists of going either forward or backward.

NCSA—National Center for Supercomputing Applications. The U.S. research facility that originally developed the Mosaic software.

Net citizens—people who use and participate in the Internet.

Net surfers—people who spend a great deal of time using and participating in the Internet.

network—any group of connected computers; in this book, often used as a synonym for local-area network (LAN).

network administrator—*see* system administrator.

newsgroup—one of the thousands of discussion groups that make up the Usenet. A newsgroup is a constant entity composed of a varying number of topic "threads," which come and go rather quickly.

offline—not logged in; using the computer without being connected to the Internet. Among Net surfers, the unfortunate condition of not being reachable by e-mail.

online—when you are connected to the Internet, you are said to be online. "Online" is used to describe your situation any time you're connected to a network of computers.

online service—one of the large systems of computers that provide news, files, and discussion areas to subscribers. Compuserve, Prodigy, America Online and Delphi are all online services. An online service is larger than, but similar to, a bulletin-board system.

packet—the slices into which TCP/IP chops all data moving across the Internet. Breaking all Internet traffic into packets ensures that it can efficiently use whatever Internet pathways are least crowded from instant to instance, and that "high-bandwidth" files don't clog up the system.

password—the top-secret set of letters and numbers you use to gain access to your Internet account on your public access provider or local-area network.

permanent connection—a connection to the Internet that's "always on" and does not require dialing through a modem. Permanent connections are used by companies and other large entities. The price (tens of thousands of dollars) is beyond the means of most users. A permanent connection is extremely fast.

player—a utility that enables you to hear sound files on a computer. *Compare* viewer.

post—to write and send a message, often to a newsgroup.

PPP—point-to-point protocol; a means by which computers can use modems to connect to TCP/IP networks such as the Internet.

protocol—a set of rules by which computers communicate with each other. TCP/IP is a set of simple but universally understood protocols.

proxy server—a server that has a copy of a program you'd like to run but don't have on your computer.

public access provider—a commercial or charitable enterprise that offers Internet accounts to the general public.

public domain—where intellectual property is said to be when no one has copyright on it. Shakespeare's works, for instance, have passed into the public domain through sheer age. Also, some computer programs have been put into the public domain. *Compare* freeware, shareware.

RAM—random-access memory, where your computer keeps any programs or information it's using at the moment. Not to be confused with hard-drive space, which is the amount of room you have to store files on your computer.

real-time—anything that takes place in the here-and-now. Life is a real-time process.

Receive Windows—the size of the packet your computer's TCP/IP connection is willing to accept from the Net.

relative URL—when writing a Web page, a link that uses only the third part (or a portion thereof) of the three-part URL of the resource or page to which the link will lead. Relative URLs are written to pages at the same domain only. *Compare* absolute URL.

reload—to ask Mosaic to retrieve again the page you're currently looking at. This is useful when you're browsing with the Load Inline Images capability turned off.

request—a signal from your computer to another computer on the Internet, asking the remote computer to send data or other information.

rights—in this context, the things you are allowed to do on a particular computer. For instance, most anonymous-FTP installations give you the right to get files, but not to put them online.

role-playing games—multi-user games in which the participants assume other identities, and occasionally skills, much different from those they possess outside the game. Many role-playing games have medieval, diplomatic, or fantastic themes. Another exercise in group imagination.

router—the specialized computer hardware that moves the packet-sized pieces of Internet traffic to their destinations.

ruled line—a design element for Web pages; a horizontal straight line across the page.

RWIN—*see* receive windows

scanner—a piece of computer equipment that translates photos and other paper-based information into a graphics file on the computer. Photos you see on the Internet were most likely scanned (if they weren't taken with a digital camera, that is).

script—a set of commands that automate something you do regularly on the computer. Many people write scripts for their dialers.

serendipity—the art and act of discovering something good without looking for it. Also, a great restaurant in New York.

serial port—see COM port.

server—a computer that supplies files and runs programs for another computer (called a client). When you log into your access provider's computer, it acts as a server.

session—a period of time spent online; also, the software's activities during that time.

shareware—programs that are put online for others to down; if you download a shareware program, try it, and like it, you are morally obligated to send its author a pre-set fee. Shareware is an alternative method of distributing and selling software; the authors retain all copyrights on their work. *Compare* freeware, public domain.

site—a computer or set of computers offering a number of Internet files and pages.

SLIP—Serial Line Internet Protocol; a means by which computers can use modems to connect to the Internet. SLIP is older and somewhat less advanced than PPP, but it does essentially the same thing.

SLIP port—*see* COM port.

sound card—a piece of hardware in your computer that enables you to play audio files.

sound clip—*see* audio file.

stack—the TCP/IP software required to run Mosaic; called a stack because the various small protocols are "stacked up" on top of each other to do their respective jobs.

subdomain—one of several sections of a domain. Large sites often divide their domains into smaller, more manageable subdomains.

subnet mask—a tool that enables network administrators to make the most of their assigned Internet addresses. The subnet mask helps the computer tell the difference between different parts of the TCP/IP address.

system administrator—the person in charge of the health and well-being of a local area network or other system of computers; occasionally, a public access provider.

tag—the HTML coding that makes Web pages look and act as they do.

target link—a point within a Web page to which other pages can link. Target links are useful to help readers find particular places on very long Web pages.

TCP—Transmission Control Protocol; see TCP/IP.

TCP/IP—the basic set of rules (protocols) by which all computers on the Internet communicate; TCP and IP are two of the components that make up the set.

telnet—a protocol that allows users to connect to remote computers and use programs on them; also, the process of doing so. This is useful if, for instance, you're out of town and need access to your Internet account back home.

text editor—a basic word processor that works with ASCII files without adding any non-ASCII formatting and coding.

text file—an ASCII-only file; more broadly, any file that can be read and understood in an ASCII file editor, such as a page with HTML coding.

title—a Web page's formal name; it may appear on the page itself but always appears in a special area reserved for the title.

top-level domain—in a domain name, the rightmost segment of the name; gives usually reliable indications as to the type or location of a domain.

UART—Universal Asynchronous Receive-Transmit chip. The UART acts as a buffer for data passing through the serial port. The new 16550 UART is necessary for high-speed modem communications on PCs running Windows; older models include the 8250 and the 16450.

uniform resource locator (URL)—the address Mosaic uses to find Web pages and other resources on the Web. Every resource has a unique URL, just as every Internet user has a unique address. The uniform resource locator includes information on the type of resource, the computer on which it resides, and its name.

UNIX—a sophisticated operating system. Vast sections of the Internet (though not all of it) run on UNIX.

upload—to move a computer file from your computer to another, or from your computer to the Internet.

URL—*see* uniform resource locator.

usegroup—*see* newsgroup.

Usenet—a large, constantly changing set of discussion groups known as newsgroups (or usegroups). Usenet has over 6,000 newsgroups on every conceivable topic. No one is in charge of Usenet, though some of the newsgroups are moderated (that is, the messages are edited and selected for publication) by a person or group.

username—your name on the local-area network or public access provider you use to gain access to the Internet. On the Internet, your e-mail address is composed of your username and the domain name of your Internet provider.

utility—a computer program, particularly one that "does something" that's invisible or trivial to you, the user. Finder (on the Mac) and File Manager (in Windows) are examples of utilities. *Compare* application.

UUCP—UNIX-to-UNIX Copy; a "sometime" connection to the Internet. Some systems such as bulletin boards use UUCP to connect to the Net several times a day, exchange mail that's accumulated, and disconnect. It's an inexpensive but limited way of gaining Internet access.

verbed—(of a word) turned from a noun into a verb; endemic in technology and in business, where people interface with computers.

video cards—a piece of hardware in your computer that controls the quality of your computer's display.

viewer—a utility that enables you to see an image file or video clip; *compare* player.

WAIS—Wide Area Information Server, a powerful type of search in which users choose keywords to sift through various databases. WAIS delivers the results of its searches as "relevance rankings" by showing the number of words in each document that match the words used in the search. This enables WAIS to guide users to documents that are a "near miss" to the search but may be useful anyway.

Web—*see* World Wide Web.

web crawler—a Web search tool. *See* worm.

Web page—any file on the Net that is composed of ASCII text with HTML coding. A Web page may contain links to images, sound files, video clips, or other files. *Compare* home page.

Windows Sockets (WinSock)—a dynamic link library (DLL) that enables Windows to handle TCP/IP connections.

World Wide Web—a hypermedia system of connecting various resources on the Internet. Mosaic relies on the World Wide Web to support the links it shows.

worm—on the Web, a program that can be used to search for specific pages. Searches are made by name, topic, location, or other criteria. (This is not related to the notorious virus-type worm.)

SYMBOLS

A

B

D

E

F

G

N

O

P

T

X–Z

Book ISBN 0-672-30627-1

HELP ME!
Caught in the Web?
Before you enter the Web, let your fingers (mouse?) do the walking through our incredible on-line (local disk) digital Web index, InfoWeb. Over 3500 national and international site names and descriptions are at the tip of your finger and are automatically linked to the Enhanced Mosaic browser that comes with this book. Looking for Sports, Business, Travel, Entertainment or anything under the sun and in the Web? ...your mouse does the walking! With on-line quarterly updates, InfoWeb is your only reliable access to complete Internet information.
Get Luckman Interactive's InfoWeb
Special Offer
Plug & Play Mosaic Buyers Only!
$19.95
Order Today!
Call (800) 500-4411

Setting Up Your Account

Before you can connect to the Internet, you must contact Portal Communications to set up your Internet account. Double-click on the Portal Internet Offer icon in the Enhanced Mosaic group for complete information.

Once you have your Portal account set up, follow these simple steps to get connected:

1. Locate the Enhanced Mosaic Program Manager group and double-click the Enhanced Mosaic icon.
2. You'll receive a message stating that Enhanced Mosaic is not yet configured. Click the Yes button to start the Quick Configuration program.
3. Next, you receive a message telling you that Quick Configure enables you to set up an account using Portal Standard IP Service. Click on the Quick Configure Using Portal button.

> **Note:** If you already are connected to the Internet through a SLIP/PPP modem connection or a network connection, choose Custom Configure Using Another TCP/IP Stack. This will disable the TCP/IP software and dialer included with Enhanced Mosaic, allowing you to use your existing TCP/IP setup.

> **Note:** If you do not have an Internet connection, and you want to use a different service provider for your connection, you must use the Custom Installation choice. With providers other than Portal, you won't be able to use the easy Plug-n-Play configuration. Contact your service provider for information on configuring the software. To read more detailed information on custom configurations, double-click on the Distinct TCP/IP Notes icon in the Enhanced Mosaic program group.

4. To the right of the Portal Phone # box, click the down arrow and choose a local access number nearest to the city or town in which you live. Once you select the number, edit it as necessary. If it's a local call, for example, remove the 1 and area code. If you need to enter 1170 to cancel call waiting or 9 to get an outside line, edit the number in this box.
5. In the Account Name box, enter the account named supplied to you by Portal.
6. In the Password box, enter the password supplied to you by Portal.
7. In the Modem Port box, click the down arrow, and choose the COM port to which your modem is attached. For most computers, this will be COM1.
8. In the Modem Speed box, click the down arrow, and choose the maximum communications speed at which your modem operates. It's important that you choose the correct maximum speed for your modem—2400, 4800, 9600, 14400, 19200, or 28800. Failure to choose the proper modem speed may result in communication errors.
9. Click the Show dialing process box so that you can monitor your call progress when you connect with Portal.
10. Click the Configure button to continue.
11. If your video system currently supports only 16 color, you will receive a message stating that Enhanced Mosaic works best with a 256-color display. Click the OK button to continue.
12. When you receive the Configuration Complete message, Click OK to continue.
13. Next, you'll be asked if you wish to start Mosaic at this time. Click the Yes button to begin, or No to exit back to Windows.

If you pressed the Yes button, Enhanced Mosaic will begin, and you'll automatically be connected to your Portal Internet account. Enjoy!

When you exit Enhanced Mosaic, it will not end immediately; it takes a few seconds to close the connection to Portal and shut down the modem.

The Plug-n-Play Mosaic Disks

The two disks included with this book contain everything you need to connect to the Internet and navigate using Mosaic. Disk One contains:

- A complete version of *Enhanced NCSA Mosaic* from Luckman Interactive
- TCP/IP software from Distinct Corporation, which allows your computer to connect to the Internet
- *Plug-n-Play Mosaic* and Enhanced Mosaic home pages.

Disk two contains Microsoft Win32s extensions, which must be installed to run Enhanced Mosaic. You'll need at least 4MB of free space on your hard drive when you install these disks.

> **Note:** By using this software, you are agreeing to the terms of the License Agreement for Distinct TCP/IP for Windows, as specified in the `LICENSE.TXT` file on Disk One.

Installing Disk One

Insert Disk One in your floppy disk drive and follow these steps:

1. From Windows File Manager or Program Manager, choose File+Run from the menu.
2. Type **`B:\SETUP`** and press Enter. If the disk is in your A drive, type `A:\SETUP` instead.
3. Click the Continue button to start the installation process.
4. Choose the name of the directory where you want to install Mosaic. To accept the default, `C:\MOSAIC`, click the Continue button. To change the name of the drive or directory, type the changes in the path window, then click on Continue.
5. The installation program will begin copying files to your hard drive. Once complete, several Program Manager items will automatically be created in an Enhanced Mosaic group.
6. Once the setup is complete, it notifies you that you need to have Microsoft Win32s installed in order to use Enhanced Mosaic. Click the OK button to continue.

Installing Disk Two

You must have Microsoft Win32s extensions installed to run Enhanced Mosaic. The installation program on this disk will automatically determine if Win32s needs to be installed on your computer. Follow these steps to install Win32s:

1. From Windows File Manager or Program Manager, choose File+Run from the menu.
2. Type **`B:\SETUP`** and press Enter. If the disk is in your A drive, type `A:\SETUP` instead.
3. Click the Continue button to start the installation process.
4. Next you're shown the directory where the files will be installed. Click the Continue button.
5. The installation program will then begin copying files to your hard drive. Once complete, click the OK button to continue.
6. You'll then have the option to install Freecell (a 32-bit card game), in order to test that Win32s works properly. Click the Continue button to install Freecell.
7. Choose the directory where you want to install Freecell. To accept the default, `C:\WIN32APP\FREECELL\`, click the Continue button. To change the name of the drive or directory, type the changes in the path window and click on Continue.
8. The installation program will then copy files to your hard drive. Once complete, a Program Manager item will automatically be created in a group named Win32 Applications. Once complete, click the OK button to continue. Windows will now automatically restart (make sure you close any open applications before you click on OK).

← *See previous page*